W9-COY-297

The Natural

order of

Things

HOUSTON PUBLIC LIBRARY

RO1137 55994

Other books by António Lobo Antunes

translated into English:

South of Nowhere

An Explanation of the Birds

Fado Alexandrino

Act of the Damned

The Natural order of Things

António Lobo Antunes

translated from the portuguese

by Richard zenith

grove press/new york

Copyright © 1992 by António Lobo Antunes

Translation copyright © 2000 by Richard Zenith

All rights reserved. No part of this book may be reproduced in any form or by any electronic or mechanical means, including information storage and retrieval systems, without permission in writing from the publisher, except by a reviewer, who may quote brief passages in a review. Any members of educational institutions wishing to photocopy part or all of the work for classroom use, or publishers who would like to obtain permission to include the work in an anthology, should send their inquiries to Grove/ Atlantic, Inc., 841 Broadway, New York, NY 10003.

Originally published as A Ordem Natural das Coisas *by Publicações Dom Quixote, Lisbon, Portugal.*

The publisher gratefully acknowledges the assistance of the Instituto Português do Livro e das Bibliotecas in funding this translation.

Published simultaneously in Canada

Printed in the United States of America

FIRST EDITION

Library of Congress Cataloging-in-Publication Data

Antunes, António Lobo, 1942–

[Ordem natural das coisas. English]

The natural order of things / António Lobo Antunes ; translated from the Portuguese by Richard Zenith.

p.   cm.

ISBN 0-8021-1658-2

I. Zenith, Richard.   II. Title.

PQ9263.N7707313   2000

869.3'42—dc21   99-40063

CIP

DESIGN BY LAURA HAMMOND HOUGH

Grove Press

841 Broadway

New York, NY 10003

00 01 02 03   10 9 8 7 6 5 4 3 2 1

for isabel Risques,

forever the best of friends

and one to whom this book

owes so much, with a kiss

of gratitude and infinite

affection from

António

Translator's Note: *I have usually left the names of streets and places in Portuguese, but* Quinta do Jacinto, *a small complex of old garden apartments in Lisbon, is translated here as "Hyacinth Park." I have also preferred, with one exception, to use the word "square" instead of the Portuguese* praça *or* largo. *(*Largo *can also, as in the case of* Largo Benformoso, *refer to a large intersection.)* Rua *is the most common Portuguese word for street; a* calçada *is a steep street, an* estrada *a main road or highway. People's names are spelled as in Portuguese, except that Iolanda appears here as Yolanda, and I have dropped a few accent marks.*

contents

the natural

order of

things

BOOK ONE

sweet odors,

sweet Deaths

I

Until I was six years old, Yolanda, I didn't even know my mother's family or the smell of chestnut trees that the September wind brought from Buraca as sheep and goats scurried up the road toward the abandoned cemetery, goaded by an old man wearing a cap and by the voices of the dead. And today, my love, lying in my bed waiting for the Valium to kick in, the same thing happens as when I used to lie down, on hot summer afternoons, in the coolness of the dilapidated graves: I feel a tombstone decoration pressing against my leg, I hear the grass of the graves in my sheets, I see the plaster Jesuses and angels threatening me with their broken hands. A woman with a hat planted cabbages and turnips between the roots of the cypress trees, the bells of the goats jingled in the ruined chapel, reduced to three charred walls, no statues, and a piece of altar with the altar cloth covered over by climbing vines, and I watched the night advance across the tombstones, congealing the saints' blessings into patches of darkness.

But yesterday, as I held your body and waited for the medicine to release me from the bombardment of memories, an ancient twilight came to mind, from 1950 or 1951, after the flowers in the garden had just been watered and Uncle Fernando, wearing an undershirt, was doing his exercises on the verandah, some cats were tussling in the yard by the kitchen, and I was perched on the garden wall, sniffing the breezes from Monsanto Park and listening to the horses of the defeated monarchists marching down the hills (as I'd learned from my aunt Anita, who was a little girl at the time) on their way to the penitentiary.

I don't know why you've never been interested in my childhood, Yolanda. Whenever I talk about myself, you shrug your shoulders, twist your mouth, and stretch your eyelids in disdain, and mocking wrinkles appear behind your blond bangs, so that I finally shut up, embarrassed, setting the plates, glasses, and forks on the table for lunch as your aunt coughs in the pantry and your father turns the TV buttons in search of the squeals of the soap opera. And yet, my love, as soon as you fall asleep, your face, scrunched against the pillow, recovers the childish innocence it had when I first saw you, in the snack bar near the high school, and your spiral notebooks and ink-stained fingers made me feel an irrational happiness,

as soon as you fall asleep and the whiteness of an elm tree with birds passes through the bedroom, I talk on without you mocking me, I hover over you and converse with your motionless hands and your defenseless thighs, and the house I lived in before I met my mother's family suddenly appears, from out of an imperfection in the mirror or from one of the drawers in the dresser where our clothes have been jumbled up with the moth nests and copper handles ever since, some months ago, you said "Come" and I presented myself, with an umbrella and two old suitcases, in this minuscule apartment in Hyacinth Park, Alcântara, to explain that yes, I'm thirty-one years older than your daughter, but my government job isn't so bad, Mr. Oliveira, and of course I'll pay the rent, the electric bill, and the butcher.

Listen, love. Perhaps you understand me in your sleep, perhaps your body stops being ironic and loves me, perhaps your eyelids, now soft, flutter if I say I'd like you to touch me and let me touch you, perhaps you rub your triangular tuft of fuzz against me, and your knees slowly open onto a moist and smooth and soft cave that imprisons my desire with the firmness of nacre. But since the summer you've ignored me, you've fallen for a classmate with flaming acne and an incipient beard, who visits us on the pretext of getting help from you in geography or math, and when we shake hands he cruelly squeezes my knuckles until they crack. Reduced to being a vague relative with a vest, a tie, and thinning gray hair, unable to do a headstand, unable to read without glasses, unable to run fifty feet because of heart murmurs, unable, in other words, to compete with that pimpled youth who's taller than me and has no paunch, no baldness, and no false teeth, whose eighteen years have defeated me, I wait with the stillness of a tarantula for night, when your body, seasoned with the oil and vinegar of toothpaste and cheap perfume, curls up on the mattress, when the rhythm of your chest becomes as secret as a boat's, and when your lips, puckered by your slumber's pouting, blow a kiss that's not for me, I wait for night, measuring its depths by your father's insomnia and your aunt's bronchitis on the other side of the wall, and I resume my tale at the point where I left off, returning, Yolanda, to the house where I lived before I met my mother's family, the house that had hundreds of hallways, hundreds of nooks, hundreds of crannies, the house, the house,

the house, my God, surrounded by seagulls and sea mist on top of a cliff, with tattered curtains and shutters banging in the wind, with a semicircular sign reading Hotel Central on the facade, and the three secret policemen, always dressed in black and raising their arms in the Nazi salute, who drank their morning barley in the small sitting room.

It's then that I remember the equinoxes that confused the wagtails, causing them to alight on the china cabinet, on the banister's flourishes, and in the torpor of my sinus troubles. I remember the storm that swept across the tiny square in front of the hotel, and on the square there was a darkish antiques shop with secondhand Buddhas and Spanish fans in the window. And I remember the garage of the albino mechanic who fixed cars in the summer, sliding under their engine bellies. The owls, Yolanda, would crash into the small window of my room, located next to the cook's bedroom with a toilet near the bed and the sound of the ebb tide forever gurgling in the drain, and the hotel's only lodgers were us two plus my godmother and the three members of the secret police, even if, in July, when the debris was cleared off the beach and a dull heat calmed the waves, the cook and my old godmother took turns sitting at the entrance, with crochet in hand, hoping against hope that a miraculous taxi would drop off a group of trembling American women, unnerved by the sinister pine trees and the backseat's worn-out springs.

If I think, my love, of that village where spiders spun desolation in half a dozen crumbling and deserted chalets teetering over ravines full of cawing birds and I compare it with this apartment in Alcântara next to the grade crossing of the railroad and the Tagus's dolphin-crowned ships that graze our pillowcases, then my legs instinctively seek the concave place between your knees, and I press my chest against your back in a plea for protection that baffles me, for it seems ludicrous to me that a forty-nine-year-old man should seek help from an eighteen-year-old girl who's dreaming of leather-jacketed archangels accelerating on their motorbikes to save her from me, an innocuous geezer flustered with embarrassment and surprise. And yet, Yolanda, don't imagine that my life in a village near Ericeira where the eucalyptus trees shed the tears of an incurable despair wasn't pleasant. It was pleasant. When sciatica didn't stretch her out in pain on her mattress, the cook played cards with me in the room with the broken boiler, while the secret policemen, planning tortures and arrests, made the floorboards creak over our heads. On certain autumn mornings the sea and the wind subsided, and there appeared a strip of sand that was soon covered by beach tents, picnic baskets, pyramids of sandals, and families in bathrobes. Mimosas sprouted from the rocks, and the kerosene lamps of former inhabitants wafted in the chalets, until a bus came and swooped up the vacationers to take them, jolting, back to Lisbon, and the waves swallowed the beach, storm clouds covered the sky, neat rows of seagulls screeched on the rocks, flocks of crazed robins flew out of the treetops, and my godmother, indifferent to the storm, took up her crochet needle and dreamed of extravagant American women wearing sandals and Panama hats as if on an expedition to the tropics.

The Lisbon night was sliced by a train running perpendicular to the streetlights of Avenida de Ceuta and parallel to the river flanked by warehouses, pontoons, cranes, derricks, containers, and freight trucks, all waiting for the lemon-colored dawn and the workmen who were already visible in the faint sunlight, walking on their way to the Tagus.

The train, my love, raced toward Estoril and Cascais (from where we live I can discern in the distance houses whose fingers hold albatrosses and steamers), and our second-floor apartment in Hyacinth Park rocked as if struck by a whirl of connecting rods, sending tremors through the shelves with clay bears, glass elephants, stuffed clowns, and the colored print of Wagner and causing the enamel box where you keep rings, bracelets, and the fake silver earrings I give you for Christmas, if I have any money left from my holiday bonus, to fall off the dresser to the floor. The train raced toward Estoril with bells jingling and lights turning on and off, it discombobulated the buildings of Alcântara, and you tossed in your sleep until finally, without waking, you turned to me and moaned like a child. Your ankles rubbed my ankles, and while I continued to talk, my mouth slyly, stealthily, cautiously moved closer to yours, I smelled your breath, smelled your hair, smelled your neck, smelled the folds in your waist, the folds in your stomach, and I was about to fondle your pubis, to feel the texture you're made of, when the cat, startled by my joyous frenzy, jumped off the bedspread, brushing against a lamp, whose shade shifted, lighting up the bedroom furniture for a second. And your elbows jerked, your body rolled over, and with it your thighs and shoulders, which slipped out of your gown's straps, and I was left alone with the bad taste of nothing, lulled by the train cars that galloped past the sewer pipes, beaches, and boats of the Tagus, lulled by the river's waves while my hands, as if praying, held the absence of your hips.

In the run-down hotel where I lived, Yolanda, before moving in with my mother's family, there were no cats, for it was too wet, too windy, too gray, and in the foggy backyard with its wild reeds and bad-tempered owls, the waves that came and went would crash against the rooms, spraying foam all over. So that stray cats, despite the cook's efforts to coax them with bowls of eels, scurried off into the eucalyptus trees, frightened by the sea's commotion and by the corpses of sailors that clutched broken rudders and peered at us from behind the hatboxes in the closets.

There were no cats, but we had a crow with clipped wings that swayed like a cabin boy and indicated latitudes to the secret policemen, who were deathly afraid that an erroneous maneuver might pitch the hotel against the rocks, opening an irreparable hole underneath the balcony windows. Each morning the crow limped around his ground-floor command post, verifying that we were on course and that there were no enemy battleships, and he was the one who shouted

"Everyone to port side, ready the boats"

when one day, inspecting the deck of the foyer, he found my godmother lying facedown on the floorboards, holding on to her crochet needle.

I heard the commodore shout, Yolanda, but inside my dream, as if the shout were part of the story in which a band of nymphs was chasing me down garden paths (the plump pink goddesses of the oleographs in the hallway skipping hand in hand through a forest or by a brook), and even when the cook came to call at my bedside her voice, seeming at first like the bushes' rustling, took a while to become real, through metamorphoses that my torso accompanied, stretching and contracting as my vertebrae softly clacked.

But I distinctly remember going down the stairs, disconcerted by the seagulls pacing in the open windows, and hearing the crow ask desperately,

"Where are the life jackets, for Christ's sake?"

and I saw the secret policemen deliberating, taking notes, ready to open fire on the wind or to arrest the clouds, as per the instructions they'd received from nobody unless from the trees' murmuring or the tables' creaking.

I remember, with the vividness of childhood memories, the tops of the pines behind the houses on the square, the honey-suckles and eucalyptus trees that hid the road from view, and the jeep from the National Guard at the hotel entrance, with an armed soldier smoking in the driver's seat. In the foyer the corporal, who before I was born had dated the cook, and a second soldier I'd never seen, both wearing gaiters and cartridge belts but with caps in hand, observed my godmother without daring to touch her, praying that the telephone would work so that they could summon the doctor from Mafra who periodically grasped my chin and cured my tonsillitis with a vigorous swabbing. The albino, intrigued, paced around in the rain, lifting his piglet eyelashes to the sky,

and the doctor, Yolanda, arrived after lunch, sensing trouble as he entered with his rubber raincoat, cod-fisher boots, and a trail of sea parrots that chirped in the seaweed. The crow, much calmer, despite the whistling of pines in the inland forest, flit-ted up the stairs muttering vernier calculations. The corporal pointed at my godmother with his pinkie, and the doctor, with knowing eyebrows, squatted to examine her, ordered

"Cough,"

and pulled from his raincoat a stethoscope with never-end-ing tubes, curled every which way in the infinite coat pocket.

"Seeing as she doesn't cough, it could be she's dead"

he concluded in a draped voice whose syllables were scat-tered by the storm just like the leaves from the acacia out back, reduced to a skeleton of water-pounded and wind-fractured ribs with pigeons crucified on its branches. The cook rubbed an eyelid with the corner of her apron, while the corporal respectfully stood at attention. The soldier, flat against the wall, gaped with open dentures at the deceased: he and I must have been the only ones who had never seen a corpse. The second corpse I saw, years later, was of a switchman who threw himself at the train I was riding in the Beira Baixa region with a co-worker, on business. I remember staring at the suicide in the gravel of the crossties and marveling at the peaceful look on his still intact face: that must have been when I stopped worrying about getting the flu.

I get out of bed, raise the blinds a sliver, and the lights of Alcântara extend to the docks and the Tagus River, dotted with rowboats searching for fish in the foam. At this hour of night, midway between sundown and sunrise, there's no traffic in the circle, and the stoplights changing from red to green command only the shadows. The March mist transfigures the buildings, imbuing them with a majesty they don't have by day, and when I think of this, Yolanda, the bedroom's silence alarms me with fears I don't quite understand, like my fear when I heard the doctor from Mafra, putting away his gigantic stethoscope, clear up the corporal's doubt:

"It's simple, friend. If she doesn't obey, it means she bit the dust. Since there are no bullet holes, just call up the priest in Ericeira, and we're set."

And so later that same day, or the next day, or the day after (since hitting forty I've had trouble with my kidneys and with dates), while an apocalyptic thunder thrashed the town and the rain washed out a piece of the garden wall, they put a part in my hair and a black tie around my neck and took me to the church in the jeep of the National Guard. We rode through a nightmare of lightning bolts that lit up cedars, walnut trees, migratory birds sobbing in the willows' long tufts, and dogs with large furry snouts that fled howling down muddy paths, frightened by the thunder. Houses of emigrants would loom, whirling, before sinking into the earth. I've never been back to

Ericeira, but since everything in Portugal stagnates and is suspended in time (except for me, forever older), I presume it hasn't changed a bit, even as Alcântara will endure for a thousand years exactly as I see it now, at three A.M. by my watch: a neighborhood of garages and repair shops proliferating over the barren terrain, and the chaos of the river's swelling, with its harsh, tunnel-like echo traveling across the asphalt to the threshold of our apartment.

And just as here in Alcântara at this hour of the night, while you and your father and your aunt sleep on the lumpy beds of the poor, just as here, Yolanda, it occurs to me how tacky the objects in the living room are and how the mildew has formed archipelagos on the walls, I also remember, as I wait for another train to rush past toward Estoril or Cais do Sodré, the cracks in the church on a hilltop with thickets and apple trees that resisted the north wind, I remember the panels with saints in the mortuary chapel and a fissure in the bricks through which the sea of winter entered and I could see Ericeira's chimneys pitching helter-skelter into the water. There was a copper Jesus hanging from the cross like a drop of water from a faucet, drapery tatters against carved flourishes, a blackbird on a rafter taking a break from the rain, the secret policemen sitting on a pew, and a sexton who winked at us with his toucan eyes. Now that no one was left in the hotel there were probably dozens of taxis arriving from Sintra, their headlights shining in the crooked rows of pines, to drop off tour groups of hundred-year-old American women shivering from the cold in their low-cut dresses. The rooms were overflowing with trunks and suitcases, a foul sludge throbbed in the bidets, walking sticks stumbled up and down stairways, door locks sprang with a rusty screech, someone fixed the boiler in the basement, which now boiled with a duodenal languor, energetic hammers destroyed the upstairs, and the crow, bothered by the noise, squawked nautical expletives on the kitchen floor. Perhaps the waters, subsiding, uncovered a strip of beach among the rocks, perhaps a skewed light revived the weeping willows and the potted magnolias, perhaps there were ships on the horizon, tankers, sloops, caravels, gliding toward Rua #8 in Hyacinth Park. Sitting on a tiny throne that wobbled, oblivious of what was going on because in eight years of life I had so far been spared the world's mysteries, I didn't notice the lady who at the end of the day would take me away with her after packing up my clothes, with the cook's help, in a duffel bag filched from the junk in the basement.

I lower the blinds as the next train approaches, and the billboards, the boxwoods, the streetlights, and the river lights start to tremble, the bedroom plunges into hopeless darkness, I walk to the bed, stepping cautiously so as not to bang my shins against the furniture, and when I lie down next to you the headboard shifts, the mattress slumps, and your body sighs with a cedar's coos. It's the moment, Yolanda, when I let myself say I love you, when I dare to fondle the curve of your shoulder, when my mouth approaches so as to feel with my tongue the feathery taste of your hair. The Valium has muffled my gestures and clouded my ideas without paralyzing my memory, it's April, and I'm leaning toward you in the snack bar where I saw you for the first time, with two girlfriends, all giggles and whispers, chewing bubble gum and drinking strawberry milkshakes, and I asked if you wouldn't mind me sitting at your table with my lemon tea for curing colds. And I sat there for an hour, anxious and agitated, while you traded photos of actors, discussed boyfriends and nail polish, complained about yesterday's philosophy exam, and showed extreme interest in an olive-skinned man with curly hair, a mustache, and pointed shoes who was drinking a coffee at the counter and leafing through a sports journal.

ב

I don't know anything, I swear to God, it's no use insisting, but hold on, wait a minute, don't go away, maybe I can remember a thing or two for your article or book if you give me a little something to help pay the rent for my lice-infested room, expensive like everything, even if it's in a rooming house for hookers on the Praça da Alegria, where between the slaps of the pimps and the guffaws of the lechers I can hardly sleep, and this goes on until five or six in the morning, when the trees begin to shake off the darkness and the pigeons descend from the Water House to contend for the food scraps left in the public gardens by choosy beggars. By day it's pigeons I see from my window—pigeons, cripples, and the unemployed all stewing their miseries in the hot sun—while at night I observe the fate of the poor girls who work the Avenida, up and down, between two infections in their ovaries and an abortion by the midwife in Loures, in a basement apartment smelling of fried fish, with little posters of saints on the walls and a grandmother groaning in a corner. You don't believe me? Write this on your pad of paper: that in the wake of the Revolution, after being locked up by the army for months without cause in Caxias, in the wing of the prison that faces the sea and the seagulls and the splendor of twilight, I returned to my ground-floor apartment outside Lisbon, in Odivelas, where I lived next door to a nurse who coaxed innocent fetuses out of women of the night right there in her living room, next to the dining table and the invalid's chair where her mother nodded to the music of a transistor radio pressed against her ear. How about that? But the real trouble was that, with the Communists having come to power, the woman and her sick mother left the neighborhood, apparently to set up shop in Paris, in one of the immigrant quarters where Africans, Arabs, Spaniards, Yugoslavs, and Portuguese spend their miserable Sundays sitting on rocks and drenching up the sky's grayness, so that there were hundreds of pregnant women waiting around the entrance to my building , balancing like storks in their high-heeled shoes and staring at one another with insomnia-ravaged eyelids. A cop with a stick finally shooed them like Christmas turkeys toward a bus stop, and the poor things, without protesting, nestled in a bus that would take them back to Lisbon, with their watercolor faces pressed against the windows. As for me, I stayed on for a while in Odivelas, without any job, any retirement, or any health coverage, staring at the fire station behind my curtains and letting my mustache grow so that I wouldn't look like the photos in the newspapers, until one day the landlord came around, called me a fascist, confiscated my furniture and the booklets for my correspondence course in hypnotism as payment for back rent, and threw me out. The guy on the third floor who used to drink beer with me in the bar and pass along some free information showered me with insults and kicks in the shins that have left scars to this day, a complete stranger came up and spat in my face, hammers and sickles and fraying placards covered the walls of buildings, workers with clenched fists shouted "Down with the dictatorship, long live socialism," and I thought, My goose is cooked, in no time at all the Russians will pack me off on a train to Siberia, where I'll freeze in a wooden shack. I went straight to a forger of doctor's certificates and driver's licenses and used the last money I had to change my name on my identity card, I started wearing dark glasses, the kind used by blind accordionists, I stopped shaving, and through a hustler who wears suspenders I found the cubbyhole where I live, in a flophouse for whores, with a clammy bed, permanganate in a corner, and turtledoves everywhere, tormenting me even in the toilet at the end of the hallway, the toilet used by all the rooms on my floor, by all the girls in the rooms plus all their clients, with the turtledoves warbling in the eaves, peering through the windowpanes, cleaning their feathers, turtledoves from the yard next door, turtledoves from Alcântara or from Chelas, turtledoves from Almada, turtledoves from the abandoned warehouses, rotten hulls, and crumbling palaces along the Tagus, homeless turtledoves, vagrant turtledoves, gypsy turtledoves, turtledoves that mock and laugh at us from the window ledge,

turtledoves unlike the ones here at Santana Park, plump, solemn, stately, patriarchal, hanging from the gutters, perched on the rooftops or in the highest tree branches, turtledoves and ducks and also, since you're taking notes, the cry of peacocks when the day starts dying, not to mention the sirens of the ambulances on their way to one of the hospitals surrounding us on all sides, the São José Hospital, the Capuchin Hospital, the Hospital of Arroios, Santa Marta Hospital, Estefânia Hospital, or Miguel Bombarda, the mental hospital, whose lunatic patients, wearing medals and stripes, walk along the flower beds and bum cigarettes at the stoplights, not to mention the vagabonds wrapped in newspapers to protect themselves from the morning dew, not to mention you and me, observing all this, each one with his soft drink and dish of peanuts in this restaurant next to the medical school, whose columns hide God knows how many cadavers cut up by students in white coats.

You're a writer and never thought of this? You never imagined yourself naked, smelling of formaldehyde, flat on your back in a marble tub, waiting for them to cut open your ribs with a huge pair of scissors? Ever since democracy caused me to lose my job as a section chief in the National Security and Information Bureau and I started eating in a soup kitchen, ever since the day after the coup when the Communists surrounded our building on Rua António Maria Cardoso while we hurriedly burned papers, peeked through the blinds, and ran down the hallways with pistols in hand not knowing what to do, I've felt certain that one of these days two firemen will wrap me in a sheet and carry me out of the rooming house as the consternated hookers look on in their panties and bras, they'll carry me out on a canvas stretcher and eventually dump me onto a stone table, among other stone tables with mutilated bodies, while men with rubber aprons use saws and pincers to rip open a child's stomach. There are times I dream of this until the turtledoves wake me up, times I hear pliers grinding my bones and I smell the soft vapor from my exposed guts, times they sew up my stomach and chest with coarse thread, and I wake up with a start, shouting in the middle of the room, and it takes me forever to realize I'm still alive, still breathing, still able to come to this outdoor café at Santana Park and watch the lunatics converse with the late afternoon swans. Doesn't this talk about dead people make you thirsty? A beer, no, I don't drink or smoke, but a mineral water would be nice, along with a cheese sandwich, because these memories give me a painful knot in the throat.

But to get to what interests you, I think a check for one hundred dollars would help my memory, because it all happened so long ago that it's kind of fuzzy, plus there's the landlord who every single night threatens to throw me out if I don't pay up by next week, and surely you wouldn't want a sixty-eight-year-old man to have to sleep on a park bench, in a nook at the ruined castle, or in the stairwell of some building, getting my backbone royally screwed, and with winter just around the corner. It's not even an honorarium, no sir, I wouldn't consider it, it's a loan, give me your address and as soon as I have an income I'll repay you, I'm in the process of setting up a correspondence course in hypnotism, all I need is some capital to print the lessons, the illustrations are what's expensive. It's a guaranteed profit maker, people send in money and I send back lessons for them to while away their evenings, wearing a turban with a ruby on their forehead, making magnetic hand movements and giving orders to their families, "Wake up," and with a little luck they'll succeed in floating off their balconies, just imagine dozens and dozens of people flitting around, and the husbands desperately shouting, "Come back here, Alice," as their wives glide toward Spain like ducks in the fall, while I, with ever more disciples, open up branches in Covilhã and in Avintes, for example, or in Viseu, think of the whole town of Viseu lifting off the ground and flying to Morocco, imagine Portalegre or Caldas da Rainha cruising toward London, you can write down that hypnotism is the transportation of the future, and besides, everyone loves to get special offers in the mail, to open up an envelope and find a man in a suit pointing his solemn finger and indignantly asking WHAT ARE YOU WAITING FOR TO BE HAPPY? THANKS TO PROFESSOR CHEOPS' HYPNOTISM COURSE, I BECAME A MAN OF SUCCESS. And speaking of hypnotism, what would go well after that sandwich is some carrot soup and a steak, because I feel suddenly weak.

But to get back to the point, yes, I recognize the face in that photo, who would ever have guessed that a hundred dollars plus lunch would revive my memory, now if you'll lay a five-dollar bill on the table I promise I'll dig him up, it's just a matter of leafing through the past, because my memory, you see, is like a scrapbook, I'll flip through and find the right page in a jiffy, show me his picture again, hmmm, he must go way back, can't you give me a hint? because he doesn't seem to be from my childhood, where what I see is a beach in the Alentejo, at Odemira, in August, with my mother limping to the clothesline among the aloes, she has a laundry basket in her arms, and the waves, ah, the waves reverberating in the incredibly blue sky, my mother reflected upside down in the clouds, hanging up long johns, my sister in the baby carriage, my father in a frame on top the buffet, with neatly combed hair and a tie, and a huge silence over the fields as far as the mountains. And the tavern, and the priest, and the houses in winter, sad and pallid in the rain, and stray dogs ranging the empty streets with their noses pressed to the ground, as if searching for the pups that were taken from them.

No, your man doesn't figure in my childhood, I never played with him, and I left the Alentejo before I'd finished school, hold on, don't get upset, be calm, let's take a look through the postcards from when I came to Lisbon and lived in Marvila with my uncle who worked for Philips as a doorman, my uncle the fat widower, forever drunk, who lived with a dog in a sixth-floor walk-up next to the Tagus, and now and then he'd clutch the stair rail, gasping and heaving, and say "Take my pulse, young man, take my pulse this instant, get the nurse over here from the Polyclinic, I feel a thump in my chest, this could be adios."

Marvila, but in the lower part, please note, where there were streetcars, little vegetable farms, stone walls, old men playing cards on the sidewalk, and my uncle, loaded with wine, yelling at his own shadow, jumping and twirling around to escape it, stomping it under foot, saying "Let me go," or else sprawled out, sleeping it off, while I learned to be a clerk in a sewing shop, and the widower pocketed my entire paycheck, which wasn't enough for his brandies in the café, so he hocked the remaining furniture, none of which matched, a couple of wobbly tables and chairs without seats that he routinely flung down the stairs, my uncle whose wife had devoted her life to spiritism and, dead from a mystical illness she contracted from an angel, now wafted through the apartment, making the teapots rattle with her jittery breath. It's possible we'll bump into the man from your photo here, in Marvila, which at that time, 1930-something and just before the war with the Germans, was a hotbed of foreign spies who wore hats and gabardines with the collar turned up and knifed each other in alleyways. Marvila, Marvila, hmmm, don't worry, it'll come, I'll bet I find him in my memory's pictures of the recreation club dances, among garlands, balloons, and humorous sayings on the wall, or in the smiles of the excursion group, with box lunches in hand as they board the bus for Fátima. If your man wasn't one of the sorry souls whose breath stank up my uncle's apartment, and he wasn't murdered by an English secret agent on a corner near the Tagus, then we're sure to run into him where we least expect, such as under a cloudy halo chalking up a cue stick in the Oriental Pool Hall, tilting his head in preparation for his next shot, or perhaps snoring with a bottle in hand, propped against a barrel next to a dockside warehouse, among the beggars hawking lottery tickets that hung like accordions from their jacket cuffs, beggars who passed the time counting swallows on April mornings and rolling their trousers up to their knees to hunt for shellfish in the sand of Chelas. No, it's no use, he's not there, either. How about a rice pudding, my friend, to kill the taste of the steak? To locate somebody is hard work, I thought we'd have luck in that smoky pool hall where absolutely everybody used to hang out, and there were wicker chairs so that former champions, now with gout-twisted fingers, could watch the tournaments with nostalgic sighs, and absolutely everybody would set his cigarette on the edge of the table, lift his heel, revealing his checkered sock, and stretch across the green felt to make the decisive stroke with his cue, I'll have a little more cinnamon, please, that's enough, you never went there? No shark ever offered you a five-to-one advantage with an innocent smile, you never got a whiff of tobacco mixed with green felt beneath tarnished lamps? I keep flipping through faces but can't find the one you want, everything's out of focus, haven't you noticed? Could it be the nicotine, or the fog from the river that's just a quarter mile away? A vitamin-rich banana or apple would no doubt cure me of my myopia, hey look, don't move, look, that guy in the striped coat talking with an old codger looks just like your man, no? Farther back, next to the door to the toilet, same nose, same mouth, same chin, am I right? Sorry, you have a point, he's blond and stockier than the man in your photo. You know how it is, you get all confused when you want something really bad. It's like when we're waiting for a woman and for some reason she's late (though women don't need any reason for not being on time); pretty soon all women start resembling the one we're impatiently waiting for, we greet complete strangers, then apologize, all embarrassed, and go back to leaning against the window of the clothing store, looking ridiculous, pathetic, and bewildered, with too many hands and not enough pockets, and that's the point we're at, my friend, hopelessly scanning Marvila's pool hall as the waiter behind the counter wipes glasses with a dirty cloth, whistling a stupid refrain.

But that guy, at any rate, is no stranger to me, I mean the blond guy talking with the codger who's wearing an overcoat and a cap and who won the three-cushion tournament of the Penha de França Sports Association in 1923, thanks to a monumental series of twelve cleanly sunken balls that's talked about to this day by people in the neighborhood. If you were born around here, then you surely remember it, even though you're younger than me, I'll bet your father told you about it, it made quite a stir, yes, the old man is undoubtedly Fausto Junior himself, the massé king, but I also recognize the blond guy, the one who's blowing his nose and sticking his finger into his nostril, how gross, you're right, here I am eating a banana and without any consideration he picks boogers from his nose and stares at us while the great Fausto Junior goes on about a complicated ricochet shot, that same guy, now in plain view at the third table, note his Clark Gable mustache, that guy, from whom the others keep a wary distance, was the one who got me a job at the state police a few months after the war. My uncle had recently passed away after throwing up a bunch of blood, and I was exempted from doing military service because of this defect in my hand, which meant I was living all alone in my spiritist aunt's apartment, a bit dazed by the whispering of the ghosts, and so, take note, it's no longer the great Fausto Junior who's talking to the guy with the mustache, it's me. The three-cushion champion has taken his chair to observe with disdain the dance of

the other pool players, and although I've changed, having gained
weight and a double chin, anyone would still recognize that it's
me, quiet and attentive, me propped on my cue stick next to
the scoreboard, me scratching my left leg with my right ankle
and biting my lip while the guy with the mustache, who rests
his palm on my shoulder and then around my neck, talks to me
in a low voice about the need to defend the nation, do you hear,
to defend the Portuguese, do you hear, to defend yourself, against
Russian invasions and tanks pouring in to destroy Odemira, to
level the pretty little pine trees on the square, to force everyone
to ride on tractors and plow stones in the fields, under the direction of traitors paid in rubles who are already conspiring, their
teeth as sharp as a vampire's, in cellars crawling with rats, vodka,
machine guns, lists of those (including me) condemned to die,
and pamphlets announcing God's funeral.

How about a coffee, sir? A coffee would surely facilitate my
digestion, which was ravaged by the swill at the prison fort of
Caxias, my intestines just won't work right, there are days I
agonize for hours on end in the john at the rooming house while
the turtledoves jeer in the window and the hookers who've just
gotten rid of their clients bang on the door, their bladders practically screaming, and I, hands pressed against the ceramic tiles,
beg my bowels to let loose into an orifice from whose depths
can be heard, as in a seashell, the gurgling of the river. The problem with Lisbon is that in every single neighborhood we bump
into the Tagus, as into a forgotten object: the Tagus that appears in the smallest of windows, the Tagus that rocks us in bed
with its tossing while we sleep, the Tagus and its nocturnal lights
that made my eyes smart when late at night I'd set out with the
mustached fellow and a couple of other co-workers to nab Communists in places where we didn't even suspect any, breaking
down doors and stumbling in the darkness toward a bed where
a frightened figure would try to get up while we searched the
bedroom, the living room, the bathroom, and the inside of the

toilet tank for weapons or a clandestine printing press, and finally we'd leave, with our victim swearing innocence and his family wailing from the doorway as we shoved him into a car parked on the sidewalk and manned by an agent wearing a cap and smoking cigarillos. And whether it was in Campo de Ourique or in Graça, whether in Alvalade, in Póvoa de Santa Iria, in Amadora, or in Benfica, whether at Cais do Sodré or in Barreiro, the Tagus was always there, with its marshes, its ships, its seagulls, and its geometry of masts, breathing beyond the last, nearly translucent row of houses. Mind if I ask you where you live? On the Rua da Madalena, near Martim Moniz, just past the shops with artificial limbs for the lame? Well, then you've noted, my friend, that there's not a restaurant around there where you don't hear the murmur of the river, where the windows don't wave in synch with the tides, where the premises don't crack from the impact of stiff currents, where the panes aren't startled by the flashing of the Bugio lighthouse. Lisbon, my friend, is a submerged city, the water closes over our heads, the clouds are just floating masses of seaweed, the mannequins of tailor shops are mermaids without heads dressed in Dacron or twilled wool and underlined with chalk where the buckram is stitched. And above all this, pure, whole, and clear, at a distance hard to measure or even to conceive of, above the coral of the rooftops, the crab dens lining the streets, and the steamship monasteries, past the mysterious algae in the trees and the eely depths of basement apartments inhabited by widows whose grief is shrouded in the wax flowers of their long-dead marriages, beyond all this, my friend, what I could use right now is a dish of plums to cool my coffee-scalded gullet, beyond all this, skirting without touching the TV antennas, the factory smokestacks, the castle ruins, and neighborhoods inhabited by canaries, functionaries, and majors, there's the Milky Way that flies away, blending in with the land around Alverca, where the river transforms into iron-smelting flames and cement factories.

Relax, don't lose your temper, I swear I'm doing the best I can, but that's how memory is, it has its own laws, its own rhythm, its own whims, we're bound to meet up with the guy when we least expect it, some place in the past, perhaps in the secret police post of Daman, where they stationed me to hunt out Communists in the monsoons, but there was nobody there except for the inspector and half a dozen mulattos that the storms hadn't carried off, or perhaps in Póvoa de Varzim, where I was promoted to being a second-class agent who rubber-stamped reports and listened to the rain, but no, I never ran into anyone there with this particular face, not in the street, not at the cinema, and not in the casino where the whirling roulette wheels were reflected in the stalactite lights, nor do I remember your man from the joke of a hotel in Ericeira, where they sent me and two co-workers, disguised as traveling salesmen, to keep an eye on an albino mechanic who participated in the strike at Marinha Grande, a hapless fellow who took refuge behind oil drums and stacks of tires to protect himself from the sun, a deserted hotel, sir, perched on the cliffs and inhabited by two old women, a little boy, and a crow that thought he was a sailor, strutting over the floorboards and squawking, "O Almerinda, my little whore, toss that shit overboard," in a rage suggesting an incurable toothache. When was that, you ask? Let's see, that must have been, no, I can tell you exactly, let me think, it was about 1949 or 1950, if I'm not mistaken, yes, it was 1950, right after I had a little problem with my superiors because of a democrat who died while being interrogated, I didn't do anything, just asked him some questions, and boom, he dropped dead on the floor, with his teeth bashed in and blood squirting from an ear. The medic, shaking his head, said "Next time don't leave any marks, just apply some electric shocks inside the mouth, they're harder to detect than punches," then the assistant director called me into his office, saying "Use your brain, for God's sake, if you finish all these guys off, we'll be out of a job," and since this incident happened just one week after another Socialist I'd been questioning jumped out a window, merely because I hadn't let him sleep for three days, I was banished to Ericeira with the mission of spying on the albino without laying a finger on him, because we already have more than enough martyrs. A real maniac, he liked to walk in the rain on afternoons when the agitated waves, spitting up birds, would climb the cliffs, reaching as high as the hotel balconies, while I and my co-workers stayed in our room writing memo after memo: "Today he spent all afternoon in front of his garage with nothing to do," "Today at five-thirty he patched a tire tube and cleaned the carburetor of the jeep from the National Guard," we were sick to death of the crow, the bad weather, and the two old women who harbored the illusory hope of filling up the hotel with tourists, of enlivening the rooms with a flurry of guests shuffling down the hallways while the thunder cracked, and we hardly paid attention to the kid who, if he's still alive, must be in his forties and who played in the basement with the albatrosses forgotten by the equinox.

Who? The kid? You mean to tell me that the person you want to write about is none other than that toddler, or are you just pulling my leg? No? Well, he doesn't look one bit like your photo. So you're interested in the toddler, I'll be damned, a kid who never opened his mouth, at least I never heard him talk, and after the hotel owner's funeral, some relatives took him to Lisbon and I never gave him another thought until now, which is only natural, he was just a kid and I had other things to think about, you know how it is, I remember how afraid he was of everything, how he never smiled, how he ate alone, I remember him staring out the window at the trawlers that would run up on the beach, just a dumb kid, my friend, and here I was trying to recall the albino when what you were interested in was the kid. No matter how good of a nose I have, tell me how on earth I your humble servant could possibly find his trail based on a photo of him as an adult, and how about ordering me a caramel pudding with lots of sauce, because this has rewhetted my appetite, incredible, just tell me where he lives and this old slyboots will discover everything you want to know for a reasonable fee, the correspondence course in hypnotism can sit on the shelf for a few months, whoever wants to fly can wait, I've had it with being broke, with your dough I can pay the rent on my room and have enough left for half an hour of oblivion with one of the sweetest, warmest girls at the rooming house, a homely chick, one of the least popular, one who's suffered, and it wouldn't even be to make love, to hell with love, it's that I desperately need an excuse to be able to cry, to lean my anguish into her neck and cry, to get away from the prison fort of Caxias, from the creaking of the latches and soldiers' footsteps on the other side of the door, to get away, my friend, from the tanks of the Revolution, from people slapping me around and weeks on end of sleeping wherever, in stairwells, in freight trucks, or on benches in Santana Park listening to beetles cracking open their eggs and swans whining like children with fever, give me a couple of crisp notes and I'll bring you the biography on this character, my dear boy, excuse me for calling you boy but you're young enough to be my son and I don't stand on ceremony, so what do you say, next week we can meet back at this restaurant, and as you calmly eat your steak I promise to give you the lowdown on this guy from front to back and back to front, today I'll spend some of your money on one of the kittens at the rooming house, I'll get my hair cut, shave my beard, take a shower at the public bathrooms by the Water House, buy a fancy shirt, button the collar, and any of the kittens will have me, I'll just knock on the door and "Hi there, come on in," and as for you, boy, finish the pudding because I've had enough, and enjoy the shade of the trees, enjoy the pigeons, enjoy the turtledoves of São José Hospital, the turtledoves of the morgue, enjoy the buildings down below and the mishmash of dockside cranes

and containers that stand high over the silhouette of the riverbank. And if you see an adult with a turban who floats in the
air without getting stuck in the gutters, you can be sure it's
not one of my students, who, since they're taught by me, migrate
like storks and ducks in autumn sailing, in huge flocks, toward
the sun.

3

Sometimes, Yolanda, when at last the bell of the grade crossing stops ringing, the dogs of Hyacinth Park—attracted by the smell of fish—race to the river, the trawler engines hush as dawn approaches, and in the silence of our apartment I can hear the diligent lacework of woodworms,

sometimes, when I realize it's morning in the faint amber of the empty mirrors, plowed by the night's tears, when your body, under the sheets, emerges from the darkness like August's stuffed chairs in a deserted house, and your nose and shoulders—born from the shadows—resemble dead corollas on the pillow,

sometimes, my love, when day has finally arrived, the alarm clock's going to ring, your father's slippers drag across the floor, rattling the cupboards, and he drinks a glass of water at the kitchen sink, while your aunt moves like a chrysalis, getting dressed in her bedroom,

sometimes, when I just lie on the mattress, silently cursing the story I tell, mere seconds before the clock will yell at me to go to work,

it can happen that I hate you

forgive me

the way our downstairs neighbors hate each other, a couple of retirees who trade insults through clenched teeth in a pandemonium of pots and pans and whom I visited one Sunday after lunch (by order of your aunt, who helps out everyone but me) to unplug a toilet with a piece of stiff wire in an apartment submerged by things, with stuffed weasels nestling on top the cupboards and a canary trilling in front of a lettuce leaf on the enclosed balcony. Squatting amid the ceramic tiles and fishing seaweed out of the toilet bowl, I could feel the old couple behind me, mutually whispering resentments through their decayed incisors, and as I flushed to test the result of my efforts, I thought I discerned, out of the corner of my eye, fingers reaching around to strangle a neck and a screwdriver boring into a thigh, jabbing straight through the terry cloth of a bathrobe. The water overflowed from the bowl in an explosive whirlpool, flooding across the living room carpet, and the couple, forgetting about eviscerating each other with ice tongs and fish knives, turned their fury against me, who with soaked knees tried to stanch the toilet tank's hemorrhage with the washcloth from the bidet. I remember slipping on the floor and falling into a rising pool, which carried away a stack of magazines to the bedroom, I remember a coffee table full of pewterware that began to pitch like a ship at the mercy of the waves, I remember the retirees up to their waists in slime and beside themselves with rage, and I remember being clobbered with a broom all the way out the door and onto the stairs, my ankles covered with low-tide debris (broken baskets, soleless boots, bottle shards, canned food, and decaying jellyfish), until I anchored in the apron of your aunt, who watched me from upstairs with arms crossed, shaking her head in disgust. Even today, my love, they talk in Alcântara of the furniture in an apartment on Rua #8 that decided to depart, one Sunday afternoon, for the Tagus River, taking with it a dinner service featuring Chinese landscapes and a government civil servant shacked up with a high school student who struggled in terror.

In the house where they took me after my godmother's funeral there were no old couples who hated each other, no pewter bibelots, and no stacks of old magazines. It was located at No. 3, Calçada do Tojal, a long, long ramp that in those days vanished amid farms and beehives (an apian buzz hovered in the air, and the day was veiled by wings) and wisteria branches that spilled over crumbling garden walls, scraping the sidewalk with their purplish clusters. Forty or fifty yards from the house stood the palm tree of the post office, and a little farther on, toward the Benfica Gates (a pair of play castles topped by time-corroded sentry boxes), the house where a bearded man played violin, making it shriek with the cruel cutting of his bow. A few months ago, on some holiday or other, I waited for a bus next to a defunct cinema at Arco do Cego and rode back to my childhood, through unfamiliar streets flanked by identical, opaque buildings, not one of whose facades I recognized, until I reached a neighborhood populated by beauty parlors and dentists' offices. Lost among street corners, I couldn't find the palm tree or the garden walls with wisteria, the buzzing of bees didn't darken the sky, ten-story buildings had swallowed the farms or else grown out of the strawberry bushes and cabbages gleaming with the blue drool of snails. After walking for miles around buildings flaunting their electric cables, I finally found a sign next to a dressmaker's shop that announced Calçada do Tojal, and yet, Yolanda, not even the ramp exists anymore—it was flattened by gigantic bulldozers. In its stead there were balconies enclosed by glass and aluminum, windows covered by aluminum blinds, and an old man walking a dog that raised its paw to the cars in the traffic circle. And I rode back to the cinema at Arco do Cego feeling like a man without a past, born already in his forties on a seat in a bus, inventing for himself the family he never had in a part of the city that never existed. And so last night, when I was telling you about my aunts, the horrid thought occurred to me that I was lying to you, inventing a nonsensical plot out of the absence of relatives and voices from my past. And I sank into the pillow, overcome with despair, ashamed of myself, listening to the words you breathe in the sheets, in conversation with a reality that I don't have.

In any case, Yolanda, the house on the Calçada do Tojal of my memory, which throbs in the nights of Alcântara next to this river I hate, was a three-story house preceded by a little gate of spears and a patch of lawn with bushes that shook their fragile limbs, and in the backyard there was a large birdcage with a lotus-shaped arabesque where a fox with suffering eyes pranced back and forth in unspeakable anguish. Years before I was born the landlord had divided the house in two: my mother's family occupied the left side, which faced the palm tree at the post office, while the right side was inhabited by a magician with a slew of children that issued from his hat—already in their teens—by a mere snap of the fingers. Every August, dressed in a tuxedo plastered with ribbons and medals, the artist traveled with a circus in the provinces, and I was astonished by the sight, right there on the Calçada, of a caravan of colorful trailers, cages with roaring lions and protruding necks of giraffes, jugglers tossing striped balls into the air, and clowns that waved good-bye to me with their unending gloves. The magician's wife, surrounded by children, waved farewell to her husband from the fence as the circus band played a festive two-step, and in the absence of the magician the children kept being born, issuing from her womb to the sound of a drumroll, with each new arrival walking immediately, math book in hand, on the way to school.

I never visited the magician's house, which was no doubt taken up by sheets of newspaper rolled into cones and containing all the flags in the world, by ropes whose knots would untie and retie with a flick of the wrist, and by star-studded boxes used for enclosing elegant women who, after half a dozen magnetic maneuvers, would pop out smiling from a different box. I was terrified of the supernatural, and when I was alone I thought I could sense, through the wall that separated the two halves of the building, a diabolical smell of sulfur and an audience clapping at some sort of trick, whose secret teetered on the dangerous line between miracle and sin. And so I felt more at ease on the side that my mother's family lived: rooms and halls wrapped in arid shadows and inhabited by photos of army officers, prints with galloping horses, and clocks with copper pendulums, chiming irregular hours, as if time dragged from fatigue around the ornate dials.

The first thing I noticed at the Calçada do Tojal was the absence of the sea, replaced by the trees' rustling and by the climbing plants softly ringing their tiny bell-flowers. A silence smelling of Siamese cats and lace doilies stagnated in the hall-ways, rising out of the vases whose water was never changed, and rays of light appeared from under the doors, revealing the pattern of the rug in the hall on the second floor, where the bedrooms were, each with a dresser, a mirror over the dresser, and a smell of crackers and lime-blossom tea. In the middle of the hall was the stairway leading to the attic, where I wasn't allowed to go, and the light from the ground floor died on the steps in a scattered dust.

Here in Alcântara, Yolanda, far from the palm tree at the post office and the farms whose wooden fences climbed all the way to the cemetery, the size of the windows and the breathing of the river prevent the darkness from instilling its threats, its secrets, and its whispers in these rooms that are waiting for the flood to take them downriver. But at the other end of town, where only the houses' chimneys could act as masts and only green beans rippled, in tiny homegrown waves devoured by hungry caterpillars, everything seemed huge to me—huge and strangely heavy, like a surprise or a dream. That, at least, is how I remember my life forty years later, now that I've grown up, have wrinkles, and my mouth glides over your neck without hazarding a kiss, now that my hands hug your waist and I feel your ribs expand and contract with your breathing, like fan ribs joined by the folds of your muscles. That is how I remember my life in the house of my mother's family, with my aunts, my uncle, and the pictures of army officers sporting spurs and whips on top the mantels, staring at me with a harshness that the years have attenuated. After dinner my uncle would take me to the pastry shop opposite the church, and while drinking lemonade I watched him talk with his bronchitic friends, who spat out their lungs into handkerchiefs in between sips of coffee. The kegs of beer emitted sighs in which the pressure of the gas fizzed. A group of painted ladies wearing artificial pearl earrings fussed with their hair around a pot of tea, and my uncle, smoking a cigarette, winked at them while puffing up like a pigeon in his enormous vest. We would end up following the trail of their perfume, and it happened once that one of the ladies, married to a veterinarian who worked in Santarém, drew away from the others while buttoning up her coat and began to walk slowly down the Estrada de Benfica, past bakeries and sewing shops, with her high heels digging into our panting chests like nails. My uncle's cigarette pointed like a harpoon at her buttocks, his elbow kept stabbing my kidneys, and I swear it's not an exaggeration, Yolanda, to say we could hear, coming from the Calçada do Tojal, the two-step of the circus band and the laughter of the clowns calling the magician to join them in their trailers, so that they could depart with the sad giraffes and the rug-worthy lions, raising the dome of their tent in forgotten villages. A little ways before the Benfica Neighborhood Council the lady from the café entered a building and switched on the hall lights, my uncle pulled on my sleeve and quickened his step, making his soles squeak, the two-step grew louder as the trombones joined in, and we found ourselves in front of her building, winking at each other and pushing on the door, when the caravan of circus trailers rolled down the street, just a few yards away from us. A lion tamer with a derby hat and a whip was perched on one of the cages, and the children rode on one-wheeled bikes, tracing complex figures on top of the ticket booth as hoops flew in the air. The car in front, which carried the ringmaster and was covered with signs, braked with a loud screech, and the vehicles all came to a dead halt, releasing balloons that got caught in the plane trees or else evaporated into the night. The giraffe probed the darkness with its neck for an antenna, while on a flatbed truck the band, led by a maestro who flogged the clarinets with his baton, switched to a soft, romantic waltz. And then, Yolanda, the magician jumped out of the fifth or sixth trailer, pulling aces and rabbits from his pockets, and ran to the entrance where my uncle and I were standing; the veterinarian's wife, trembling amid the potted plants on the stairs, let her coat drop to the floor and stood there almost naked while the midgets clapped; the magician, followed by a purple spotlight, climbed the stairs and took her in his arms; she, hanging on to his shoulders, raised her hand with a swirl like a trapeze artist at the end of her act; they climbed on to the truck of the bearded lady and the trained donkey that could tell the future; pajama-clad spectators, woken up by the music, threw streamers from their windowsills; at a sign from the ringmaster the caravan started rolling away to the luminous weeping of rockets, a rain of confetti, the yawning of tigers, and the tightrope walkers' gasps; the maestro began a military march, molding the notes with his fingers; and the caravan disappeared into the night until nothing was left on the street but an illusion of music, spotlights searching for artists who were no longer there, spectators shutting their windows to go back to bed dreaming of acrobats and trained dogs, and my openmouthed uncle and I all alone on the sidewalk, shaking off streamers the way you shake off my kisses when I dare to touch your cheek in an irresistible surge of affection. We stood there for a few endless minutes while the universe around us fell back into place. The circus lights, hanging like apples from the trees, slowly died out, and things resumed their customary, humble, everyday order. The streetlights returned, the sign of the bakery shop hiccuped in its fluorescent tubes, the first bat of the night attacked the moths flitting around the light over a tiny jewelry shop, my uncle lit another cigarette, declared in a voice that betrayed the bitter seeds of his disillusion,

"One thing there's plenty of in the world is women,"

and we walked back toward the Calçada do Tojal under a warm drizzle, until the sight of the bougainvilleas and the humming of the bees calmed my spirits. I was lulled to sleep by the hours of the clock and dreamed of the officers in the silver-plated frames, even as here in Alcântara, when I finally fall back against my pillow, next to your disdainful body, I dream of our wedding reception in a room full of your girlfriends, each one blowing a wad of gum into a pink bubble, while the karate champ slaps his friends on the back and your family, off to one side, commiserates in joint resignation.

Unlike my uncle, my two aunts, who taught catechism to boys pledged to a future as deacons, refused to frequent the pastry shop, which they regarded as a kind of antechamber to hell, full of lascivious men drinking mineral water while discussing women's bottoms and soccer. My aunts stayed at home, occasionally running a feather duster over the furniture but otherwise sunken in the shadows of the sofas, deaf to the barking of the fox that paced around its cage in anguished fright. They were both sisters of my mother, and neither had married. One of them, the older one, was called Dona Maria Teresa and never smiled, and if she were alive, Yolanda, she would disapprove of my foolish decision to live with you. But it's possible that the other one, Dona Anita, who went to fetch me in Ericeira and always worried about my colds, breaking into my room at every sneeze, as if propelled by a spring from downstairs, would have forgiven me with a wrinkling of her turtle nose, which ended in a two-pronged piece of cartilage. Perhaps not even my uncle would have approved, bothered by your diabetic's hyacinth-scented breath and by your daily need to test in the bathroom, with a cardboard strip, the color of your urine. And yet, darling, my decision wouldn't be affected by their opinion, because I love you, even as I'm not affected by the smirks of your girlfriends or the snickers of the waiters when we eat out, on Sundays, at the seafood restaurant by the traffic circle, where the crabs and crayfish bump into each other in an aquarium, their pincers bound by string and their glass-bead eyes rolling upward, just like Dona Maria Teresa's eyes when I asked her, several months after they'd brought me to Benfica, on an afternoon when she was spraying water on the plants to revive them, what had happened to my parents.

Even as today, Yolanda, your illness bewilders me with its fits of trembling, its fainting spells, its sweating, its scent of crushed flowers, and its intense, underground communication with death, aging you on the inside, as if your heart, your stomach, your liver, and other organs, ancient and rotten like those of heroes lying in crypts, were decomposing under the victorious youth of your skin, so too my parents, when I was a child in Ericeira and then at the Calçada do Tojal, were a complete mystery to me. No one ever mentioned them, there was no photo of them among the porcelain vases decorated with sycamore leaves, the officers in their frames and the silver-rimmed ovals with children on tricycles against a background of broom shrubs and plump grandmothers, and I imagined them living in Africa or in Macao, surrounded by Chinese in front of boats with vellum sails beached on a riverbank. When after dinner I lay in bed and listened to the Spaniard's sheepdogs, unable to sleep, I would hear in the wind the low tide of their voices giving me advice that I couldn't understand. Dona Maria Teresa would roll her lobster eyes in silence, Dona Anita complained I was too skinny and gave me cookies that tasted like chalk, and my uncle Fernando winked his eye at the ladies and talked about his brother Jorge, the major, arrested for conspiring against the government and imprisoned in Tavira, in a seaside barracks, where the foam dampened the sound of the bugles. I'm sorry that you, born in Mozambique the year of the Revolution, can't understand the time during my youth when on Sunday mornings men would don the uniform of the Portuguese Legion and march up and down Lisbon's streets. I'm sorry, since it separates you from me, that you never knew the processions, the anthems, the speeches, the cafés overflowing with uniforms that belted out war songs around tumblers of brandy, while functionaries of the state police took note of suspected Communists in their little memo books. Even Uncle Fernando, son of a hero who led a brigade during the monarchist uprisings, would lower his tone of voice and regard the agents with a kind of grudging respect, forgetting the ladies who gaped in awe, with toast in hand, at the medals of the patriots. Long before you were born, Yolanda, in a city of boas, blacks, and Protestant missionaries, Lisbon was a merry-go-round of proud and useless militiamen, hordes of canon priests, and Freemasons wasting away in prison forts, while I, wearing breeches and a beret, was learning the rudiments of war during school recess. Lisbon, darling, was masses on the radio, ubiquitous altars to St. Anthony, beggars and blind people's harmonicas on the street corners, in fact never were there so many blind people as then: blind people leaning against walls, blind people with accordions slung on their backs and feeling their way down the sidewalks, pitiful blind people outside chapels where the Blessed Sacrament was on display, blind fado singers accompanied by hustlers with sideburns who received donations, aggressive blind people who sold knick-knacks on church steps, blind people proudly holding their chin up at street crossings, blind women cuddling blind children who never cried, blind drunks zigzagging among the potted palms in taverns, blind people hovering in the air, like angels, hanging from open umbrellas, blind people and beggars and Gypsies in wooden carts worn out by the world's endless roads, in search of an empty lot for pitching their tent, but mostly just blind people staring at nothing with their cloudy pupils, thousands of blind people filling the lanes, the alleys, the squares, the grungy courtyards surrounded by the dark shops of cobblers and blacksmiths, blind people drinking water at the fountain for mules, blind people talking to each other in their world of shadows, blind people and beggars and Gypsies on the farms of Tojal, stealing the bees' honey, legionnaires and blind people and the ladies in the pastry shop and the secret police and the rallying cries of Sunday's patriots, and I asking my aunt, "What happened to my parents?" and she rolling her eyes upward, without interrupting her crochet, blind people fumbling at our gate or wandering across our lawn, having mistaken the address, and at that moment, Yolanda,

blind people

there was a tremor in the wineglasses, in the leaves of the houseplants, and in the tree of my blood as I heard for the first time

blind people

the sound of footsteps in the attic.

4

Hold on, calm down, wait a minute, friend. Before you get upset, look me straight in the face and tell me if you've seen anyone with a turban and a ruby on their forehead flying over Lisbon's rooftops. No? Well, that's because I completely neglected my correspondence course in hypnotism to dedicate this entire past week to investigating your man, questioning, spying, traipsing all over the place and taking photos, working full-time except for a couple of quick breaks with one of the girls at the Praça da Alegria Rooming House, a chubby girl the way I like, who helped me forget my griefs with specially priced caresses and a back massage, and at least half a dozen turtledoves, I kid you not, sang on the windowsill as they watched me convulsing in the tousled sheets like a tuna out of water. Her name is Lucilia and she has a wandering left eye. She's a mulatto who came from Angola on a boat of destitute victims fleeing from the civil war, and there's something in her, I'm not sure what, maybe it's her smell, that reminds me of the cotton fields before sunup, when the mist that hangs over native villages weighs on the trees as on a chair arm and the sunflowers turn their stalks toward the light. Speaking of which, I still owe her some money for the last time we were together because I ran out, "Sorry about that, Lucilia, I promise to pay up on Monday," and the roly-poly, lying on the bed smoking, with her left pupil having wandered off to the wall while her good eye smiled at me, said "Don't worry, Mr. Portas (Ernesto da Conceição Portas is my name), we're not going to let that spoil our fun, everyone has problems, just relax," and so give me a little more dough up front, friend, for this sweet but unlucky girl, exploited by a black pimp with headphones who every now and then, to show her who's boss, and I understand his point though I think he takes his arguments too far, smashes her face in, and I see the poor thing all bruised up, with stitches over her eyebrow and Band-Aids on her chin, limping among her co-workers on the Avenida, all vying for clients. Which is why, to tell you the truth, I didn't even feel like making love the last time we were together, because if my nerves get rattled just from her being cross-eyed, imagine how they react to the adhesive tape, the swelling, the purplish marks, a gash over her mouth, and so we just talked about this and that, she on her side of the bed and me on my side, I didn't even undress, while the turtledoves stared at us in bafflement, their foreheads pressed against the windowpanes. Lucilia explained to me that although she had a white girl's upbringing and finished the first year of high school, she'd ended up working in a bar in Carmona, with a fruitcake Italian at the piano, and I, in turn, told her about the workings of the state police, about how we risked our necks for almost nothing to defend national security, about the injustices I suffered because of the Revolution, which tossed me into the ranks of the unemployed, just like that, without any consideration for all my hard work, without so much as a measly pension, so that I quite frankly can no longer believe in gratitude, if in fact I ever believed in it, look around and all you see is indifference and selfishness, the way people have treated me, for instance, assaulting me on the street, insulting me, calling me a murderer and a scoundrel, spitting in my face, kicking me out wherever I go, leaving me homeless, penniless, friendless, with all my belongings in hock, and Lucilia, teary-eyed, because these hookers are all softies at heart when the right chord gets touched, said in a drippy voice, "It's just like in a movie," and pulled a pint bottle out from under the bed to get even more emotional, alcohol's good for tears, she offered me a sip of something that burned, and I spent half an hour hiccuping so hard it frightened the turtledoves until there were none left in the window, which filled up instead with the rooftops and gutters of the Praça da Alegria, and I thought I even saw a cousin of mine who's interested in levitation floating around the square of Príncipe Real, while my worried mulatto sweetheart lost no time in slapping me on the back, saying "Is that better, Mr. Portas? Is that better, Mr. Portas?" with one eye on me and the other, bizarrely indifferent, on the ceiling. She wanted to get up and fetch some of the other girls, but I motioned her not to bother, "Stay here, sweetie, where are you going?" and she continued to clobber my back while drinking from the pint bottle to calm down, so that by the time my hiccups had stopped and my breathing was back to normal, which seemed like an eternity, Lucilia had imbibed so much that not only did she talk sheer nonsense, she started belting out a French song in such a loud voice that her black pimp, alarmed, broke open the door, rushing in with four or five kinky-haired friends who wore tennis shoes, printed shirts, glittering rings, and brass bracelets and worked in construction, to judge by the dust on their trousers, so that I buttoned my shirt collar, straightened my tie, emitted a final hiccup that brought the memory of the alcohol to my tongue, and walked to the door with whatever dignity I could muster, keeping as far away as possible from the Cape Verdeans, who glared at me with their backs to the wall and without saying a word, and when I was already in the hallway, no longer under threat, I heard the first pedagogical punch, which must have hit her square in the teeth, for she immediately shut up, and then came a hailstorm of educational kicks, accompanied by a paternal scolding in a rudimentary Portuguese. Today after lunch, before coming here to meet you, I crossed paths with Lucilia in the lobby of the rooming house; no longer drunk, she had a bandage around her head, Band-Aids on her nose, a surgical collar around her neck, one of her legs in a cast, and bruises on her feet that caused her to walk with difficulty, supported by a crutch that curved into a bow with each step. She didn't look at me (it's hard for me to tell when a cross-eyed person is looking at me, and I usually shift from one eye to the other, undecided, searching for the midpoint between the two pupils), but I watched as she climbed the stairs to the fourth floor with the speed of a lobster, dragging a leg without any sound of complaint as she slipped out of sight. She was accompanied by the black pimp, who had his hands in his pocket and looked as if he were taking his crippled lamb to pasture. But perhaps one of these weeks, after the girl recovers from her injuries, I'll return to her room to lie on her bed and talk about what life has done to us, expelling her from the bar in Carmona, from the farmers' eager hands, and from the apartment she shared with the Italian who inundated the shelf in the bathroom with hair-coloring lotions, and transforming me, who slaved for thirty badly paid, life-threatening years for the sake of our country's welfare, into a professor of hypnotism by mail whose students can hardly get off the ground and who now sits with you at an outdoor café in Santana Park, where the swans begin to stir as evening approaches.

Have you noticed the shadows descending from the Archbishop's Palace, the branches of the plane trees merging into one mass, the pigeons migrating to nearby backyards, and the ambulance sirens emitting a different tone? You can write down that the sunset frightens me, friend. I've never been comfortable in the dark, I feel like turning all the lights on until morning arrives and to sit up in a chair, fending off sleep, which is why in the state police I volunteered for all the night jobs that my co-workers didn't want: interrogations, stakeouts, searches, guard duty, wiretapping, and interminable surveillances (using binoculars and a tape recorder) of couples who typed out pamphlets and communiqués or mimeographed circulars against the government, inciting insurrection among an alienated people that crammed into buses after a long day's work to return to outlying towns suffocated by factory smokestacks, any job, my friend, that would save me from darkness and its mysteries, which have oppressed me ever since childhood. And so I've learned over the years to sleep during the day, with the blinds raised to keep out the shade, with the turtledoves of the Praça da Alegria entering my room and perching on the dresser or on the bedposts, and I wake up with a splitting headache, with bird shit on the floor, and with a final feather hovering over my lips, waiting for me to stop breathing so that it can die in my mouth.

I know you're the one who's paying, you don't need to remind me, I'm getting there, I'll tell you all about your man, if you think that since last week's lunch I've spent my time on anything else, you're wrong. Have you found any leaflets about a hypnotism course in your mailbox, mixed in with the gas bill, the glut of political propaganda, and the letter from a cousin who immigrated to Luxembourg and complains about his harsh and insensitive boss? Of course you haven't, my friend, because I haven't sent any such leaflets to anyone, which proves, in case the honor of my word weren't enough, that I've even been shirking my duties as a professor since I started working for you, I haven't even gone to my post office box to pick up my students' queries and written exercises, and just think of the responsibility, imagine if one of my students foolishly makes his mother float in the living room and can't get her back down, with the distressed woman desperately trying to hook the console tables with the handle of her umbrella, demanding in vain that the family do something, her son using a stepladder to give her her lunch as the perverse daughter-in-law opens the door to the balcony, on the hope that the old woman will float away, protesting and calling for the police in the autumn of Campo de Ourique, or imagine a guy hypnotized only from the waist up, spinning around in a trance without being able to come to a halt, wearing out the carpet in a hallway in Telheiras. Teaching entails a lot of responsibility, especially for such a delicate topic as hypnotism, I feel terribly guilty for neglecting my disciples in order to work on your behalf for next to nothing, since what you pay me doesn't even cover expenses, and I've been spend-

ing twenty-four hours a day on this job, all because I took to
you, my bad luck was that I took to you, and it doesn't happen
very often, I can promise you, not with the guy in your photo,
for example, photos are so deceptive, you imagine a certain kind
of person that has nothing to do with the real article, who in
this case is a short guy with a large bald head, no neck, badly
dressed, employed by the National Tourist Office, where from
nine to five he numbers photocopies at a desk with no horizons
beyond the file cabinets. I think he's there only because they
forgot about him, his existence being so superfluous it's as if he
didn't exist, he could fall over, bam, from a stroke or a heart
attack, and his co-workers would keep right on reading the newspaper as if nothing had happened. As far as anyone can tell, he
never has adventures or gets into mischief, he hasn't even had
an affair with the switchboard operator, a tall platinum blonde
with the cigar of her headphones sticking out of her permanent,
at ten after five I saw him file away what he was working on,
place the photocopies in a wire basket, grab his coat from the
chair, and leave the building without using the elevator, without saying anything to anybody, without asking the guy at the
desk next to his to join him for a coffee before catching the sub-
way, and once outside, with briefcase and umbrella under his
arm, he waited at the bus stop for the bus to Alcântara, and all
the while I, who rode with him, enduring the same shoving, the
same trampling feet, and the same jolting traffic without him
ever recognizing me from Ericeira, I, who followed him to
Hyacinth Park, a subdivision of low-rent garden apartments with
numbered streets, I, who watched him step on a porch, push a
door, and disappear like a caramel when you get to the end of
it, kept asking myself why it is that you, a writer, a man who
sells novels, who appears on TV, and whose name is in magazines, are interested in a loser like that, a guy who lives on Rua
#8 in a crappy building undermined by vapors from the river
and by the sewer stench that peers through the holes in the wall

like an animal with nowhere to go. A dump on Rua #8, for Christ's sake, a hovel for pensioners and housemaids, with crumbling plaster and leaky plumbing, the gate off the hinges, a couple of honeysuckle bushes crying out for help to the ocean's indifference, minuscule windows, a washbasin where the water comes out in spurts, what do you want, young man, with a trash heap like that, are you sure your mind's working all right, what kind of book can you make out of a story like that when squalor's what this city already has too much of? Yesterday I dropped everything I had to do in order to catch the streetcar at Cais do Sodré, I rang the doorbell, flashed the corner of a card to the aproned woman who examined me from the doormat, and said I was a safety inspector for municipal apartments, "What kind of apartments?" asked the woman suspiciously, fearing eviction or a fine, "Municipal" I answered, stepping forward while the aproned creature stepped aside, and my eyes beheld a wooden hat stand with mother-of-pearl inlays, a 1965 calendar with an Austrian landscape and all the months intact that served to cover the water meter, a tiny sitting room whose chairs were arranged around a prehistoric television, bedrooms where I could make out only the bedspreads, and a patch of yard in the back, squeezed between two stone walls and containing a dozen lifeless vegetables and a walnut tree whose walnuts rattled with a melancholy sound. The woman observed me, trying to figure out which way my municipal temper was leaning as I studied the cracks in the ceiling and the fungus infection on the walls, as I checked the electric sockets and the insulation of the wiring, clicking my inspector's tongue, as I entered windowless rooms imbued with sweat, essence of cleaning products, and supermarket perfume, walking sideways to avoid stumbling on slippers and chamber pots and wondering what could possibly be interesting about poverty, what could possibly have led you to choose these embittered people, full of fear and the resentment of the hapless, from among the tens of thousands of embittered souls that inhabit this shitty town, in which the sun spangles the misery with a robe of light. I took my leave of the woman, who from the threshold kept repeating "You didn't find anything wrong, did you? You didn't find anything wrong, did you?" And I left Rua #8 of Hyacinth Park just as a passing locomotive shook the buildings' foundations and Alcântara looked as if it had been traced on the tissue paper of twilight by a pencil that piled up cornices, all galloping toward the Tagus. Near the Avenida de Ceuta I saw a dog in heat, a steamy mongrel bitch craved by a swarm of small and large, variously shaped and colored dogs, which jumped over one another, drooling with desire. I applied a swift kick to the bitch, which ran away howling, followed by the suitors that took turns trying to mount her, a little later I spotted them on a grassy slope, and as I arrived back at the rooming house it seemed as if I could again see the animals, on their way to Lapa, with the bitch slowly leading the way, carrying the burden of her nature, and the other dogs behind her, baring their teeth and stopping to urinate against park benches, it seemed as if I could see them trotting around Lisbon with wilted penises, the way you trot, if you'll excuse the comparison, after that booby in Alcântara, and the way I trot outside Lucilia's room, putting my ear to the door and seething with jealousy when I hear her stimulatory sighs and the huffing and puffing of clients, either that or imagining her spasms of pleasure when the black pimp beats her up, the way I trot in a tizzy over a mulatto girl whose feet are covered with corns, I a grief-stricken man going on seventy and with high blood pressure making a complete fool of myself by getting worked up over a hooker who likes to get roughed up by the first guy who comes along, who wriggles with delight at each punch, who goes into a wild orgasm when her kneecaps get creamed, I, who when I worked for the state police had all the women I wanted, I just pointed my finger and presto, I even slept with a Communist gal, in a jail cell between two questions, and I didn't even have to suggest it, I merely asked "What are your contacts, young lady?" and she, brashly smiling with her hands on her thighs, "Come a little closer and I'll give them to you," and now I, an old man who's lost his patience and pep, agonizing over a slut who guzzles turpentine and rubbing alcohol and plies the street at night to round up customers, two dollars for every ten minutes, when I could be peacefully figuring out crossword puzzles or thinking about the gross wrongs I've suffered at the hands of socialism, I, who should be worrying about my students who forget their turbans and magnetic maneuvers, thereby condemning themselves to an unhappy earthly destiny, walking as you walk, young man, battering their feet against the pavement instead of gliding happily, weightlessly, whichever way the wind blows. For you and me, my writer friend, there's no hope, we're like the mutts wagging their haunches as they chase a bitch all over Lisbon, with the difference that I'm at least attracted to a woman, good or bad, whereas you're obsessed with a guy who's utterly and irremediably worthless and whom ninety percent of the population would pay not to meet, a washout who's pushing fifty and lives in a pigsty called Hyacinth Park, shacked up with a diabetic girl who shoots up insulin, is young enough to be his granddaughter, and thoroughly despises him, supporting her with a salary so pitiful God only knows how they make it to the end of the month, her and her father and the aunt who showed me their decrepit apartment while in the unit next door a couple I didn't have the pleasure of meeting argued in a loud swirl of insults, their decrepit apartment with a dinky backyard, the presence of the river behind the stone wall, the trains from Estoril and from Lisbon passing each other on the railway separating Alcântara from the embankment, I, my friend, meditating on all this without being able to grasp it, putting facts together, taking them apart, putting them back together, thinking, There's something here that escapes me, something that doesn't add up, what could possibly be interesting about the geek in the photo, about his diabetic sweetheart, about Hyacinth Park? And then, while shaving this morning before coming here to meet you, it suddenly dawned on me, and I stood stock-still in front of the mirror, which is actually just a piece of mirror, with shaving cream covering half my face, it dawned on me, with my razor in midair, that your man doesn't exist, that the walnut tree doesn't exist, that the father, the aunt, and Hyacinth Park don't exist, that not even Alcântara or the Tagus exist, it dawned on me that you paid me a few bucks to work on a bizarre mystification, that you invented this story for your book, confess it, that you obliged me to lose the time I owe myself and my students on a cock-and-bull story, and now who will compensate me for the problems I'm going to face because of haywire hypnoses? Who will defend me at court if people in Lisbon start disappearing? It dawned on me—and my bladder is about to burst, and I probably still have shaving cream in my ears, because I was so excited with the discovery that I didn't take a piss or wipe my face with the towel—that there are no turtledoves, that there is no Lucilia, no Praça da Alegria Rooming House, no black pimp, that there's no secret police, that there were no Communists, that my past never existed, nor Daman, nor my apartment in Odivelas, nor I myself, that this almost hamless ham sandwich I'm chewing on right now at this table doesn't exist, even as you don't exist, my friend the writer, and that we're meeting each other, take note, not in nonexistent Santana Park with its equally nonexistent peacocks, beggars, and lunatics, but suspended in a kind of limbo, talking about nothing, surrounded by rooftops and trees and people without substance, in an imaginary Lisbon sloping down toward the river in a chaotic precipitation of invented lanes and alleys.

5

Yesterday, Yolanda, when I took off from work to go with you to your appointment at the Association for Diabetics, and we left very early so as not to miss the doctor

(so early that the river's night entered with its ship lights into the city's day),

yesterday, as we walked toward the traffic circle of Alcântara to get a taxi, it seemed that morning was vying with the shadows on the wall along the Tagus and that it was just possible we would see a trawler drifting down the street, with the captain at the helm and the light in the stern reflecting off the asphalt,

even as it was possible that the apartments in Hyacinth Park were sending plaster roots into the water,

and I loved you for letting me live with you in the miracle of a sunset or a sunrise, the seaweed tangled in the trees and the tankers looming like cathedrals, with saints, candles, and altars in the hold, and the notes of a Gregorian chant rising with the fumes out of the enormous smokestacks. I loved your narrow shoulders, your nose that was runny with a cold, your voice that got cross with me, your skinny legs beneath your raincoat, I loved your body's fragility and the way you walked, bent forward by the February wind, and I loved

forgive me

your disease, which gave me the chance to accompany you, in Lisbon's early hours, as if we were a couple, although you blamed me for your cold and the lack of public transportation, although you demanded I find a taxi in the fog that had diluted the automobiles and you shouted that you hated me as your eyes flashed with fever and your eyelids blinked above the fringe of your scarf. I ran around the traffic circle in search of a cab, prevented from crossing by the buses that kept coming off the bridge with a wag of their haunches, and as I gesticulated I remembered the consternation of Dona Maria Teresa one afternoon, many years ago, on the Calçada do Tojal,

(and on that morning in Alcântara, indifferent to your ire, my childhood rose before me, as the bones of martyrs rise from their graves)

when the fox escaped from the birdcage, crossed the gravel path, entered the house barking, and knocked over the little tripod tables with military engineers that were photographed in France during the war and that fell onto the floor without protest, staring at us with their frozenly heroic eyes.

The fox, helplessly yelping and not knowing what to do, scurried into the living room in a whirlwind of fur, and my aunts, busy knitting doilies in worn-out armchairs by the faint light that entered through the curtains, stood up in unison, using their needles to shoo away the animal, which bumped into a pendulum, setting off a hailstorm of carillons and hiccups of cuckoos, and finally, Yolanda, after you'd sneezed for the third time, pulling Kleenex from your purse, there appeared a green taxi light sailing in the traffic circle behind a hearse, and I, eager to please, oblivious of the traffic, skipped across the asphalt, threatened by splashboards, horns, and insulting expletives, the fox turned around in a circle, dragging with it a tablecloth and a porcelain vase that shattered on the floor, the taxi stopped next to us, its hood trembling as you opened the door and called me an imbecile, blaming me for future pneumonias, warning me at the top of your voice, "Don't you dare touch me," and you plopped into the car seat, blowing your nose, Dona Anita ran over to the tablecloth to try to save a silver shell and a crystal heart but tripped on the heater cord and grabbed on to a chair that fell on its side like a stiff corpse, you pulled on your clothes, saying, "Your rear end is crumpling my raincoat, dummy," delivery vans ironed by the fog passed us without letup, the stoplights wavered in the brume, the sewer smell increased, and from the lowing of boats

I could tell the river was close by, a second chair fell onto the rug that turned round thanks to the fox, the heater began burning a set of curtains that writhed, scattering ashes across the floor, "A bucket of water," pleaded Dona Maria Teresa, afraid that the majors on top the chests of drawers would go up in flames. "Sorry," I answered, raising my buttocks while closing the door where my overcoat had gotten caught, Dona Anita, sitting on the ground, groped for her glasses, and the fox snuck up to the second floor, already homesick for the cage out back and the garden wall from where one could see, in the evening, the flocks on the heights of Tojal, tended by shepherds who talked with their sheep in a language of whistles. A column of cars squawked behind us, and in the dissipating fog that unveiled streets, apartment buildings, and a café whose metal blinds were being rolled up, I discerned, toward the Avenida de Ceuta, a policeman's glove motioning as the lighthouse snored, the car engines roared, and the fox's paws slipped on the steps,

"So where to?" asked the driver impatiently while drumming the wheel with his fingers.

"Well, that's just great, you wrinkled my skirt," you complained while exhibiting a piece of the fabric, "I'll be a wonderful sight at the doctor's."

The charred curtains lifted off their hooks and flew around the room, strewing carbonized shreds, while the heater began devouring the rug under the dining table, which was graced by a tray of bananas and oranges that no one ever touched, but at close range we felt their swooned odor. Dona Maria Teresa went up the stairs in pursuit of the fox, and Dona Anita, who had found her glasses, less one of the lenses, contemplated the military officers with an infinite desolation, oblivious of the heater that burned one after another of the rug's swirling figures, listening to the gentle rustle of leaves soothed by the night's arrival and the absence of harsh winds. The cars behind us turned on their headlights, the policeman's glove, with a whistle between the thumb and index finger, became frenetic, and the scattered fog revealed new streets, streetcar tracks, and a hint of color in the chimneys and rooftops.

"To the Association for Diabetics, we need to be there before nine," I told the driver, who was already sick of us and who shifted in his seat, making apologetic gestures to the policeman. "If we miss the appointment, we'll have to wait at least two more months."

"At least the pictures of Dad weren't broken," said Dona Anita by way of consolation while picking up shards. "At least nothing happened to the photos from Verdun."

"The Association for Diabetics, you should have told me right away," sighed the driver while shifting into a despondent gear and merging, on the clear morning that echoed with soft hues as the last cloud slid toward Algés, into the shoal of vehicles that moved around the traffic circle, where the policeman's glove could no longer locate him. "If I get fined because of you, you'll be sorry."

The sun grazed the palm tree at the post office, one of the heater coils, exhausted from chewing up wool, broke with a loud pop, losing its red glow, Dona Anita, who because of the missing lens cocked her head to the left, like a one-eyed toucan, was taking inventory of the shards with the tip of her shoe, from upstairs came the sound of the fox's scurrying, of small shrines crashing to the floor and pulverizing terra-cotta martyrs, and of Dona Maria Teresa shouting "Call the Legion and get Fernando over here fast, before the critter decides to go up to the attic," but we passed the policeman without his glove (preoccupied with a moped crossing the roadway) taking notice of us and cruised toward the Praça da Espanha with our backs to Alcântara's trains and the Tagus's ships, the sound of the lighthouse died out, and we were greeted by domiciles without walls, then a shantytown. Billboards on both sides of the road streamed past us, and your angry profile traveled through the bleakness of Lisbon—cinemas, shops, garages, and buildings all glaring with bad taste—without ever looking at me. The driver kept illegally switching lanes to get around trucks, and Dona Anita, heeding her sister's words, dashed to the phone, which sat on top the directory and a notebook with the phone numbers of the butcher, the seamstress, and the baker, while a Saint Expeditus tumbled down the stairs, losing a limb with each bounce, and I tried to find the words that could excuse me for having wrinkled your dress, for having crumpled your raincoat with my rear end, for constantly disturbing your life with my ineptitude, and after a half an hour or less, Yolanda,

as the sun slid down the palm tree and the inside of the house looked more and more like a bombed city, in spite of the resistance put up by the colonels from the trenches of their tortoiseshell and silver-plated frames,

I heard boots marching up the gravel path that separated the gate from the front door, I heard voices, coughs, orders, a key fighting with the lock, and Uncle Fernando, dressed in his legionnaire's hat, riding boots, spurs, and a drawn pistol, appeared in the living room with a dozen rifle-carrying militiamen, who paid their respects to Dona Anita, engaged in trying to reconstruct a plaster of paris Molière, and then scattered throughout the rooms, shooting at random in search of the fugitive fox. The driver, after insulting a streetcar whose trolley wheel had slipped off the wire, leaving it stranded in the middle of an intersection, stopped the taxi and turned off the meter in front of the Association for Diabetics, where a bevy of patients, rubbing their hands in the cold, were gathered at the entrance, and I reached my hand into my pocket to pay, felt nothing, and realized that in our haste I'd left my wallet at Hyacinth Park. All I had on me were a few coins mixed up with slips of paper and boxes of matches in the pocket of my overcoat. You grabbed the door handle to get out of the car, the cabdriver waited, taking notes on a pad, one of the militiamen's shots hit the dining room lamp, which shattered on the floor, Uncle Fernando told the patriots, "That's enough roughhousing, the animal's upstairs," water from a pipe started gushing from behind the drapes, drenching the rug and spreading toward the kitchen tiles, and the driver calmly laid his pad of paper on the dashboard, turned, and said in a compassionate voice:

"So you forgot your wallet, right?"

The diabetics filed through the front door of the Association, which was squeezed between buildings undergoing renovation, a woman with a white coat and cap peered out a window, and I, while rechecking the contents of my pockets, imagined offices full of surgical instruments, pads for writing prescriptions, and shabby desks, waiting rooms crammed with people and a No Smoking sign taped to a bulletin board, microscopes, guinea pigs, Bunsen burners, and throughout the whole building, in the doctors' offices, the waiting room, the laboratory, the hallway, and especially in the bathrooms, the diabetic scent of chrysanthemums, penetrating the brick and mortar through cracks in the plaster. And it occurred to me, love, that there are times I'm not with you—at work, on my lunch break, in the lobby, in the middle of rubber-stamping photocopies, or on the bus going home—when I find your chrysanthemum odor on my body, in my clothes, or in my breath, and I feel so close to you it's as if I lived in you, my desire for you is so strong it's as if you were my only nourishment, my nation, my city, my home, as if your blood lit up my voice and I walked, in Hyacinth Park, guided by the incense of your eyes, toward a young female's breast that awaits me. The driver cracked an endlessly wide smile:

"And you naturally have no identification on you, am I right?"

At these times, Yolanda, and only at these times, when my fifty years retreat and for a while I'm free, easygoing, nimble, confident, strong, unafraid, secure, then my life acquires a morning freshness, a taste of August, a texture that soothes, mellows, and justifies me, so that my nerves relax and I can sleep, not in the nest of your affection but at least in your willingness to have me there, lying at your side without pain or torment, as under the sycamores' shower of shadows in summer, breathing the sweet smell of chrysanthemums.

"So I give you my address, and this afternoon you'll run right over to Cabo Ruivo to pay what you owe, is that it?" asked the cabdriver, who by now had turned completely around and had his hand on my knee, squeezing my bones. "You have no ID to prove who you are, but I can rest easy, because as soon as I get home the first thing I'll find is an envelope with my money and a tip waiting for me in my mailbox, because you're the most honest person in the whole wide world, is that the idea?"

The diabetics, wearing long sad coats, continued filing into the Association for their appointments, a fellow with a bow tie leaned into the window and asked "Are you free?" and the legionnaires quit firing at the India Company tureens and the military photos to dash up the stairs behind Uncle Fernando, who yelled, "Keep the critter from going up to the attic, keep the critter from going up to the attic," brandishing his pistol that distended and recoiled, pulverizing the plaster flowers that trimmed the ceiling.

"Whether I'm free or not," answered the driver without loosening his grip on my knee, "depends on this joker."

A wardrobe fell to pieces until it finally landed against the arch in the living room, reduced to a heap of boards and wire and wooden hangers. Someone turned the crank on the gramophone, which played the Italian national anthem in a version full of wrong notes, the boots ran back and forth overhead, another wardrobe suicidally hurled itself down the stairs, a voice shouted, "That son of a bitch fox bit me," and the driver, who was crushing my cartilage, suddenly stopped smiling:

"You have thirty seconds to quit with the shenanigans and pay up. And you, little girl, can keep quiet, because the matter's between me and your daddy."

"He's not my father, he's my godfather," you said with a mixture of rage, distress, and shame, as your breath made the backseat smell like a funeral parlor. And I instantly shrank in size, offended in my love for you, holding it tight against my chest like a gift no one wants.

"Godfather and goddaughter, how charming," declared the driver while wringing my thigh muscles and using his free hand to rummage for his cigarettes and lighter on the dashboard. "Well, listen up, little girl. If your old man doesn't cough up what he owes, we're going straight to the police station, and maybe the chief can even marry you."

The music from the gramophone became so shrill that it drowned out the shouts, the shots, my aunts' and uncle's fear that the fox would slink up to the attic, and the rage of the legionnaires in the hallway. The house shook with the anthem's base drums, Dona Anita, whose bun was coming undone, seemed to move to the drums' rhythm, the heater was liquefying a papier-mâché doll, patriotic reinforcements burst through the door with bayonets that destroyed whatever photos were left, the doctors examined X-rays and blood samples while the nurses filled syringes with insulin, the patriots went up and down stairs with grenades dangling from their belts, the man with the bow tie, playing along with the cabdriver, suggested the justice of the peace for the wedding, and amid all the confusion Uncle Fernando, with his legionnaire's cap resting on his nape, appeared in the living room holding the fox up by its tail, and I backed away in fright, to the corner cupboard with glasses and goblets, confronted by the nothing in its eyes.

Yolanda, darling, my life's only Sunday, I love you. I love you and understand, I dare to presume I understand, your impatience and your fits of anger, your intelligence alternated with stupidity, listlessness with impetuousness, innocence with malice, your refusal to talk, your childish whims, your aversion to me. My age and my bone spurs are like a wall between us that keeps you from appreciating me, separated as we are by years of experience and fears we never shared and can never share. And yet, my love, I understand so well when in the evening your face darkens, becoming veiled, when you sit at the table in a grouchy mood to eat your aunt's chicken or bream, when you toss down your napkin, push back your stool, and lock yourself in your room without explaining or excusing yourself, staring at the river beyond the trains, the seagulls, and the cranes whose metal arms stand out so distinctly in the falling night.

Yolanda, I love you. I love how you transform the prohibition against sweets into a personal decision, a proud resolution. I love your pupils that are beginning to cloud over with cataracts, your kidneys that suffer in silence, the complaint of your pancreas. I love you with the infinite, enraptured commiseration of passion. I love you when you sweat in your sleep, and I drink every drop of you, my avid tongue passing over you pore by pore. My life, with its still unresolved anxieties and mysteries, with its childhood marked by the absence of my parents, the magician neighbor, and the attic where footsteps echoed, has ceased being an enigma for me since I met you, so that my past is as clear and vivid as yesterday's scene in the taxi, in front of the Association for Diabetics, which ended when a nurse came out, confirmed who we were, and lent us the money for the fare, to the great disappointment of the bow tie, who had hoped for bashed-in cheeks and billy clubs flying in the air. The past is so clear and vivid that I don't need to close my eyes to see, once more, Uncle Fernando descending the stairs holding the fox by its tail, followed by his band of rifle-carrying patriots, my aunts who died long ago from obscure maladies, the devastated house—without light, with water dripping behind the drapes, and with bullet holes in the walls—that has given way to a beauty parlor or a butcher shop, and the horn gramophone that is so very real I presume you must hear it whenever you suddenly stop speaking, your spoon suspended over the soup like a flamingo's foot over water, the gramophone that again plays the anthem with a fanfare of trumpets, sending waves of music over the shattered chests of drawers.

6

Be patient, my friend, I just didn't have time this week, but I
haven't forgotten your case, I swear, I was planning to work on
it twenty-four hours a day, and when I say twenty-four hours a
day I mean twenty-four hours a day, even if, as in this case, I'm
badly paid, I even bought a monthly bus pass to follow your man,
plus a tape recorder and a roll of film, here are the bills, the shopkeeper said there's no hurry, and right here in my pocket is a
list of the neighbors who need to be questioned because his relatives have all disappeared, so you can see I was full of good intentions, but lo and behold, that's how life is, you never know
what'll happen, my room was invaded by every turtledove in the
world, not five, six, nine, or ten, but dozens and dozens of them
filling my room, write it down on your pad, I opened the door
and heard a symphony of coos, I couldn't even see the bed there
were so many wings, beaks, bird eyes, bird feet, fanned tails, and
feathers that lifted and lowered without being blown on, my first
thought was to flee, to abandon my suitcase, toothbrush, and
clothing, turn the key in the door, run down the stairs to the
street, and not stop until I reached the ferry boats at Commerce
Square, but a woman's voice called my name from out of the
feathery confusion, and it was her, it was Lucilia, smiling at me
from the mattress, which was covered with dust and speckled
eggs, the black pimp had gone to his mother's funeral in Cape
Verde, and she was alone, imagine, free from having to work
the Avenida at night, alone and at peace, free from getting beaten
up, insulted, and shouted at, alone, Lucilia, my humble ideal
and dream sprawled out on my sheets, drinking her rubbing
alcohol and handing me the little bottle, and there were more
turtledoves on the windowsill, more turtledoves in the gutters,
and more turtledoves in the room, white and blue and gray

turtledoves, not the usual turtledoves of the Praça da Alegria, turtledoves strutting on the floor, on the seat of the only chair, on top of the only table, turtledoves on my mulatto girl's breast, her face, her smile, her thighs, turtledoves galore, my writer friend, calling me to the pillow where every morning I suffer the scourge of my colitis, turtledoves everywhere and Lucilia waiting for me, making signs with her pint bottle, sticking her tongue out at me, making faces that disarmed me, playfully mocking me, Lucilia, free of her pimp, waiting for me, talking with me, daring me, placing her thumb on my belt, on my zipper, removing my shoes, unbuttoning my shirt, undoing my belt buckle, kissing me, pulling me against her, saying

"Relax, Portas,"

running her hands across my back, my buttocks, the hollows of my knees, and I, worried, pushing away a bird's tail with my hand,

"And if the black guy show up?"

and my sweet girl, all cocky, swigging from the bottle,

"He won't be back for at least a month, funerals last forever in Cape Verde,"

and I, more at ease, imagining hundreds of blacks dancing on an island around a coffin, suggesting

"How about going down to the café next to the firehouse and getting me a grilled cheese for lunch?"

me giving her orders, you understand, me spending her money, me, after years of leading a dog's life without anybody, now suddenly with a woman all to myself, at my service, doing whatever I wanted, showering me with affection, and so surely you, a writer, can appreciate that at my age, when one no longer expects anything, it was only natural that so much happiness made me forget about the booby in your photo, about the monthly bus pass, about the tape recorder, about the list of neighbors to talk to, it was only natural for me to lie around in my pajamas, or rather, the black pimp's pajamas, real snazzy ones that Lucilia brought me from her room along with a pair of pom-pom slippers, and she shooed the turtledoves out of the room, cleaned the bird shit off the floor, off the bedspread, and off the sheets, with her good eye concentrated on what she was doing while her other eye strayed, until finally she returned to her place next to me on the bed, and I finished off the sliced bread, used my tongue to pry the last bits of cheese from my molars, sucked the crumbs and margarine from my fingers, and said, with seeming indifference,

"An orangeade would hit the spot right now,"

me taking the place of the orphan who at that moment was presumably dancing on the beach amid coconut trees, surrounded by three hundred male cousins and four hundred straw-skirted female cousins, beseeching the idols to look after his mother's soul, me giving the orders with my mouth full of bread,

"Tonight you work the Avenida until five A.M., so that I can at long last buy a decent coat,"

with my hand poised to deliver a punch, because there's nothing like a good smack to seduce a woman, a nice hard blow and they tremble with passion. "Romeo, lovey-dovey, cupcake, sugar," and other idiotic endearments, and more cuddles, more presents, more nuzzles, more footsies, and the turtledoves pecking at the window, which I'd shut so that they couldn't enter, the turtledoves in search of Lucilia, who receives an old gentleman in the room at the end of the hall or else returns to the Avenida, offering herself to those who get off work at six, so that, being so busy with my mulatto sweetheart, how could I find time for your case, my friend? Now and then I'd trip over the camera and think

Oh shit, I still haven't talked to the neighbors, tomorrow I'll do it without fail,

but I ended up using the film to take shots of me with my mulatto honey at the zoo, she and me in front of the lions' cage, for instance, and I'd ask a stranger,

"Mind snapping a photo? Just press this little button,"

and we smiled arm in arm, our backs to the bars. If you're interested, I can show you Lucilia feeding little fish to the walruses and peanuts to the monkeys, I can show you Lucilia and me handing a coin to the elephant, Lucilia and me drinking sodas at the snack bar next to the sliding boards, I forgot all about the secret police, all about prison, all about the Communists, and I even forgot about you, but what do you expect, those were days of sheer ecstasy, perfect happiness, utterly miraculous, I could have died in peace, because I'd reached paradise, I even thought of proposing marriage to Lucilia and of using what she earns at her job plus my earnings from the correspondence course in hypnotism to rent an apartment in Birre, a one-bedroom with imitation marble floors looking out onto dozens of other one-bedrooms with imitation marble floors, I thought of introducing her to a brother of mine who has a tobacco shop in Cacém, and this I actually did, we took the bus out there on Monday morning, me wearing a necktie and Lucilia wearing a tiger-print outfit that left men drowning in the foam of desire that formed in her wake on the sidewalk, we walked holding hands into the shop full of cigarettes, lighters, newspapers, magazines, school supplies, and useless odds and ends, and I immediately spotted Augusto, similar to me but balder, attending a customer from behind the counter, we walked forward, but my brother, with a pencil behind his ear, didn't notice us, we stopped right in front of him, I cleared my throat, and peeped

"How's it going, Augusto?"

and my brother, whom I hadn't seen since democracy took over this country, raised his chin in the direction of my voice and gawked in arrested fascination at Lucilia's glandular marvels, which were accentuated by the tiger and a whalebone bra, at the fantastic curvature of her thighs, at her earrings resembling miniature pineapples, and at her kinky dyed hair. Lucilia sighed so as to widen her V-neck, while the customer, a short and homely woman wearing support hose, stared with jealous indignation, because a couple of high schoolers were already peering in from the street at Lucilia's rear end, and my brother, whose pencil trembled in his ear, finally noticed me, whereupon his lips instantly hardened,

"If you've come to ask for money, save your breath, because I don't have any,"

and the breasts of my mulatto sweetheart, who had pulled a tiny mirror from her purse and was painting her lips violet, made her blouse's hooks snap one by one, while her mouth, opened taut to receive the lipstick, embraced the world in a promise of pleasure that overwhelmed my brother, me, and the spectators at the shop entrance, and that extended throughout Cacém and beyond, exciting the mechanics in the workshops of Rio de Mouro and the workers and foremen in the small factories of Mem Martins, all possessed by a desire whose origin was a mystery to them,

"I didn't come to ask for money, Augusto, I came to extend to you an invitation"

I said

"you're the only family I have left,"

and now, my friend, it wasn't only her blouse but her skirt that threatened to come undone, unable to contain the abundance of her hips and the gullied bulge of her pubis, and I imagined Lucilia's legs, with their star-spangled stockings, devouring the tobacco shop in Cacém, I imagined my brother retreating in panic to the back of the shop, sticking his hands out like shields, begging

"No, no, no,"

I imagined the high schoolers dropping their notebooks and fleeing in terror toward Carcavelos, and Augusto removed the pencil from his ear, placing it on the counter,

"An invitation, what kind of an invitation?"

Lucilia, who looked less cross-eyed in the dim light, opened her purse to put away the lipstick and the little round mirror with the Belém soccer team insignia on the back,

"An invitation?"

repeated Augusto while shaking his head,

"And just how much will your invitation cost me?"

and I just wish you could have been there, because even I couldn't believe how violently that meek and gentle creature reacted, her kinky hair rising up like the crest of a cockatoo, while her breasts pointed like daggers at my brother, who quickly tried to sugar-coat his question with a smile,

"If you think we came here to mooch off you, then you can fuck yourself. Let's get out of here, Portas, this creep makes me sick."

And her fanny shook, her nostrils shook, her wiry hair shook, and the pineapples shook loose from her earrings, while I, with a hand on her shoulder, tried to calm her down,

"Take it easy, love, Augusto didn't mean to insult us, he just wasn't aware of our plans, that's all,"

and Lucilia, ignoring my advice, knocked a stack of newspapers and magazines off the counter, repeating

"You creep, you creep, you creep,"

and she began slugging Augusto in the cramped, stuffy tobacco shop, a neighborhood business, the kind with little round signs in Magic Marker taped on the window, a grungy shop that my brother and his wife inherited from her father and that he then inherited from her when she keeled over from an aneurysm while buying fish at the outdoor market, the sardines scattered over the wet ground, Augusto, who had no children, lived alone from then on in the Villa Gomes of Cacém, and the feisty mulatto, her good eye full of hatred and her bad eye with a large and round, evangelical expression, insulted him

"You louse"

until, remembering the pimp's technique, I gave her a kick in the shins and stood between her and my brother, shouting

"Quit it, Lucilia, or I'll bash your teeth in,"

the gentle eye shifted toward me without seeing me, the eye of hatred glanced at me and then went out, Augusto, liberated, checked to make sure he hadn't lost either of his mother-of-pearl cuff links, knelt to pick up the papers and magazines off the floor, and asked with his face at the level of my ankles,

"So how much do you want?"

and what immediately came to mind was the Villa Gomes next door to the Villa Home Sweet Home and the Villa Antunes, what came to mind was my brother in the kitchen taking pain pills for his stomach, what came to mind was the squalid end of his life, no different from mine, so that an intense feeling of solidarity softened my heart, and I bent down to whisper with commiseration, affection, friendship, devotion,

"That really isn't what I came for, Augusto, but now that you mention it, give me whatever cash you've got in the register."

Have you noticed what a beautiful day it is, the mulberries so still, the cats stretched out among the potted flowers? Even the pigeons are calm today, uninterested in the retirees' shabby jackets, scarecrow hats, and stubby cigarettes. A swell afternoon for this time of year, a swell afternoon for the lunatics from Miguel Bombarda Hospital, sticking out their palms to truck drivers waiting at the intersection for the light to change, and a swell afternoon for us, warming up our rheumatism in front of the medical school and the morgue, where the deceased lie in drawers waiting to be cut up by huge knives, while we're still healthy, still whole, still alive. What a treat to be able to sink our false teeth into this taste of spring, this breeze of May, this freshness like a river. A beautiful day, young man, the kind that shoos away sickness and sheathes us, as it were, in a kind of zeppelin. A day almost as beautiful as the day before yesterday, when, clad in the black pimp's pajamas, I decided to stay in bed with Lucilia, to cut my nails and listen to the radio, not in my room, which was still dirty from the turtledoves, but in the mulatto's chamber of pleasures, lined with mirrors that had lost their power to give back the world. Lucilia, curled against my tummy, drank from her pint bottle while I dozed, feeling my flesh against her plump flesh, which throbbed with the blood of wild forests. The doors of the rooming house's cubicles, nearly every one with its benefactress, regularly slammed like the doors of cuckoo clocks, downstairs the proprietor's voice railed, and the bell at the firehouse summoned generous men with helmets to hasten to one or another calamity. The radio music lulled me into a daze, the croissants from the pastry shop weighed in my stomach, I'd put the munificence of Augusto in the bank to earn interest, and with a dozen new shirts and my rent paid up, I felt happy, invulnerable, rich, and far removed from the world's disasters, when I heard a light tap on the door, I said

"Come in,"

thinking it would be one of the cross-eyed's colleagues, Elizabeth or Mafalda, who worked in the adjoining cubicles and who sometimes came to show her a skirt or to complain about the weird demands of a client, the doorknob turned, and the black pimp, who'd let his mustache grow in the huts of his island, appeared on the threshold and eyed us with his usual impassivity. The mulatto dropped her pint bottle and jumped out of bed, her deviant pupil more skewed than ever as she pleaded

"I'm sorry, Alcides, I'm sorry, Alcides, I swear the guy paid."

I, stepping on a calf's hide, hurriedly searched for my underwear, the other blacks appeared behind the pimp in their construction clothes and lined up against the wall, I put on my socks and shoes but couldn't find my shirt, my stomach started to ache, and I don't know why, but I felt like vomiting, the black pimp pushed Lucilia away with a swift smack, and she fell down on her back, gasping

"Don't leave me, Alcides, don't leave me."

One of the pimp's friends lit a cigarette, and the smoke momentarily concealed his features, I went out into the hallway, queasy and dizzy with fear, pressing my hands against my stomach to puke my soul into the toilet, and behind me I heard shouts of love from Lucilia, whom the orphan was pulling by the hair onto the bed.

What a truly swell day it is for this time of year, my friend, what peace among the dead in the morgue as we leisurely, luminously enjoy the sun, what a hankering I feel for another soda, another sandwich, another dish of snails or sunflower seeds, to accompany our free and easy conversation, while the man from your photo, with raincoat and briefcase, returns to Alcântara and his diabetic girlfriend's scorn: now we see him on the bus, now he's crossing the traffic circle, now he's walking up the ramp of Hyacinth Park, now he's rummaging for the key among the change in his coat pocket, now he's entering the apartment, greeting the aunt and the girl's father, who don't answer his smile, now he's walking toward the tiny bedroom where the diabetic is immersed in her history book, accompanied by a classmate who rests an arm around her shoulders, now he's setting down the briefcase next to the bed, staring at the girl and her friend without noticing their hands with chewed fingernails joined on top of the open notebook, and now, my friend, he goes to the backyard, where there's a stone bench against the stone wall and a walnut tree whose branches sag toward the ground, now he's dusting the bench with his handkerchief, now the Lisbon night is falling all around him, now he's blending with the wall the way my voice blends with the first croaks of the peacocks here in Santana Park, now he's sitting there expecting nothing, thinking nothing, feeling nothing, quiet, just quiet, old, and very still, so still he doesn't even notice the train from Cascais that leaps over the squalid gardens of Hyacinth Park and crosses his body, taking away—in the stream of train-car windows—the dreamless silence of which he is made.

7

Don't take it badly, because you know I love you, but sometimes, Yolanda, especially in winter and before my month of holiday leave when I walk around the house yawning, not knowing what to do, while you go with your girlfriends to the beaches at Caparica, returning in the evening with a sunburn and a straw basket full of lotions, towels, and pebbles from the ocean,

sometimes, when I feel more tired, tense, and enervated than usual, or when my paycheck won't cover the household expenses and I leave IOUs in the payroll office,

then I toy with the idea of packing my suitcase and stealing away from Hyacinth Park to start up a new life (what a strange expression, to start a new life, when you're pushing fifty) in another part of town, far from the river, far from the trains, far from your hard-heartedness, far from your father's harping, far from your recriminations and ruthless lack of affection, to start a new life in another part of town, in Campo de Ourique, Campolide, Alvalade, or Portela, dragging myself into unfamiliar cafés, eating in diners where I don't know the menu, answering newspaper ads for marriage partners and meeting, with carnation in hand, women as lonely as I am, so that we can unite our desperation, after the justice of the peace, in beds whose springs squeak at the least sigh, inciting Molièresque raps on the wall from indignant neighbors: a prelude to the kisses of our old age.

It's August in this summer as scorching and endless as a shout of fear

(my fear of losing you, my fear that you'll die, throbbing in my fingers like a bird's heart)

and I'm thinking of packing my suitcase, Yolanda, as I thought of doing when I got so sick of hanging out all morning

and afternoon at the Paradise of Pedrouços café, reading magazines and watching the waiter sweep sawdust around the floor
and into a bucket, that I took the bus to Caparica to look for
you, sweating in my idiotic jacket among teenagers wearing
shorts, and I walked from beach to beach with my socks inside
my shoes and my shoes dangling from my fingers, looking at
the ocean to my right and to the restaurants and pine forests
that proliferated on my left, seeing you in virtually every silhouette, in every girl who came out of the water or rubbed oils into
her skin next to a surfboard, in every female torso sculpted by
the sun, with breasts exposed, like figures on ships' prows. With
my head protected by a handkerchief tied at the corners and my
trousers rolled up to keep the Dacron dry, I never felt as out of
place as in that violent surfeit of colors that highlighted the
absurdity of my apparel before hundreds of suntanned gods. I
ended up sitting on a rock at the side of the road and holding
out my hand with the shoes, to see if one of the vans passing by
would give me a lift back to town. A car with a foreign license
plate, in which sandal-shod Germans sang loud and lively folk
songs, picked me up when my jaw was already drooping toward
the asphalt with the resignation of a dying man and dropped
me off at the traffic circle of Alcântara, before the iron roots of
the bridge and a tanker that was sliding downriver like a swan,
arching its symmetrical wings. Weak on my legs and with my
head still wrapped in the handkerchief, I reentered Hyacinth
Park, followed by the ire of the tailor, who grumbled from the
door of his shop about the daytime drunks that went overboard
on the wine, shamelessly ruining the neighborhood's reputation.

Just between us I confess, darling, that I went back two or
three more times to Caparica, in my suit and with my handkerchief, to wade again through the sand in my cumbersome patent-
leather flippers. I never found you, nor did I expect to find you,
nor at heart did I even want to find you. I merely wanted to
revisit the waves that wash ashore the streets, groceries, statues,

and processions that constitute our nation. I wanted to see my homeland emerge as the tide goes out, a land of resigned women, roosters crowing in the distance, trainloads of emigrants, and gold chains around its olive-skinned neck. I wanted to hear the voices that roll in from the sea with the clouds, the fig trees, the sparrows, the fir trees, and the acacias that scatter pollen across the beach, giving rise to ships and the mystery of blood in the veins of Portuguese marble. I wanted to see my parents. I swear I'd really like to see my parents, for it's now, afflicted by gallstones, that I really miss them, Yolanda, lying here at your side, without daring to touch you. I'd like to feel them next to me, alleviating my torment with their grown-up serenity until I would doze off, protected by their silhouettes that would be there in the morning, smiling at me out of the tender familiarity of their affection.

And so, Yolanda (don't take it badly, because you know I love you), sometimes I feel like fleeing to Campo de Ourique or Campolide, to Alvalade or Portela, as when, in my childhood, condemned to watching my aunts crochet day after day in the house on the Calçada do Tojal, I dreamed of running away to the barracks of the Legion, in Amadora, to sing military marches against the Communist threat. Uncle Fernando, glowing with patriotism and anise liqueur, would return on weekends from these exercises in hatred, sit at the table, wedge the napkin in his shirt collar, and yell for his soup, and I considered him

(and still consider him, when I remember him winking at the ladies in the café)

capable of single-handedly stopping a column of Russian tanks bound for Lisbon's government buildings.

The Legion's barracks that defended the world, my love, was an ordinary building on an ordinary street, near a coal depot where young men with blackened hands and faces filled up bags with charcoal and almost opposite the headquarters of the United Wine Lovers Excursion Group, from whose windows came the clacking of billiard balls and the loud chatter of drunks. The shop attendants from the coal depot, the alcoholic pool sharks, and the militiamen with their useless, ammo-less guns crossed paths on the sidewalk, so that not infrequently an excursionist would wander into the barracks with his cue stick, climb up the stairs pushing heroes out of his way, burst into the office of a commander unfurling maps on his desk before general staff members standing at attention, chalk his cue stick without noting the strategic points indicated by pins, and sink a paperweight right off the table.

And so I ran away to the barracks of the Legion, Yolanda, attracted by bugles, booming drums, and liberating cavalry charges, I ran away as the shapes and sounds of dawn were taking over the city, even as they're doing right now, while I talk to you and the whistle of the first train pierces the night around Caxias, I reached Pedralvas and continued on toward Venda Nova and beyond, breathing the scent of camellias wafting over the garden walls, hearing battle cries and military orders. My blood throbbed to the ticking of Tojal's clocks, and I imagined the Russians landing in Leixões, eager to desecrate cemeteries, knocking angels off the tombstones with the butts of their rifles as your father knocks down chairs when he returns from the toilet, his knees feeling in the darkness for his bed, and you turn in your sleep, moving farther away from me, burying your hair in the pillow.

I arrived at Amadora, love, already homesick for my aunts, already worried about how upset they'd be, about their phone calls to the police, the National Guard, the hospitals, and I was frightened by the last dogs and the first roosters as the moon swooned, while on the side of town away from the ocean the sun dilated amid the poplars, pulling from out of the shadows (which were no doubt full of Communists with machine guns hiding behind corners and ready to shoot me) a tiny public garden with swings, hedges, and a star-shaped weather vane that twinkled in the light. Just as I'm forever getting lost in Alcântara, Yolanda, so on that Friday morning I kept going in circles, always returning to the park with swings, never finding the Legion's barracks on the streets of Amadora, whose shops were opening up one by one, with the employees on the thresholds, opening wide their mouths and stretching their limbs to shake off what remnants of sleep still stuck to their skin. People on their way to work trotted to bus stops with umbrellas, clouds from Mafra or Sintra gathered in the east, the Russians were setting up barricades on the road to Lisbon, adjusting the sights of their cannons and using walkie-talkies to communicate with one another, and I, passing for the tenth time in front of a still closed hardware shop with bottles of turpentine in the window, kept expecting a company of militiamen to run out of nowhere, singing combat songs and armed with guns and bayonets that would chase the Communists into Amadora's fields, where the night stubbornly persisted, doubly so in the thickets where owls languished, frightened by the absence of darkness, as here in Hyacinth Park, my love, when I finally forget you and fall silent, defeated by the light's relentlessness, seeking on my half of the mattress a soothing spot for my aching muscles, but before long you sit up in the sheets and shake me, complaining that I snore and ordering me to bring a vial of insulin from the drawer for your first injection. It's in these moments, preparing the syringe and listening to your sarcasms, that I think of packing my suitcase and leaving you, that I feel like walking on the beaches of Caparica, even in winter under the January drizzle, like walking on the sandy strand without stopping, without hurrying, without tiring, all the way to the shacks at Fonte da Telha, where bands of beggars bustle about among the weeping willows, lighting paraffin stoves on which they place rusty cans.

I eventually found the Legion's barracks by following a coal depot employee who, like an earthly angel, shed a charcoal dust, even as bread vendors leave, on the doorsteps of their customers, a halo of flour resembling stardust, and there it was, in the peacefulness of nine in the morning: a three-story building with a flagpole on the facade and a sentry at the entrance sporting a prehistoric rifle and a forage cap that covered his eyebrows like a poodle's fur. I could hear drunk men talking and balls colliding in the United Wine Lovers Excursion Group, the scale of a fife warned that a knife grinder was coming, and a parrot jabbered away on its perch, as my aunts scanned the directory for the phone numbers of hospitals, the Russians took their positions in the garden with swings, ready to invade the nation, submarines patrolled the coast, and battleships and aircraft carriers docked at Arrábida, capturing those in Panama hats who were unlucky enough to be fishing for crabs on the cliffs, "There's no one here by that name, madam," replied the nurse, "have you tried the morgue?" and the grinder, blowing his fife, pushed his cart toward the barracks, the now perpendicular sun revealed the cracks in the gables, "The morgue," insisted the nurse, "try the morgue, madam, because everyone we have here is alive," and at that moment a Communist snuck in through the kitchen door and decapitated Dona Anita with the carving knife, the footsteps in the attic became quick and alarmed, Dona Maria Teresa dropped the receiver, put her hands over her mouth, and stared at her sister, "The morgue," suggested the nurse, "be sure to contact the morgue, and be insistent, describe your nephew in detail, threaten to write the newspapers, because there are always at least six hundred unclaimed corpses, just imagine: six hundred corpses in a cupboard," a second Communist brandished the family Chinese vase to finish off the aunt who was left, and before the porcelain shattered over her head I ran to the sentry (although it was hard, Yolanda, to believe in a barracks that amounted to a four-room apartment with kitchen and bath) shouting

"The Russians are killing my aunts, the Russians are killing my aunts"

in such a desperate voice that the knife grinder let up on his fife and stared at me, forgetting the pedal that made his grindstone go round.

But even if I wanted to, and I swear I don't, I could never leave Hyacinth Park, I could never let you, your father, and your aunt eat the dahlias in the backyard, with only their skimpy social security payments to subsist on till the end of the month, I could never be the cause of you quitting school to work as a cashier in a supermarket or as a clerk in a clothing shop so that your family could eat sardines on Wednesday and pot roast on Sundays, and so that you could buy new shoes every six months at the sales on Calçada do Combro, and you'd have a side job doing housecleaning on Saturday to pay the water bill, gas, and electricity, not to mention the landlord threatening eviction because of the back rent. I can't leave: I'm tied to you like a bat to the night, I revolve around your body tracing pointless ellipses, and I pay the water, I pay the electricity, I pay the gas, I pay for your clothes, for the roast beef, the fresh whiting, and the butter, I deal with the landlord about the rent, I promise to fix the kitchen sink and to replaster the walls, I promise you'll turn down the radio to keep the neighbors happy, I promise your father will stop insulting the widow downstairs who complains that our hanging laundry drips on hers, I promise and I pay, Yolanda, I pay and I promise, for the joy of living with you, or rather, for the privilege of having you sleep at my side, embalmed in the odor of chrysanthemums, avoiding contact between my body and yours, irritated by my idiosyncrasies, by the tone of my voice, by how I get undressed and by how I sneeze, by my glasses, by the knot in my tie, by how I eat, by the threadbare shirts and slacks I wear because I don't even have enough money left over to buy clothes at the flea market. I won't let you eat the dahlias, even as the legionnaire wouldn't let go of my arm but dragged me upstairs and through a tunnel full of typed papers to the commander's office, where a man wearing an unbuttoned hussar's jacket and propping his elbows on a desk covered with dossiers, telegrams, and newspaper clippings, murmured into the telephone

"Pussycat"

with an ecstatic smile.

"Excuse me," apologized the sentry, "sorry to interrupt your work, but this boy just arrived at the barracks and swears that the Russians are killing his family."

The commander, flustered, whispered into the receiver

"Don't go anywhere, not even to the hairdresser's, I'll call you right back, pussycat, an emergency has come up,"

buttoned up his hussar's jacket to gain time, looked at one or two telegrams, made sure his pistol was in its holster, and leaned back with the serene composure of the brave:

"The Russians? What Russians, Saramago?"

A truck was blocking the street, dumping sacks of coal onto the sidewalk, and the bituminous dust, entering by the window, danced around the furniture in search of a surface for depositing its particulate glimmer. A billiardist, leaning on his cue stick as on a shepherd's staff, sang on the second floor of the United Wine Lovers, which I imagined to be decorated with enamel spittoons and a gallery of brandies, the Communists were bolting mortars and other artillery to street corners where housewives lay dead, their shopping baskets lying next to them, and so I alerted the commander,

"They're less than two hundred yards away, their tanks have brought traffic to a halt in Venda Nova, if you don't do something they'll stick me, my aunts, and the person who paces in the attic on a cattle train to Siberia," and the commander, Yolanda, livid with fear, turned to the legionnaire and ordered in a nervous undertone,

"Call all hands,"

and while the likewise livid sentry ran out shouting down the corridor

"Hey Viegas, hey Viegas"

the hero leaned toward the phone, dialed a number, redialed, and whispered in a moribund echo

"Stay locked in your apartment, pussycat, because the Russians are killing left and right and have already captured City Hall."

But in all seriousness, Yolanda, I have no desire to pack my suitcase and leave. I was just kidding when I talked about moving across town, to Campo de Ourique or Campolide, how could I live with a sixty-year-old woman in Alvalade, with a sixty-year-old woman in Portela, with a widow who would do everything to please me, who'd always ask me

"What do you want for lunch, love?"

always get jealous, always buy me clothes, always be so ready to agree with me that her submission would get on my nerves, that Sunday outings with her to buy cheese pastries in Guincho would make me scream with impatience and the urge to batter her with the jack, to sink a screwdriver into her stomach, or to strangle her neck, that the mere idea of accompanying her wordy solicitude to the movies would inspire me to swallow a bottle of pills or stick my head in the oven? I have no desire to get married to a menopause's hot flashes, to ovarian cysts, to hands speckled with old-age freckles, to a bevy of women friends involved in tortuous romances with bureaucrats whose pacemakers tick electric passions under their thermal shirts. Let me stay here, in Alcântara, on the edge of your bed like an innocuous animal, let me converse with your slumber, let me die of love for you as the legionnaires wanted to die for the nation with their breechless rifles and carnival pistols, fainting from terror in their march against the Russians, while their commander, who had pushed his desk against the door, was sitting on the floor, gripping the telephone, and swallowing tranquilizers as he mumbled, trembling,

"I can't go to our love nest because of the Communists, pussycat, the whole of Portugal is depending on me, just think of the responsibility. As soon as I capture Stalin I'll come right over, but meanwhile, as a precaution, shut yourself in the pantry and hide the money and rings I gave you in the dishwasher."

BOOK TWO

the Argonauts

I

There are those who fly in the air and those who fly under the earth, although they're not yet dead, and I, daughter, belong to the latter group, having flown at a depth of a thousand feet with a lamp on my forehead, surrounded by blacks, in the tunnels of the Johannesburg mines, pushing ore-filled wagons along perspiring walls, and sometimes, while sitting on a rail eating canned food for lunch, I could hear the deceased floating—with their wedding clothes and endlessly sad flowers—far above me, almost next to the sun, separated from daylight only by their tombstones and crosses, the deceased who did not dare to descend as far as we did or to go up with us in the elevator which at day's end discharged us on the surface, still with picks in hand, coughing into our handkerchiefs, pulling goggles off our heads, and suddenly seeing not lamps, shadowy caverns, and sheets of dampness in the tunnels, but the trees and houses, with one room and a shower, of the neighborhood they'd built for us to sleep in and whose lanes were scoured by packs of dogs.

In Johannesburg, when I flew under the earth amid a flock of black men, each with a pickax and a light on his helmet, it initially seemed strange to me that the departed didn't take advantage of the elevator to return, in their wedding clothes and with spikenard in their arms, to the city where they were born, to sneak in through the kitchen door and peek into the pots on the stove. In Johannesburg it surprised me that they didn't want to go back to sleeping in their unmade beds or to working in the breweries or ceramicware factories, twirling their tuxes and bridal gowns amid co-workers who wouldn't even notice their smiles, until I understood, daughter, the dead people's fear that their families—already used to not having them, to missing them, to not being burdened by their final illnesses—would no

longer receive them now that their money and furniture had
been divvied up and the contents of their private letters divulged,
the fear that the family would refuse to receive the censure of
their silence, and perhaps it is because of this discretion, this
reserve, this fear, that your mother won't leave her plot in
Lourenço Marques to come and be here with us, with you, me,
your aunt, and the sucker who pays our rent and groceries so
that he can see the pans rattle on their nails when the trains of
Alcântara rush by.

In Johannesburg, in 1936, I flew under the earth pulling
gold out of the walls for fourteen hours a day, and on Sundays
I took a break from being a bird, I sat in a chair in the canteen
verandah, with a dozen bottles of beer to help me forget Monção,
listening to the insects that buzzed in the grass and gazing at the
clouds that arrived from the sea, while kids drummed on cans
in the black encampment patrolled by policemen on horseback,
and in my memory the Minho region was a terra-cotta Christmas manger, with its river that flowed through willowy slopes
and separated me from Spain, with its tiny villages, the stone
houses with jalousies and coats of arms shimmering in the sun,
and oxen whose flanks sweltered in the August heat on fields
that would soon be plowed, and the beer bottles were emptied,
the African night snuffed out my childhood, and I rose from
the chair, stumbling on the cans, stumbling on the policemen's
horses, and stumbling on the encampment's refuse and stench
as I sought the shack of a mixed-blooded Senegalese woman who
was older than me

(back when people older than me existed),

a woman who cleaned offices at the mine's administration
building and who received me on her mat surrounded by oil wicks,
protecting me from homesickness for Monção, from thunderstorms, and from liver trouble with the palms of her hands.

I had been flying for ten years under the earth, far below
the roots of mango trees and the fancy suits and shoes of the

departed who hovered close to the sky of tombstones that kept me from ever seeing the stars, when a cousin of mine, a warehouse manager for customs in Mozambique, got me a job in Lourenço Marques as a longshoreman, loading and unloading crates of fruit, machine parts, broods of penguins, and midget prostitutes for the bars catering to colonists in the vicinity of the beach, where the gin-laced water made the fish tipsy. I never again flew under the earth in Johannesburg, but when I doze off in the living room after lunch, sometimes I still hear the dead who didn't dare rise to the surface.

I never again flew under the earth, because on a Sunday in November at a poor people's wake in a hovel on the island I met your mother, drinking vermouth next to a coffin in which the dead man's hands clasped a rose on top of his stomach while we smothered in our flannels, passing the bottle back and forth and talking while gazing, through the open door, at the baobabs that sprang from out of the low tide and at the flowers now hidden now unveiled by the waves, dripping dew from their stems. One week later I was married to the corpse's daughter, who spent all her time at the window, contemplating the Indian Ocean's trawlers and freighters and the whale that had gone off course and beached on the shore, where it was transforming into a structure of teeth and bones. She contemplated the trawlers and freighters day after day without talking to me, without talking to anyone, without answering questions, interested in nothing, forgetting to eat, to bathe, to comb her hair, to change her clothes, to sweep the house, forgetting you crying in your crib and your bottles scattered on the floor, and forgetting my needs as a man, until she was finally hauled off to an insane asylum on the northern edge of town, where the maniacs, wearing nightshirts, were tied to posts just like goats in the Minho region. I visited the asylum three or four times, on Fridays when returning home from the docks, and a nun led me to a basement where I found your mother staring through cracks in the wall at the sea, at the Indian Ocean's trawlers and freighters en route to Timor or Japan, staring at the sea in a cellar full of patients to whom attendants applied cupping glasses behind folding screens. She didn't ask about you or about me, she didn't complain about anything, didn't talk, didn't even veer her gaze when I stood right in front of her, and now that I'm old and death is gnawing my backbone and hardening my arteries, it occurs to me, when she comes to mind, that we all fly as best we can, however we can, I pushing mine cars through tunnels under Johannesburg, your mother in a nuthouse, drilling holes in the walls with her eyes to see the trawlers, you in the gillyflower cloud of your disease, and the clod who lives with us strolling in the backyard, disheveling the cabbages with the tip of his shoe and sniffing out the night with his idiotic smile.

We all fly however we can, or so I see it, I whose legs are so bad I don't even leave the apartment, I who expend miles of effort just to make the trip from my bedroom to the bathroom and back, I whom no friend, no godson, no former co-worker, and no cousin ever comes to visit, I who argue the whole blessed day with my sister to make sure I'm still breathing, to make sure I can still talk, to make sure I'm still alive, we all fly however we can, and perhaps your mother has kept on flying down in Africa since we left her to come to Lisbon, in the brouhaha of independence, perhaps she still flies among the freighters of the Indian Ocean, perhaps the civil war has spared the hospital on the northern edge of town where patients are tied to posts just like Minho goats, perhaps the whale's bones and teeth are still there on the beach,

the whale I sometimes dream about after supper, in front of the TV, imagining the waves of Lourenço Marques and the hovel on the island, imagining your grandfather, with his hands clasping a rose on top of his stomach, and us standing nearby, smothering in flannel, passing the bottle back and forth and talking while staring, through the open door, at the baobabs that sprang from out of the low tide, at women squatting under the palm trees, and at the vastness of the sunset,

because as faces and voices collide on the screen and I hear you yelling in your room at the ninny who lives with us, I simultaneously dream of the baobabs, daughter, as I also dream of the willows in Monção,

as I also remember taking leave of your mother the day before I set sail for Lisbon, I remember taking a taxi through a plundered Lourenço Marques, looking out of the backseat window at the furniture on the streets and feeling completely indifferent, because I never liked Mozambique, I never liked all those blacks, the heat, the rain, I never liked the sudden fevers, the geckos, the snakes, or the silence following the storms, they could bomb wherever they liked, including the port, including my neighborhood, including my own possessions, and not one nerve would twitch with regret, because to hell with Mozambique, to hell with mango trees, to hell with the colonists, to hell with everything,

and so I walked into the hospital full of glee, thinking, Any day now Africa will be finished, hooray, any day now it'll vanish from the map with a bang, the nun with sandals came to get me at reception, I approached your mother, who had gotten thin and whose hair was starting to go white,

I approached your mother while repeating to myself, Any day now Africa will be finished, hooray, and the nun, speaking Spanish, scolded an old lady who had wet her bed, I heard the grenades downtown that were transforming Lourenço Marques into a scene of ruins, the old lady was wheezing with the aid of an oxygen bottle, I said to your mother, "I'm going to Portugal, Noemia," and she kept her eye on the wall, observing the trawlers with all of the interest that she never showed me,

I said, "I sold the house, Noemia, I'm taking our daughter with me," the old lady tensed her limbs, shook with a gasp, and became still, the nun unhooked the oxygen, another crazy woman, on all fours, tried to rip her mattress, and I said to your mother, "This is the last time I'll see you, Noemia,"

a cannonball whistled over the hospital, the ceiling light went out, and to myself I gloated, At last Mozambique will vanish into thin air, and meanwhile they'd already whisked the old lady out of the basement, and meanwhile the nun was scolding another madwoman who was shrieking, and neither your mother nor I was sorry to separate, she thinking only of the sea and I dying to get out of there, though I did reach out my arm to shake her hand or caress her shoulder, and I did think about giving her a kiss, it wouldn't be that hard, a measly kiss, we did after all live together for twelve years, and perhaps, daughter, she's still there in Africa, perhaps she's the one who now gets scolded for wetting her bed, perhaps she's the one they'll unhook from the oxygen, I didn't shake her hand, I didn't caress her shoulder, and I didn't kiss her, I walked to the exit without nostalgia, without regret, though I did, who knows why, turn around on the first step and look at your mother, staring at the wall with her usual intensity, counting up the trawlers on the wharf.

We all fly however we can, that's my theory, and I came back to Portugal to fly under the earth, but in the Minho there are no tunnels where one can push ore-filled wagons, there are no canteens, no neighborhoods for workers, no sounds of cans being drummed on Sundays, just small farms that grow onions, coriander, tomatoes, just water singing in the moss. Not in the Minho, not in Trás-os-Montes, not in Lisbon, and not in the Algarve, because there's no room in this country for flying under its statues and bridges, and yet, after a lot of searching, I did find in the Beira region an elevator to the earth's core, so I put on my helmet, pulled the lever, and was taken by rusty pulleys and cables down an unlit shaft, arriving at a platform where my steps echoed as in an empty theater. The light on my helmet revealed tools, spools of wire, pieces of track, and a mining car lying upside down in the lividness of an icy morning. At the mouth of the tunnels, wolframite rocks stubbornly waited for the shovel that would remove them, the walls were covered by the beards of lichens that thrive in soulless tunnels, and there was a second elevator, obstructed by a foreman, on which bundles and sacks were being loaded. Prevented from flying, I returned to the surface by the jogs and jolts of an ailing motor, unnerved by the cries of the bats that my helmet light frightened, and I stepped out onto an open land where olive trees leaned toward a churchless village with granite-paved alleys in between the buildings. The carcass of a small truck was decaying on a path, a partridge disappeared into the woods, the clouds were sailing to Spain, a boy grazed cattle among thistles, and a perfectly still kite flashed its aluminum wings. Walking downhill, I found a tavern where farmers got drunk without a word, a tavern with two casks and a blackboard where the wine debts were written in chalk, I bought a liter of brandy from the runty barman who was busy beating a mouse with his broom, I scrambled back up the slope and leaned against the truck's mudguard, at the entrance to the mine. The calves approached, asthmatically sweating, a tractor roared on the other side of the hill, and the kite suddenly swooped down on a group of startled chickens. I finished off the bottle, threw it into my bag, reached the door, put on my helmet, switched on the helmet light, jumped onto the elevator platform without a pick or any ropes at my waist, and vanished down the shaft, determined to fly as fly can under the earth.

ב

My brother's convinced he flies in Alcântara as he used to fly in
Africa, in the Johannesburg mines, and I mentioned the problem when I went to have my kidneys checked at Public Health,
saying

"It's a terrible nuisance, doctor, sometimes he grabs a shovel
and tries to dig into the living room carpet so that he can crawl
into the earth like a mole,"

but the doctor, laying down his hammer for tapping knees
and his stethoscope for hearing the heart's tears, said

"Don't worry, Dona Orquidea, it's just arteriosclerosis, be
grateful he only thinks he's a bird, imagine the fix you'd be in if
he thought he were a hippopotamus, always in the bathtub,
eating bunches of turnips,"

and I, worried about the apartment, because social security's
too meager for new rugs,

"I could deal with it if it were just the holes, even if I sometimes catch him in the backyard at night, wearing his helmet
and digging next to the walnut tree, but I have to contend with
the neighbors, who can't sleep with him beating the rake against
the floorboards, and every month the landlord warns that he
doesn't want a tenant who makes a well so deep he could fall
through and reach the other side of the planet,"

and the doctor, while writing out a prescription,

"Give him these pills at lunch and dinner, Dona Orquidea,
and I guarantee that his birdish tendencies will disappear immediately, he'll sit in the living room without flapping a finger,
as still as a terra-cotta cat,"

and I, already on my feet, smoothing my dress and hunt-
ing for the umbrella I always lose when I go out,

"And besides flying, he's got it into his head that his wife's still alive, counting frigates in a mental hospital in Lourenço Marques, when everyone knows that she died of sugar in the blood the day after my niece was born,"

and the doctor, who was stuffing X-rays into an envelope and writing notes on my chart,

"Make an appointment at the window for three months from now, Dona Orquidea, your kidneys are looking great, the worst that can happen is a tiny stone in your urine, and don't worry about your brother, I wish I had a wife who counts frigates instead of the one who lives with me in Miraflores and is such a pain in the neck that it's me who ends up seeing ships,"

so that I left Public Health feeling somewhat reassured, I went to the pharmacy to get my vials and the pills against birds, which cost so much and came with a sheet of instructions so long that they must be good, and when I arrived at Hyacinth Park, with my umbrella open in case it began to rain, I found my brother wearing his lighted helmet and hoeing the pavement in front of our building, giving orders to invisible blacks and shouting to me, still at some distance,

"I won't quit until I've dug a thousand feet deep, sis, can't you hear the mine cars down below?"

when all I could hear was the sidewalk vibrating from the train whistles, the pebbles rolling in the Tagus, and the peeping of the seagulls, when all I could hear then was what I hear now: ammonium crystals jingling in my bladder and a buzzing in my ears that no specialist, not even at the private clinic in Belas, has been able to cure, and my brother, putting on his diving mask and hoeing the asphalt,

"A thousand feet, sis, no more than a thousand feet to reach the tunnels, I could do it in a trice if other people would join in and help," and there were already people at the window, people who laughed at him, children who drew crosses on the asphalt and eagerly advised,

"It's not over there, Mr. Oliveira, you have to dig here, I feel a tickle in my feet from the miners' voices, I feel a tingling in my knees every time one of them coughs,"

and so my brother hoed up and down the street, trying at the corner, then at a gate, then under a car, as instructed by the youngsters, a kidney stone suddenly lodged in my ureter, seizing my thigh, and so I stopped short, placing my hand on my lower back to relieve the pain, while the kids pointed to one place, then another, and still another,

"Dig harder, Mr. Oliveira, dig harder, there's an injured miner on a stretcher,"

the owner of the fish shop, whose apron exuded the smell of the entire ocean, walked out and stood still on the threshold, stupefied to see my brother waist high in asphalt, hoeing the gutter as directed by the imps, and I, frantic,

"Hold on, Domingos, while I fetch a glass of water for you to take one of the doctor's pills, they're just iron and calcium, word of honor, plus Indonesian ape glands to strengthen your muscles,"

and then, when only the helmet and my brother's neck were still visible, the blade struck a pipe, struck it again, yet again, the owner of the seafood shop took a step backward, warned

"Watch out"

in a shout that dissipated an aroma of crabs and squid, the spectators hung out the windows, the stone in my ureter dissolved in my blood, I pleaded

"Domingos"

as I fumbled for the pills, I don't know whether for him or for me, the pipe finally burst, and a gush of excrement, sludge, and urine rose from the street's intestines, spattering the rooftops, the chimneys, the balconies, and the dahlias and spreading across Hyacinth Park in a volcanic torrent that carried the butcher's van, the cement mixer at a construction site, and the chairs from the café all the way to the Tagus, while my brother continued to dig underneath Alcântara to reach the ore wagons of the mines that only he perceived and to save the injured miner invented by the schoolchildren.

The city government spent two weeks repairing the sewers, with architects and engineers orchestrating an operation that left half the city without phones or electricity and cut off power to the Cascais train line, the neighbors filed suit against my brother, but the doctor from Public Health, the one whose wife made him see ships, signed a declaration swearing on his honor that anyone who flies under the earth is ill, swearing on his honor that subterranean birds, even with a human form, had never been known to exist. The dissatisfied neighbors, who stopped talking to me, insisted with the judge, saying that even their bottles of perfumes sprayed a fecal mist and that the power shortage had obliged them to light kerosene lamps inside their televisions to be able to watch the soaps, my brother swallowed six pills a day and drooled nonstop in his bed, uttering incoherent phrases about elevators and gold and pickaxes, about mining camps and canteens and a mulatto woman from Senegal whose every pore was a mouth that kissed him, but the doctor, whistling to himself as he examined the crystals of acid I'd brought in a jar and sticking an X-ray into a frosted glass square, said,

"Rest easy, Dona Orquidea, it's a result of the treatment, when the patient starts talking about mulatto women, it means he's almost cured,"

and I, who had read the leaflet that came with the pills and had even memorized the side effects, which included losing one's fingernails and microcephaly, said,

"But that's not what's written on the package, doctor, what it says there is that the patient's head is liable to shrink," and he, with his back to me, absorbed in the negative of my viscera, following the trajectory of my urethra with a pencil,

"That's in France, Dona Orquidea, it's the French whose brains are prone to shrink at the drop of a hat, in Portugal an appetite for mulatto women is the first sign of improvement, whoever doesn't think about mulatto women dies, and speaking of mulattos, the situation of your left kidney is looking very black, you'd think that all the marble from Estremoz had converged there,"

and I, nervously grabbing at my waist,

"So now what?"

And the doctor, sticking in a new X-ray, deciphering a lab report, and underscoring the outline of my ovaries with a pencil,

"So now, Dona Orquidea, either you get a job as a marble tabletop, or we operate and you become a millionaire by selling all the stones you're carrying around, in fact the other kidney, not to be outdone, looks worse than a night watchman at midday, the truth is I don't know which one we should start on first,"

and I, with my nerves in tatters, now grabbing myself on both sides,

"And will the operation put everything right?"

and he, shrugging his shoulders and calling a co-worker on the intercom,

"Hey, Aires, come take a look at some kidneys that aren't even fit for an autopsy,"

he flipping through analyses, checking my blood pressure, and patting me on the shoulder,

"You can always take comfort in the fact we all have to die sooner or later,"

so that I left Public Health imagining my final agony, the bile I would vomit, the tubes that would run through my nose and mouth, and the excruciating pain I would endure with Christian resignation, I was so pale that the receptionists at the window and the patients in the waiting room recoiled from me with fright, and when I reached Hyacinth Park, convinced that no one would go to my funeral and that they wouldn't even remember to put my name and picture in the paper, the picture from my ID card where I look younger, when I reached Hyacinth Park, envisioning no flowers and just one taxi, with a broken exhaust pipe that would make loud pops behind the hearse, I was approached by a plainclothes policeman who said

"Sign here,"

because the trial of my brother, accused of puncturing the city, was the very next day, my brother who lay in bed drooling, so overwhelmed by the effect of the pills that he would implore the wardrobe

"Give me a massage, Solange, because the mine really did me in today, a massage, Solange, because I've been pushing mine cars all day long,"

and I, despite my imminent death, as foretold by the Public Health doctor, took the policeman to my brother so he could sign the summons,

"Next to the x"

said the policeman while fumbling in his pocket for his pen, and Domingos, without lifting his head from the pillow, asking me with difficulty as saliva dripped onto his pajama collar,

"Is that the foreman from Johannesburg?"

and the policeman, who had found his pen and held it out along with the typed pages that came from the court,

"Cut the crap and just sign, I've got twenty-one more to deliver this afternoon, and I knock off at six,"

and my brother, struggling against the pills, aimed his drowsy pupils at the policeman, sought me around the room with his gaze, stared back at the policeman with a sudden glow in his face that I remembered from when he was young, at the Saturday night dances in Monção, and replied with scorn, in a voice that filled the apartment with the weight of its authority,

"You can shove your signature straight up you know where,"
and the next day we all sat before a judge in Boa Hora, me in my painful patent-leather pumps, with my mind on the operation and the jar for stones in my purse, my hapless niece, the good-for-nothing who sleeps with her, and my brother, who was wearing ropes at his waist and a lit helmet on his head and who had to be helped by the rest of us, since the antiflying pills made him weak, the next day we all sat in a chamber with a high desk on top of a platform and rows of benches like in the collapsible cinema of Esposende, where the movie mingled with the sea, and the actors' voices had an aquatic tone, and suddenly a man dressed in a long black cassock said to a man dressed in a short black cassock,

"Bring in the first witness, Tavares."

In Esposende, at the cinema by the beach, the movie and the sea were the same thing, the same sound behind the canvas wall, and not just the movie and the sea, but also the pines and weeping willows, the bathing huts and the wind, I forgot about the night and the wind, about the fishing boats and the foam on the beach, I forgot about the cold, in August, thirty-six years ago, when my boyfriend lay on top of me and pulled up my skirt, and I felt his hands searching me, breaking elastic bands and pinching my flesh, hurting me, I felt his hands find me and open me, exploring the canal between my legs, I felt his breath on my neck, felt his voice repeating my name, felt a juice flow out of me onto the rockroses, spreading its odor all around me, and while the images jelled on the screen, equal to the sea in Esposende, equal to the wind and the willows and pines and the night, jelling on the screen as black as the bathing huts, as black as his face when he got up and waved good-bye, I just lay there against the canvas wall, quartered and naked inside, speechless and with an absurd, inexplicable need to cry. I saw him three weeks later in my father's shop, and he didn't smile or even speak to me, he left his money on the counter, took his pack of cigarettes, and vanished, leaving me in Esposende, near the water's thousand secrets, to think about what the cinema owner had taken from me, this thing that was only worth something for having ceased to exist, me in Esposende, listening to the waves, listening to the sound of the waves against the hulls, listening to the weeping willows, me in Esposende thirty-six years ago, more naked than I've ever seen myself, before or after, and me the day before yesterday, already an old woman dying of kidney disease, listening to our neighbors from Hyacinth Park explaining to the judge that my brother, with express intent to harm the neighborhood, spent the entire afternoon breaking up the asphalt with a hoe, in front of one building after another, until he finally hit the sewer and inundated them with refuse that to this day hasn't been completely eradicated from inside their cupboards and that even seeped into their safes, mucking up their savings and love letters, "He caused me at least two thousand dollars' worth of damages just in painting and replastering, not to mention the broken stove and hot-water heater, can you imagine living without a stove?" "What he ruined for me was my grandparents' tea service, it stinks so bad I can no longer use the teapot when I get a cold or when my engineer godson visits me at Easter with his family and a box of fancy biscuits, if he went to my place now, he'd flee in horror, and so here I am, with only this one tooth left and nary a biscuit," "The big problem for me is that I can no longer get close to my wife without immediately sniffing a toilet odor, with the result that I sleep on the living room sofa and now have a crick in my back that won't let me get a good night's rest," "What makes my life hell is the water getting cut off, I spend the whole day with two buckets at the fountain in Alcântara like an idiot, and I'm a sergeant charged to defend the nation, if the Spanish should invade us, we'll be up shit's creek," "What I miss is the telephone, I can manage without water or electricity, but without a phone how can I put in my song requests at the radio station?" and me remembering Esposende as the judge nodded assent, thumbing through a legal code, and after dozens of complaints and a whole afternoon of indignation and protests, the clerk in the short cassock craned his neck and bellowed, looking at us,

"The defendant shall rise,"

and I elbowed my brother, who was switching his helmet's light on and off,

"That means you, Domingos,"

and he, adjusting his miner's goggles, without budging from the bench,

"I don't feel like working today, sis, the blacks'll have to fly under the earth on their own,"

and the judge, leaning over the bench and fanning himself with his crapes,

"Say what?"

and my brother, untying the ropes from his waist,

"I'm not working today, not even if they're paying overtime, what I need is a good long nap in Solange's bed,"

and the judge, jotting down furious verdicts,

"Solange?"

and my brother, as if patiently explaining the obvious to a mongoloid,

"Solange, the mixed-blooded cleaning woman who lives in the only brick house at the end of the barbed wire, next to the reed plot, a tall woman, on the thin side, who's carrying my baby and whom I've forbidden from hanging out with the other blacks,"

and the judge, with his hand cupped to his ear,

"Huh?"

and my brother, with the beacon on his forehead brightly shining,

"What do you expect, for Christ's sake, haven't you ever noticed how sloppy they are, and how bad they smell?"

and the man in the short cassock, concerned about the judge, who was wiping his forehead, on the verge of passing out,

"That's not the issue, buddy, forget about the blacks, forget about their smell, what we need to settle are the sewer mains you burst in Alcântara, the residents of Hyacinth Park are demanding fifty thousand dollars in damages,"

and me in Esposende, thirty-six years ago on a Friday night, at the beach, leaning against the canvas of the traveling cinema, with the water just a few yards away and the movie mingling with the sea, and the weeping willows, and the pines, and the wind, the Esposende wind hurling the sand from the dunes against the fishermen's shacks, me lying flat in Esposende,

in Esposende,

my womb opened, my blood exposed, rocking to the rhythm of the tides, me shivering from cold and from heat as the man whispered in my ear

"My God"

me in my father's shop

in Esposende

straightening the bolts of cloth without answering my stepmother's questions, nodding my head yes, shaking my head no, watching them take down the canvas and pack up the benches of the traveling cinema, piling everything into a truck and leaving for Póvoa, early in the morning, me looking at the reels of film and the projector, wrapped in burlap, me looking at him, wearing a cap and sitting next to the driver, vanishing around the first street corner, me staring at the patch of sand where the cinema had been and where the grass would start to grow again until it covered the shame of what I no longer had, and my brother, veering his helmet's light toward the man in the short cassock,

"What mains, what damages?"

and the judge, dazed by mines and mulatto women, using a finger to relieve the tightness of his collar,

"The sewers you exploded in Hyacinth Park, the shower of excrement you unleashed over half the city,"

and the doctor, beaming as he pulled on my sleeve and clicked his pencil on a lighter area in the X-ray,

"Here, Dona Orquidea, a stone that's at least as large as a millstone, I don't know how you can walk with this inside,"

and the guy with the short cassock, hopping up and down on the platform like a sparrow,

"Witnesses have testified that the feces ruined a wine depot in Poço do Bispo, the firemen claim that the feces reached as far as Ajuda,"

and the doctor, shoving my forehead up against the kidney,

"A millstone, Dona Orquidea, congratulations, the only thing I can't figure out is why you're still alive,"

and the judge, by this time too rattled to lick his thumb,

"A devastated wine depot, two feces-engulfed churches, a day care center where the filth rose up to the wet nurses' waists, Prazeres Cemetery with half its corpses afloat and its gates closed to all the widows, and the stoplights at Cais do Sodré all gone haywire, City Hall is demanding a million dollars in damages,"

and the doctor, offering me candies, offering me cigarettes,

"May I show you this contract I drew up, Dona Orquidea? For over a month now I've been obsessed with the idea of turning in my stethoscope and us going into business together, with me getting fifteen percent of the profits. We'd show off your kidneys in a tent, with special prices for baptism parties, golden wedding anniversaries, and Christmases for cripples, Orquidea the Marble Woman, and after a year, if you survived the mills, we'd each own our own house with swimming pool, our own yacht, and our own Van Gogh,"

and my brother, diminishing the intensity of the light on his helmet,

"A million dollars is serious money, I never dreamed shit was worth so much," and me, feeling a tiny stone in my bladder and thinking about Esposende, about the sea and sand, about the grass that drank my body's juice next to the cinema's canvas wall, that drank the blood of what I never realized I had until I lost it, thinking about Esposende, about the pine trees and the wind and the man getting up, shaking off the pine needles, lighting a cigarette and walking away, and I decided that when we got back to Alcântara I would quietly, secretly, stealthily fetch the pickax from my brother's room, fetch the lighted helmet and the ropes, go out to the backyard where the walnut tree rattles, and start digging in a flower bed until I'd dug to where the mine cars screech on the tracks, a thousand feet deep, so that I could fly under the earth, among the blacks and next to the waves, to recover what was stolen from me one Friday evening, thirty-six years ago.

3

I had just made the decision to return to Johannesburg because I don't like Portugal, I don't like Lisbon, I don't like Alcântara, I don't like Hyacinth Park, I don't like not having tunnels, canteens, and mine cars full of ore, to return to Johannesburg because I missed Solange and the oil lamp that enlarged her face, scrambled my dreams, and prolonged until dawn her tender caresses, when the doorbell rang and a man carrying a tape recorder strapped around his shoulder, unable to fly, said to me from the doormat, "I was an agent for the secret police, Mr. Oliveira, and if you'll answer just a couple of questions about your daughter and son-in-law, I promise not to trouble you further."

As soon as lunch is over and I'm by myself, because my sister has been going almost daily, with a bottle of pee, to have her kidneys analyzed by the doctor, I roll down the blinds, hang blankets over the windows, put on my helmet, take up my pickax, and sit down in my chair in the total darkness, imagining the sounds of the earth below me. All alone in the building, I try to make out a foreman floating with outstretched arms and squawking gruff orders. But Lisbon's exaggerated sunlight, which lasts all evening and won't let me sleep, and its river, which dances on the ceiling, prevent me from descending to the earth's core to push gold-filled wagons and to eat canned food for lunch on a stair step in the tunnels. So I end up pulling the blankets off the windows and rolling up the blinds, defeated by this light that hates me, and I just sit in the living room, listening to the Tagus. As in Monção, as in Esposende, as in the Beira region, as in every corner of this country, where everything leans toward the sea, where the waves are even felt in the tousled tufts of wheat, and I ask myself how it's possible to live in a place that's noth-

ing but low-tide debris, the waves receding and leaving behind
a convent on the sand, the waves receding and leaving behind a
bunch of streets, a pillory, and a square, the waves receding and
leaving a hotel, a prison, a neighborhood, an open-air mass, a
wake, the waves receding and leaving us, at the table, eating the
fish and collard greens of our dinner, the waves receding and
leaving me to myself, searching for Johannesburg in the empty
apartment, searching for Sunday beers at the canteen where I
always remembered my childhood, where I always remembered
the rockroses, the weeping willows, and the chinaware oxen of
the Minho, the waves receding and leaving behind a man on the
doormat with a tape recorder strapped around his shoulder,
unable to fly, wanting to ask a few questions and looking suspiciously at my helmet and pickax, and since I was tired of not
having anyone I can tell all this to, since I was tired of the sun
and anxious to break the news that finally, my friend, I'm going
back to Johannesburg and Solange and the mines, stealing pas-
sage on a ship like the first time, I'm going back to the wagons
that haul rock from a thousand feet below, I said "Come on in,"
led him to the living room, offered him the armchair, sat down
on the sofa, thought for a second that the mulberry tree waving
its leaves in the window was the canteen owner handing me a
bottle, banged my pickax on the carpet, and said, "Don't you
agree there's too much sea, don't you find Portugal to be a waste
of water?

"The first time we sailed to Johannesburg, me and the
cousin of a cousin of mine, we didn't even see the Atlantic, nor
even any dolphins, because we kept hidden, fearing all the while
that a sailor might spot us amid the crates where we repressed
our coughs, repressed our sneezes, repressed our nausea and urge
to vomit, and we didn't even see the waves when after five or six
days the first mate tapped us on the shoulder and said, 'Come
with me, you bums,' for it was by interior stairways that we were
taken to a cubicle without portholes that swayed more than all

the rest of the ship, and a cabin boy would bring us cauliflower for lunch and cauliflower for dinner, so that we puked up stalks into enamel pails for the rest of the voyage. One morning the hull bumped against wooden posts that creaked, the motors stopped turning, and we were kicked off board and onto the docks, 'Scram, you scoundrels,' and we found ourselves amid a flurry of containers, caged parrots, and blacks, mainly blacks, stumbling as we went on our weakened legs, shoved by forwarding agents, stevedores, and passengers, toward the Indian neighborhoods on the outskirts of a city we didn't know, a city that was still far away from Johannesburg and the tunnels where I would fly for years, you in the secret police and I one thousand feet under the earth," and the man with the tape recorder strapped around his shoulder, eyeing the pickax that banged on the rug, answered "I don't know a thing about what happens down below, but I can make my students rise above the rooftops, I'm a professor of hypnotism by mail."

This guy doesn't know diddly, I thought, because to fly over trees and houses is a cinch, sparrows do it all the time, you just run a few steps, leap up, grab on to a sliver of wind and, presto, climb the clouds into the sky, everybody in the north used to fly when I was little, on feast days the band would fly behind the priest and the platforms with holy statues, the brothers of the Sacred Host—uplifted by wine—would fly past the balconies covered with banners and flowers, and the little angels with fake wings and the barefoot penitents also ascended, their hands folded in prayer, until they disappeared like helium balloons into the June afternoon, to fly over trees and houses is a cinch, in the Minho region the sheep and goats always flew when I was a kid, and it was in the air, suspended, that cows grazed the smoke from the grass burned on the threshing floor, and my grandmother fed corn to the chickens with her skirt as high as the tops of the plum trees, to fly over trees and houses is a cinch, I remember my sister flying in Esposende around the collapsible canvas cinema by the beach, even when there was no film, the man who worked the projector would come out, smoking a cigarette, and talk with her, they'd sit in front of the fog because in Esposende there was no sun, just a kind of army green moonlight that lasted for months, and my sister and the cinema owner would lie in a rockrose patch, my aunts whispered, my stepmother whispered, my father, with a pencil in his ear, unrolled bolts of fabric in the shop, and my sister, ignoring them, flew above the screen on which the actor kissed the actress and mouthed words whose sound came ten minutes later, and once the loudspeakers quieted and the cinema left town, the sea continued to batter the cliffs, the wagtails continued to perch on the crags, the trawlers still arrived and departed, devoured by the fog, and my sister still lay in the rockroses overlooking the water, they were rockroses, yes, they were rockroses, rockroses, rockroses, and she with her thighs stark naked, as if the man with the cigarette were going to come out of the projection booth that was no longer there and touch her breasts, touch her tummy,

rockroses,

as if the man with the cigarette were lying at her side and whispering his craving into her ear, as if the man with the cigarette, kneeling in the roots and leaves, were unzipping his trousers for her to measure with her own fingers "my desire for you, love, make me grow in your hand, make me grow against your breasts, your neck, your chin, your eyes, don't stop now, darling, help me, please, make me feel like a man," while my father unrolled bolts of fabric in the shop and I spied on them, gritting my teeth and unzipping my trousers too, behind a ruined wall or the trunk of a pine tree,

rockroses,

my sister hugging him and I hugging myself as I watched them, my sister getting aroused and I getting aroused as I watched them, my sister uttering moans and I keeping quiet as I watched them, so that when the cinema, the canvas, the benches, the reels, and the man with the cigarette left for Póvoa, I felt as orphaned and alone as my sister, both of us scouring the rockroses, rockroses, rockroses, both of us scouring the sea, both scouring the trawlers in search of a half-smoked cigarette, a piece of cap, a figure that would rise out of the night and break away from it, shaking twigs and needles from his trousers to change the reel of the film, making the screen fill with silhouettes out of synch with the sounds of their steps and voices, we were both orphans of Esposende's cold, listening to the drone of the lifeboat, the drone of the lighthouse, the two of us side by side on the sand watching the waves' despair, if I hid behind the ruined wall or behind the trunk of a pine, I'd see no more than the forlorn weeping willows, the trawlers' lights, and the beach, "To fly over trees and houses is a cinch," I argued, "blackbirds, owls, and crows also fly, and so do the brothers of the Sacred Host, but to fly under the earth, my friend, without breaking any bones against the edge of a wall, only I and the blacks of Johannesburg succeeded in doing (as Solange can tell you, she keeps me honest), whereas my brother-in-law's cousin, after less than an hour,"

rockroses

"had to be rushed back to the top, given oxygen, and taken to the mine infirmary, half a dozen beds where failed birds agonized with helmets on their heads and picks on their chests, like crucifixes on corpses, and where he raved without letup, saying 'I don't want to be a sparrow, I don't want to be a sparrow, I don't want to be a sparrow, I want to be a junior pharmacist in Valença,'" and the secret policeman with a tape recorder who wrote booklets to teach hypnotism to people afraid of tunnels, protested, "You're obsessed, Mr. Oliveira, you obviously don't understand anything about parapsychology, study my lessons, if you like I'll mail them to you COD, two dollars per lesson, and with every twelfth lesson you get a free gift, try wearing a ruby on your forehead and then come talk to me."

But there was nothing to talk about, I thought, because what on earth can one say
rockroses, forget the rockroses
to a man who never lay in Solange's bed, feeling her tenderness and submitting to her authority? And so I got up from the couch and fetched, in memory of Johannesburg, some cold beers that the fool who pays our rent sometimes buys for me so that I'll let him sleep with my daughter, I opened myself a bottle and watched the foam run like tears down its neck, then a second bottle for the instructor of magnetic movements, who raised his hand in refusal, "I don't drink or smoke," and I said "Around here everyone drinks but my daughter, who's diabetic," I held the mug against the light to observe the bubbles break away from the glass, the policeman hesitated, to encourage him I swung my pick against the floor, slicing off what was left of the rug's fringe, even as the foreman in Johannesburg used to swing his pick when the blacks were afraid to get on the elevator, I took a sip and was transported, as usual, to my Sunday afternoons some twenty-five years ago in the canteen of South Africa, looking at the grass, looking at the workers' gypsum-and-mud huts, before I met my wife, who counted frigates, leaning out the window during her father's wake in their hovel on the island, and through the thick, refractive, overlapping layers of twenty-five years' time I saw the hypnotist, frightened by the pickax, grab his mug and take a nervous sip, suppress a burp, take another sip, turn red in the face, widen his eyes, turn pale, grow larger, empty the bottle, and then finish off what was left in mine, whereupon he asked if there was more in the kitchen, because beer helped, "You don't have to get up, I'll find it, the refrigerator's this way, isn't it?" And in a voice that acquired weight and authority, he argued, "If you realized the benefits, such as migrating to Morocco, passing over the Alentejo region and enjoying the landscape like the ducks in autumn, I bet you'd become a convert to hypnotism by mail, you'd buy a turban and see I'm right, because under

the earth, where everything's pitch black, cramped, and damp, and it feels as if we've been locked in a trunk for centuries, what horizons are there?"

Sitting in the canteen of Johannesburg, still young and without a bum leg, the lamp on my forehead glowing as I wait for nightfall to visit Solange, and simultaneously sitting in Hyacinth Park, exasperated by the river and the exaggerated sunlight, looking at the hills, buildings, and factories on the far shore, looking at Montijo, or Alcochete, or Almada duplicated in the water, looking at the window and, beyond it, the sewers and the trains to Cascais that make our floorboards shake, our tureens crash to the floor, and our pictures tilt on their hooks, looking at the starving stupidity of the seagulls, so voracious that they shriekingly devour their own shadows in the wakes of ships, looking at the window and seeing black miners all around me, likewise with glowing lamps on their foreheads and with mugs of cane liquor that yellow, like sulfuric moons, the evening mist, looking at the window and hearing the children in the workers' neighborhood drumming on cans, the dogs scampering, and the patrolmen's horses neighing, I thought, Everything pitch black my eye, everything cramped my eye, all damp and stuffy my eye, locked inside a trunk like hell, enjoy the landscape how stupid, "It's obvious from the way you talk that you've never gone twenty feet below ground, much less a thousand, a thousand feet, my friend, imagine the pressure on one's chest, the pressure on one's soul, imagine a world of tunnels that end who knows where or why, or if they end at all, because maybe they hook up to other tunnels, maybe there are infinite branches of tunnels with echoing mine cars that no one pushes, pickaxes no one uses, foreman's orders that no one remembers," and the policeman, getting more insistent, "After the Revolution, the Communists, the traitors, the profiteers who took power threw me into the prison fort at Caxias for the sole crime of having loved my country, and during those months when I lived off bread and water,

Mr. Oliveira, literally bread and water, I learned what it means to live below ground and I can promise you it's dark, it's cramped, it's stuffy, it's damp, months and months of cold soup and sprouted potatoes and hearing the sounds of deep wells and doors in corridors that perhaps hooked up with yours, that perhaps united Portugal to Johannesburg, the prison in Caxias to your mine worked by blacks, and perhaps, while I slept, there were helmeted blacks, all dirty and smiling, who emerged from under the flagstones of my cell, so I can assure you that the last thing I ever wanted to do was fly under the earth, all I wanted was to be let out, even though I had no job, no retirement, and no health coverage, because you know how the democrats are."

And I, opening bottles, filling our mugs, using my shirt-sleeve to wipe the beer that spilled on the table, "A labyrinth, my friend, a veritable labyrinth, just think of all the surprises in a labyrinth, there were even tree roots in the tunnels, trees are even worse than teeth, which reach through our gums to our ears and neck, as we all know, but we look at a tree and never dream how far it goes in search of the deceased and the world's silence that sprouts as fruit on its branches,"

and the policeman, forgetting the tape recorder strapped around his shoulder, forgetting his questions about my daughter and the guy who pays our rent, "I got booted out of government service, I who was the terror of the Bulgarians, and that's when I came up with hypnotism by mail, I thought that showing people how to fly over the city would be a gratifying job, because who doesn't like to float over rooftops by means of just a turban and some magic sentences?"

and I, now feeling less pain in my leg and realizing, by the lights turning on in the miners' neighborhood, that it was time to leave the canteen and pay a visit to Solange in the little brick house at the end of the barbed wire, shot back, "Gratifying and easy, my friend, extremely easy, because even with my bum leg I could, if I wanted, go outside and start flying above Lisbon," and the policeman, staring hard at me from the other side of the table, covered by a forest of empty bottles, "Oh, it's easy, is it? You think it's easy even without having studied to become a medium? Then let's go outside and test your powers,"

and I, standing up and zigzagging toward the door, grabbing on to the suddenly slippery, swaying, elusive walls, saying in a huff, "How much would you like to bet, my friend, how much do I get if you lose?"

and the policeman, holding on with both hands to a chest of drawers in the beer-induced storm, "A night with Lucilia, Mr. Oliveira, a night all to yourself with Lucilia and the turtledoves, to forget how shitty life is in the Praça da Alegria Rooming House,"

and I, who don't know Lucilia, I with poor Solange wondering where I am, I with my supper getting cold in a hovel in Johannesburg as I listen to the dogs and the kids drumming on cans, I who hate winning easy bets, "Forget Lucilia and the turtledoves, my friend, because I've already got more women than I can handle, one who's counting frigates in an asylum in Lourenço Marques and another who's fixing supper for me just a few minutes away from here, hold on to my shoulder, we just need to go down the stairs and we'll be out on the sidewalk,"

and the policeman swimming in my direction like a frogman, in the sea of buffet corals and reef chairs that the living room had become, "The hat stand, Mr. Oliveira, if we reach the hat stand, we'll be saved,"

and I, despite my wooziness from the beer, now grabbing hold of the doorknob, now turning the key, now pulling the latch, adjusting the helmet on my head, feeling the freshness of twilight on my neck, and discerning, in the growing darkness, the garland of headlights on the bridge, "Hurry up before my daughter gets home from school and my sister from the doctor's, since they'll forbid me from flying," and the policeman, trampling on the dead dahlias in the flower beds, "Let me just throw up and take a piss, getting rid of some beer to lighten the ballast,"

and I, leaning on my pickax, pushing on the gate, looking out for my sister and daughter on the slopes of Hyacinth Park, and homesick for Monção, as always happens when I leave the canteen, "Now show me what you can do, pal, let's see who can go higher,"

and so we spread our arms at six o'clock in Alcântara, at six o'clock in Johannesburg, leapt into the air, and slowly climbed to the heights of the windows, the balconies, the TV antennas, and the chimneys, frightening the seagulls and feeling out the direction of the wind as we hovered over the traffic circle, he clutching my neck, puffing alcohol into my face, "Is this or isn't this better than being underground, Mr. Oliveira, stop quibbling and be honest: is it or isn't it better?"

We flew high above the river, Lisbon shrinking under our stork bellies, and as we got ready to head south I spotted down below, in the whirl of Alcântara's traffic, the fool who pays our rent and gas bill, plodding home from work like a mangy dog, dressed in a raincoat and carrying a briefcase. I flapped my arms more slowly, pointed him out to the policeman, shouted "There goes my son-in-law, didn't you want to ask me some questions about him?" And the professor of hypnotism by mail, twisting his torso to avoid a cloud, answered with a caw that was instantly scattered by the wind, "There's time, Mr. Oliveira, there's time. First let's go to Odemira with the other pigeons to eat corn, and tomorrow morning, after we return to Lisbon and I've talked to Lucilia, we'll see."

4

The doctor handed back the analyses, shaking his head in disappointment,

"I'm afraid your kidneys are better, Dona Orquidea, the left one's working fine and the millstone has begun to dissolve,"

and I, sorry to displease him, felt ashamed of his crestfallen voice and of the nurse's despair over my improved health, ashamed of the sadness in their faces due to my autopsy's postponement, and so I claimed, in an effort to cheer them up,

"But it hurts me more and more, doctor, I have to take pills at night to get to sleep, I even use my brother's antibird pills, fancy that,"

while the doctor, still shaking his head, filled out a prescription, the nurse silently censured my progress, voices and footsteps echoed in the hallway, the oceanic murmur of patients in the waiting room came and went in plaintive puffs, and the sun shed its light on the objects in the office (the stethoscope, the scale, a chart of shrinking letters forming nonsense words to test the nearsighted), stripping them of mystery and causing the chrome tools of suffering to gleam.

"To destroy the stones inside you through negligence, Dona Orquidea, is as perverse as being born with an uncommon talent for the piano and refusing, out of spite, to play," chided the doctor in a hurt tone of voice.

So I left Public Health blaming myself for having let down the doctor and inwardly vowing to make cliffs grow in my belly, cliffs like those in Viana, covered with tenacious grass, cliffs like those along the Douro River, with terraced vineyards and the streambed glistening below, and I went home determined to transform myself into a mountain range of schist, into stratified slate, into basaltic formations, swearing that in less than a month I'd get hooked up, already semicomatose and surrounded by surgeons, to the blood-filtering machine in the hospital where I was interned with jaundice seven years ago, in a bed next to a window through which a row of plane trees dropped leaves onto my shivering skin. As I climbed the street to Hyacinth Park, still with no sign of evening, I felt a sharp pain in my side, and my thigh stiffened as if a calcium crystal were beginning

what luck

to stop up my ureter. I quickened my step in the hope of depositing a heartwarming mica sliver or granite chip into the chamber pot, and I suddenly saw that our front door was open, the hat stand overturned, the living room furniture in complete chaos under torn-up drapes, the table covered with beer bottles, and there was my brother, with helmet and pickax, accompanied by a stranger of roughly the same age, both of them sitting on the carpet and dripping with vomit, boastfully asking each other: "You want me to fly higher, my friend?" "You want me to fly higher, Mr. Oliveira? Notice how Odemira looks from up here. Let's go and eat some corn at the bandstand in the middle of the square." "I guarantee you it's harder to fly under the earth."

At first, when I saw the two men waving their arms back and forth, knocking over my chinaware vases, I thought, It's because of the wine, it's the same blasted wine that caused my father, in Esposende, to brandish a shotgun and shout amid the fabrics, "Either you clear all the lizards and spiders out of my shop or I'll shoot everybody dead," my stepmother, in tears, would phone the firemen, who would plead from the threshold, without daring to enter, "Hand over the gun, Mr. Oliveira, and we'll get rid of the geckos for you," and my father, "Get back, you scoundrels, get back, you dogs," while firing two cartridges at once, filling the shop with gunpowder, then he reloaded the gun and advanced along the beach, aiming straight at the windows, "Get out of there, frigging Spaniards, I want all you damn Spanish back in Madrid, where you belong," and I, on all fours behind the counter, thinking in panic, If he hits the cinema owner, we won't have any more movies in Esposende, no more romantic dramas, no more Zorro bending down from his horse to kiss the viscountess, if he hits the cinema owner, there won't be anything left to blend in with the sea. When he'd used up all the cartridges, my father would lift up his trouser leg and say, in a suddenly soft and whiny voice, "Help me, Orquidea, before the mice eat me, look, there's one climbing up my leg," and I'd raise my head an inch or two over the counter, the firemen would tackle him amid a whirl of insults and flashing hatchets, and the triumphant fire chief would swear, "I'll give you mice, buddy, I'll give you better than mice, you're going to spend the night with the bedbugs at the police station to dry up, and in the morning the judge, who's been throwing the book at everyone since his wife left him, will do whatever he legally can to banish you to Africa."

And so, when I saw the empty bottles and my brother talking to the other man in the bandstand of Odemira, pecking at the pigeons' corn with their chins in the carpet, I initially thought their behavior, like my father's, resulted from alcohol, except that instead of geckos, spiders, and rats, they invented birdseed and bread crumbs, but then, after hearing them talk about winds and clouds and about having glided for an hour over the fields of Grândola, I began to doubt myself and to touch the walls to make sure that I wasn't also flying and alighting, like them, in the trees of the public square, until my brother noticed me standing next to the buffet and elbowed the other guy, flapping his arm, "Time to take off, pal, time to fly away, because my sister has arrived."

It can't be from the alcohol, I thought, because drunks aren't interested in bandstands, no drunk gives a hoot about bandstands, what drunks worry about are ants and tarantulas crawling in their clothes and the ghosts they fight against all night. On Sundays, after the matinee, the cinema owner would guzzle a quart of tangerine liqueur, and all he felt like doing was beating me up for no reason at all, so that if, for example, I made the mistake of talking about storks, he'd fly into a rage, saying "Storks? What do you mean, 'storks'? Have you flipped your lid? Here I am having a serious discussion and you bring up birds." So that perhaps, I thought, they're not inventing but have really been traveling around in the air, and the guy with my brother, lifting his lips from the carpet, said, "But if we're in the Alentejo and your sister's in Alcântara, how could she possibly find us?"

and my brother, pointing at me with his pickax, "I don't know how she got here, maybe she flew here like us, maybe she studies hypnotism by mail, all I know is that it's Orquidea, yes sir, I've known her face since the day I was born,"

and the other guy, searching for me with his blinking woodcock eyes and focusing on the photo of my mother among the port glasses on the sideboard, "Which is your sister, Oliveira? Is it that old white-haired lady who's tossing us bread crumbs?"

And I scowled at my brother for having brought home such a stupid friend, because my mother was twenty-nine if that old when she died in the Minho region, on an August morning, we were playing on the threshing floor and my uncle Aurelio, with his hat in his hand, called us from the kitchen steps, there were dozens and dozens of sparrows in the trellised vines, the sun gilded the grains of wheat on the bricks, and the dog, wounded in its hindquarters, was indifferent to the rabbits behind the chicken wire, while inside the house they had tied shut my mother's jaw with a handkerchief and made her lie down, fully dressed, on top of the bedspread, and I couldn't understand why, instead of her slippers, she was wearing my father's blue-and-brown shoes, the ones he used for processions, so I shoved aside my godmother, went up to the bed, and said "Mommy," and nothing, said "Mommy, I'm hungry," and nothing, shouted "Mommy, give me a slice of bread," and nothing, screamed

"Mommy, if you don't wake up, I'm going to smash the saint next to the candle," and she kept sleeping, her head lying perfectly still on an embroidered pillowcase, my uncle Aurelio came up behind me and put his hand on my shoulder, "Calm down, sweetie, calm down, the priest will be along soon," and I, clutching my mother's Sunday dress, "You bitch, you nasty bitch who ignores her own daughter," and the next day,

rockroses, so many rockroses, "my heart's desire, I love you" as I cursed her in tears, repeating "Bitch, you bitch, I swear over my dead body I'll never speak to you again, you bitch," they shut her in a coffin and she didn't say no, and we walked behind it to the cemetery of Monção, and I can still hear the bells when I remember that day, I can still see my cousin Afonsina, who never married because she was born hunchbacked, covering my face with a veil to protect me from the sun, and I pressed my ear to the coffin so I could hear my mother say "Put on your father's cap, dear, it's hot outside," I still remember the gravediggers, and the priest blessing crosses under the poplars, and as they dropped my mother in a hole I said "Stop it, you bastards," they poured over the lid a pouch of lime, whose white cloud danced for a long time amid the tombstones and flower wreaths,

not rockroses, not broom shrubs, but flowers, flowers, red flowers, blue flowers, white flowers, I think magnolias, I think marigolds, I think daisies, flowers, flowers, ribbons, and bows with silver and gold letters, flowers, flowers like I'd never seen, the rockroses were later, in Esposende, the rockroses were next to the sea, in February when the movies from the collapsible cinema blended with the waves and your body got up from mine, "See you later," with a cigarette in your mouth,

the priest closed the book, handed the holy water to his assistant, removed his stole, and wiped the sweat from his temples, my father took us back to the house, which had always seemed tiny, cramped, and stuffy but which had grown during our absence, the furniture lined up against endless walls, and after lunch, without my mother to worry about my skinniness and to make me eat this, eat that, I went back up the slope to the cemetery, found her among the tombstones, and said "Mommy, I haven't eaten a thing all day" to get back at her for her absence, her silence, her disdain, and my brother, who instantly forgot about her, going straight back to the threshing floor to play with the wounded dog, chasing butterflies, stared for a second at the photograph before sinking his lips back into the carpet, saying "I don't know who she is, probably some old bag from around here, because my sister's a brunette who crouches in the sand, gazing at the sea of Esposende."

It can't be from the alcohol, I thought, because they don't fuss, or fight, or see animals, or beat me up, it's not necessary to call the fire department to stop them from destroying the shop with a shotgun, they're both calm, peaceful, eating corn off the floor, it can't be from the alcohol, because alcohol enrages, and I thought this until my brother's cohort pulled from his pocket a length of satin cloth, which he began to wrap around his head like a bandage, saying "As soon as I put on this turban and chug another beer, because I'm dying of thirst, we can leave Odemira and jaunt over to North Africa, it's been at least a month since I've seen ostriches and camels."

While my brother's cohort secured the turban with adhesive tape on the nape of his neck and stuck a saucer-size ruby between his eyes, I tried to count the bottles on the table, getting up to twenty-eight before I lost track, and I began to suspect that it could after all be from the liquor, because there are people whose liquor is strangely gentle, people whose booze is peaceful, when I first came to work as a housemaid in Lisbon, my boss, a Swede, would spend his weekends sitting in front of a mirror with an assortment of whiskies, and he didn't demand anything, didn't bother anyone, he was just happy to sing the folk tunes from his native land, on Monday morning I'd bring him a fizzy tablet in a teacup, he'd drink it, shave, and say in a perfectly normal voice "Today, Orquidea, I'll have soufflé for dinner," and drive off to work, vanishing so quickly that if I went to the mirror, I could still see him crooning country dances in the glass, since, as everyone knows, the reflections of drunk people take hours to fade away, so that long after they've left they still look at us from out of polished surfaces, round faced in teapots, skinny in knives and forks. Yes, there are people whose liquor is strangely gentle, people who quietly, contentedly ferment like flies in vinegar, and perhaps this was the case with my brother and the lover of camels, perhaps they were of the same race as the Swede, who is no doubt still singing folk songs in the mirrors of all the houses he's lived in, and I was worried about them traveling at night without anyone to look after them, so that despite the stones in my urethra and kidneys and despite the crystals in my bladder I announced, "Without me my brother, whose leg's in bad shape and who has a daughter to raise, isn't leaving Hyacinth Park, so if you want to go anywhere, reserve a seat for me on the bus,"

because it's much easier to agree with a drunk than to argue with him, so that when my father complained about mice, I kept my mouth shut and beat the floor tiles with the broom, if he said "Get these lizards and grasshoppers off my clothes," I ran the brush over his jacket, and if the cinema owner had calmly asked me "What's this about storks?" I would have readily answered "Storks? Did I say anything about storks? I was distracted, forget about it, storks, that's crazy," and the proof I'm right is that the guy with the turban, looking at me from beneath his ruby, turned to my brother and said "Now there's the kind of woman I like," and to me, "I'll bet you're the best student of my correspondence course in hypnotism, have you read the latest illustrated booklet, which shows beginners how to fly backward like hummingbirds?"

and I to myself, with the millstone weighing in my gut, No doubt about it, they've gone bonkers, the beer made them go bonkers the way my father went bonkers at the end of a squid dinner to celebrate my stepmother's birthday, he finished the rice, stiffened his body, raised his arms over his head, and said "There! I'm an acacia tree," "Huh?" marveled my uncle, who castrated animals for a living, "I'm an acacia," insisted my father as he climbed onto the tablecloth, "In May my branches will begin to bud." "My husband thinks he's a tree," explained my stepmother to the pharmacist, "Do you sell injections against trees?" and I added, "He's forgotten all about the shop and the fabrics, he spends the whole day perched on a table and pleading 'Don't prune me, don't prune me, that branch there is healthy,'" and the pharmacist said "I don't know of any drug for fighting trees, have you tried in Oporto?" and my father, sending roots into the tablecloth, shooting branches toward the ceiling lamp, and dropping pollen from his hair, asked us to open the window because he missed the early evening breeze, but after a week we had to bolt the shutters, "Sorry, Dad," because during the night bats were flying out of the hollows of his trunk, and when his breath was just a tiny cold north breeze he had to be sawn in half to fit in the ambulance, and my stepmother, wiping her eyes, lamented to the family, "To be an acacia is a dreadful disease," the doctor called us aside, saying "If you plant him in the yard and fertilize him with care, he may improve," and my brother, pounding his pickax on the carpet, said to the guy with the turban, "Hummingbirds, shmummingbirds, flying is a cinch with the aid of a little beer, just a few sips was enough to get me from Johannesburg to the Minho region, what's hard is to travel below ground, like miners and the dead,"

and I agreed, "Of course," thinking of my dead mother swimming beneath the poplar trees in Monção, alone in the darkness, as when we wake up in the morning completely disoriented, not knowing the time, not knowing where to reach for the alarm clock, my mother, who has also died in the photos, like all the deceased, for when you look at a picture you understand immediately whether the framed figure is alive or dead, the expression is so different, the gaze so different, more distant, hazier, sadder, I've never had the courage to go back to Esposende, much less the Minho, where I'd have to fight not to hear my mother's voice asking if I've thinned, if I'm avoiding drafts, if I eat my soup, and if I ever returned to Esposende it would be to remember, next to February's waves, the man with the cap and cigarette who died, I know he died, because his eyelids have wilted in the photograph, don't argue, don't marvel, don't ask me how I know, but I know, I know because of his wilted smile, his smile in which I soaked my affection the way people soak bread in their morning coffee, I know, I know because his eyes suddenly looked troubled,

rockroses rockroses rockroses rockroses rockroses rockroses rockroses, the juice of my thighs, the blood of my thighs on the rockroses

because the photo pleaded "Help me," because for the first time it pleaded "Don't go away, Orquidea," and I, who never knew his name, who never had the courage to ask him what it was, answered

(and the dunes, how speak of the dunes where in the evening dogs howled?)

"I won't go, I swear I won't go away, I'll sit on a rock and talk with you while the drone of the lifeboat descends into the water," and the professor of hypnotism, straightening his turban, said to my brother, "Anyone who flies over the clouds can fly below ground like the blacks, if there were a mine here in Odemira, I'd show you,"

and my brother to me, "Go get me a beer, sis, I'm tired of being a pigeon, look in the cupboard, where I hid a few bottles behind the shoe polish,"

and the other guy, "A thousand feet below ground or even two thousand, Oliveira, it's all the same, and I don't need an elevator, I can get down to the tunnels with a few flaps of my wings, then back up, then back down, pushing a dozen mine cars while I'm at it,"

and my brother, supporting himself on the furniture as he stood up, "Easy to talk, my friend, but I'd like to see if you really have the guts,"

and the medium, likewise standing up, after pecking at one last kernel, "Then hand me your pick and I'll start digging,"

and the rockroses, whirling with the pine trees, the wind, and the sea, sailed over Alcântara's traffic circle and the slope of Hyacinth Park, I heard the trawlers' engines and the captains yelling orders as the sea, the pines, the wind, and the rockroses passed over the stairs, the doormat, and the hat stand in the foyer, a fisherman wearing rubber boots ran in through the window, the waves frothed against the sofa, and the living room was filled with a fog so heavy that I could hardly make out my brother and his cohort saying farewell as they vanished under the floorboards.

book three

journey to china

I

I've been here next to the beach for centuries, but I've never heard the sea, as I never heard the footsteps coming up the gravel path when they came to get me, on a Sunday after lunch. They rang the bell, my sister Maria Teresa looked up from her crochet and asked "Who could that be at this hour?" My brother, who was laying out cards for a game of solitaire, put down the deck and his cigarette and walked to the door, saying "Probably a beggar, but I don't have any change," the bell rang again, at the same time as the telephone, I picked up the receiver and the voice of Colonel Gomes barked "Get out of there on the double, Valadas, they're on their way to arrest you," and three soldiers suddenly stood in the foyer, accompanied by a civilian with a pistol, "Please come with us, Major, there's a car waiting for you."

I'd always thought things might turn out badly, but not that fast, and not in that way. We were still only in the planning stage, we still hadn't decided which units to contact, we were just eleven officers who met in each other's homes, Commodore Capelo assured us that the chief of staff knew of our plans and approved, we were extremely cautious in our overtures among the ranks, with no mention of politics, no criticizing the prime minister, just a few demands on behalf of the military, just the desire for a larger role in the state bureaucracy, because don't forget, my dear brigadier, that this is 1950, do we or don't we have a say in this nation, and we waited for a show of interest, for some kind of response, the idea was to rally the troops and sound out the units, but some opportunist ratted on us to the ministry or the state police so that he could get a promotion for distinguished service and enter the good graces of the regime, maybe it was Commodore Capelo, maybe it was Colonel Gomes, the same colonel who was shouting over the phone "Leave your house immediately, Valadas, we have a man waiting in Penafiel who will take you to Spain, they've already nabbed Barrela and Monteiro," and the civilian, "You can put down the receiver, Major, this is no time to be murmuring sweet nothings, you'd think my invitation had taken you by surprise."

My sister Anita began to cry, my sister Maria Teresa, marking the last stitch with her fingernail, got huffy, "What do you think you're doing?" and the lieutenant who commanded the two enlisted men politely answered "Nothing special, ma'am, we just want to have a friendly chat with the major, we'll bring him back tonight as fresh as a daisy, it seems there are a few wise guys who'd like to overthrow the powers that be," and my brother, who was born a half-wit and thinks only of manicurists' asses, moved his paunch forward and announced "I'm a legionnaire, and if you don't leave Jorge in peace, I'll go straight to headquarters in Amadora and get all the men to riot."

I was so busy wondering who had ratted on us and who hadn't that I didn't even notice the civilian walking toward me, snatching the phone, listening for a second, and saying, almost with pity, "Surprise, Colonel, we're already here, we've got the bird in our hand, no use wasting your breath, because the man in Penafiel works for us, and if I were you, Colonel, I'd go to the balcony and take a peek, you have visitors waiting for you on the sidewalk." The phone on the other end immediately hung up, and the civilian, waving his pistol, said "Put on your coat, Major, because it's cold, I've never seen such a deceptive spring, my poor wife gargles and gargles but still keeps on sneezing, I'd give anything for a night of peace and quiet."

The lieutenant and enlisted men went through the drawers, flinging around towels, shoving aside dishes, and flipping through bundles of letters, while I watched my sister Anita cry and remembered our last meeting, in the garage of an air pilot in the reserves, wondering, If it wasn't Gomes, could it have been

Alexandre? I never really trusted Alexandre, his father is palsy-walsy with Salazar, it was the commodore who insisted he be part of the group, could it have been the commodore? My brother said "Leave those letters alone, they were written by my parents and they're personal, don't crumple the flowers in the envelopes," and the lieutenant, poking a fork into the soil of a flowerpot, "Take it easy, this is just a routine inspection, no one's going to hurt your belongings."

The phone rang again, the civilian motioned us with a raised hand not to answer, my sister Maria Teresa—whose fingernail still marked the last stitch as she marched toward the soldiers, unafraid of their rifles, "What do you think you're doing?"—froze with one foot in the air, the civilian waited until the fifth ring to pick up the phone and snarled into the receiver "Yes, that's right, no resistance at all, but the turncoat colonel made a call here, yes, we'll be on our way as soon as we finish searching, tell Captain Alexandre that the police couldn't be more grateful, he can count on us for whatever he needs, take care, Commodore, hope to see you soon."

The commodore and Alexandre in cahoots is too much, I thought, How stupid of me, I should have suspected that cock-and-bull story about the chief of staff's approval, I should have suspected those meetings at Capelo's beach house in Caparica, everything laid-back, no precautions, his daughter serving snacks and vermouth, Capelo wearing sandals and his shirt unbuttoned, all jovial, confident, "So let's get rid of the fascists, how about it, let's finish off the dictatorship in Portugal, it's been five years since Hitler committed suicide and we should commemorate the event, I believe our nation, in spite of everything, is ready for democracy, don't you?" Alexandre nodded his head in agreement, Monteiro nodded agreement without removing his eyes from the legs of the daughter serving vermouth, Colonel Gomes tried to moderate the commodore, "Watch your words, João, don't drink any more or you'll lose control," I, leaning over a balcony with geraniums, looked out at the ocean, and the commodore answered "I guarantee we're going to overthrow Salazar, Carlos, I guarantee I'll have three ships in front of Commerce Square in the wink of an eye," and the wife, a nice woman, slid open a glass door, stuck out a smile, and said "Good afternoon, don't get up, how about some lobster salad?"

I should have suspected right away, I should have told my buddies, I should have gone to navy headquarters and said "Listen, Commodore Capelo, this was all a trap to find out who's loyal to the government, today we're going to inform on you to the secretary of state," I should have seen him turn white, wipe his forehead, hesitate, and finally stammer "But that's crazy, everything I've done is with the minister's knowledge and consent," and I, walking to the door, would say "Well, Commodore, I'm relieved to know you're as patriotic as we are." I should have spoken in private to Colonel Gomes, "I hate to break it to you, but your childhood friend is an informer for the government, I just saw him at navy headquarters," etc., etc., telling him to warn the others and to draft a letter swearing his loyalty to the regime and suggesting, without citing names, that all enemies of corporativism be dismissed from the army, as we simultaneously spread the word in the barracks that there were officials who defended the idea of democracy over clandestine cocktails at Caparica Beach, but the commodore's enthusiasm was contagious, his daughter's legs were gorgeous, and everything always seems easy in summer, "Let's have no ceremony, here we're all cadets," proclaimed the old man as he started in on the lobster, white wine in hand, and I was fool enough to fall for it, to believe in his wife's smile, to believe in their daughter, and now one of the soldiers was ransacking my grandfather's desk, rifling through paid bills, notebooks, dead memories, wan regrets, the dust of the past, and my brother to the civilian, "What fucking harm did the deceased do to you that you have to paw through their stuff like that?" and the civilian, pressing his pistol into my brother's gut, "Lean against the wall and shut up, if I had a paunch like yours, I wouldn't prattle on in front of a gun."

Even the fox got nervous, bumping into the wire walls of its cage, and even I got scared when the lieutenant suddenly froze, to listen, forgetting my grandparents' junk, "I thought I heard footsteps overhead," and from the corner of my eye I saw my sister Maria Teresa quickly knock over my godmother's Bambi, which shattered on top of the backgammon board, the sound of footsteps faded, and the civilian, pushing me outside with the tip of his pistol, "Don't get carried away, Lazaro, it's not likely they have Lenin holed up in the attic, come on, let's go, they're anxious to hear from the major back at the bureau."

I remember that the soldiers wouldn't allow my family to say good-bye, I remember the telephone trilling without letup, softer and softer as we walked down the gravel path toward the gate, I remember the civilian sitting in the front seat of the Ford and puffing on a cigarillo while telling the lieutenant all about his wife's cold, her handkerchiefs, lemon teas, linseed poultices, aspirins, I remember us stopping on Rua António Maria Cardoso, in front of the bureau, I remember them ordering "Get out," and at that moment my sister Maria Teresa was calming down the footsteps in the attic, "It wasn't anything, nothing happened, just lie down and try to rest," my brother was taking the bus to Amadora to shout at his fellow legionnaires "Jorge's been arrested, our country is run by a bunch of lunatics," and I, after corridors and stairways and offices, sat in front of a desk where a bald man, attended by an Indian with goiter, tapped his pen against the wooden surface and exclaimed "Well, at long last, Major Valadas, what a pleasure, I've been dying to meet you."

The commander of the Legion barracks, who was whispering over the phone "Of course I love you, cupcake, of course I love you," was concerned about my brother, "Calm down, Valadas, move those files off the sofa and lie down," my sisters took a taxi to the home of a director-general cousin in hopes he could save my neck, my brother, whose mustache twitched in panic, said "They've thrown Jorge in the clinker, Frederico, you're a powerful man, you know a deputy, so what will you do to straighten out this mess?" the director-general cousin opened wide his arms, "I can't make any promises, Teresa, the cabinet just got reshuffled and I don't know who ended up in the Interior, but I'll do my best to find out what's up with Jorge," and the bald man, examining his pen, "Treason, bribery of military personnel, attempted overthrow of the prime minister, this is serious stuff, Major Valadas, there are countries where people are executed for less, even if I interceded on your behalf, I wouldn't be able to help you,"

and for hours and hours, I don't know how many, because they took away my watch and the ceiling lamp eternalized time, he asked questions and I muttered replies, trying to figure out his strategy, I wanted to pee, I wanted to eat, I wanted the lobster salad and the legs of the commodore's daughter on the terrace at Caparica, I wanted the mess hall in Tomar, with Margarida, "Tomorrow I'll let you know something, maybe I'll have some good news," promised the cousin as he whisked my sisters toward the front door, and the bald man abruptly dropped his pen and snapped at the Indian with goiter, "Let him have it, Nicolau, this customer doesn't want to cooperate."

The man with goiter applied a swift kick to my chair, then a second kick into my groin, the lamp swayed, the desk flew toward me, then retreated, and instead of pain I felt a strange peace, while my sister Anita, on the landing, asked "At three o'clock, Luís Filipe, can we come around at three?" and the director-general answered "At three, okay, leave a message if I'm not here, sorry to be in such a rush, but my son-in-law's family is here visiting," Nicolau massacred my shoulders, knees, chest, "You piece of shit, trying to corrupt the army,"

and I, far away, in a beach chair on the commodore's terrace, sucking out the contents of a lobster claw and talking with the young girl, almost touching her face with my fingers, far away from the commander of the Legion, who said "It's probably nothing, they made a mistake, it'll work out," far away from the bald man's questions and Nicolau's rage, immersed in an ocean of happiness, tenderness, innocence, where my mother again smiled at me, assuring me without words that none of us would ever die.

And so I've been here for centuries, next to the beach, but I've never heard the sea. Next to the beach, I know, because of the seagulls' cawing, the iodine color of the air I breathe, and the motors of the fishing boats I hear at night in this barracks I inhabit, a barracks in the Algarve, in the town of Tavira, whose bridge I was so fond of, and the square called Fatinha, when I was a corporal. Centuries without visitors, without mail, without newspapers, oblivious of the world, centuries with a lieutenant colonel opening the door every now and then, "So is the room service of our hotel acceptable, Major?" as I keep thinking, I miss the commodore's daughter, I miss Caparica Beach, I miss the lobster salad, what happened to Colonel Gomes, to Barrela, to Monteiro? The doctor at Rua António Maria Cardoso had me interned in the Fort of Caxias with six broken ribs, badly gashed eyebrows, and two displaced vertebrae, I heard the bald man's voice, three or four feet from me, explain to the doctor, "Nicolau got a little worked up, I wish my other agents had his mettle," my brother insisted with the legionnaire, "I've always backed the regime, Frederico, I've always hated the democrats, and there's no way Jorge, who has my same blood and spent fifteen months in Timor, could ever be a conspirator," the director-general cousin was never at home, even though his car was parked out front, the housekeeper told my sisters "The director-general went to a meeting at Commerce Square, the director-general went to a dinner at the Uruguayan embassy, the director-general just left for Italy on a business trip, try again next week, try in about two weeks from now, try again next month," they took me on a stretcher to an enclosed yard where a group of policemen played ball, then they stuck me into an army ambulance, my back was throbbing, my teeth were throbbing, there were spongy caverns in my gums, as soon as we started moving I asked "Where are we going now?" and a corporal who was taking my blood pressure said, "We're on our way to China, pal, didn't they tell you that you're going to China? China, yes, and it takes a long time to get there."

Caxias was next to the beach, like Tavira, but without the breath of Africa at night, just the smell of sewers and the river turning into sea. In the bed to my right an old geezer refused the soup, refused the capsules, and resisted the shots, which they administered anyway, in between slaps, jabbing the needle through his pajamas, while I, with a metal collar around my neck, memorized the islands that formed a demented explorer's map on the ceiling, and as soon as I was able to sit up they ordered "Get dressed" and took me back to Rua António Maria Cardoso, to the office of the bald man, who still tapped his pen against the desk and was still attended by the goiter-afflicted Indian, "Now that you've recovered from the flu, Major, how about telling us the names of the officials who contacted you?"

only this time, at his side, sat Commodore Capelo himself, not with sandals and his shirt unbuttoned, but in uniform, severe, with three rows of medals, "Just look at you, Valadas, all shabby and disheveled, a disgrace to the military,"

and the bald man, "Your Excellency the commodore is absolutely right, this official is unpresentable, look at his clothes, look at the scars on his face," and Commodore Capelo, "That's how lunatics and renegades are, and to think that I introduced him to my wife and my daughter,"

his daughter, whom I ran into at the movies one Saturday, she was with some girlfriends, and as she left the theater she dallied just long enough for me to grab her arm and ask her if she'd join me for a cup of tea, and on the following Sunday we went to see an American comedy, I bought seats in the last row, and after the intermission, as soon as the lights were out, I gave her my hand, her name was Alice, I could feel her skin's warmth through her skirt, and if I sniff my hands, I can still smell her, if I close my eyes, her shoulder leans against mine, she was a pharmacy student, her boyfriend was a cadet, but she wanted to marry me,

and the bald man, accelerating the rhythm of his pen against the desk, "That's serious, Your Excellency, a slob like this contaminating your home,"

Alice fabricated a weekend at a girlfriend's house in the country, and we went to Buarcos, she'd had her hair done up and her nails trimmed, she was gorgeous,

Do your remember the small hotel, do you remember the sea that gnawed the rocks all afternoon?

we saw a sick sea swallow squawking among the rocks, you ran toward it and it flew away,

and Commodore Capelo, "Extremely serious. We want what's best for our loved ones and unwittingly open our doors to scum like this,"

and Nicolau, crushing my testicles with his heel, "Names, you bastard, cough up some names," and the legionnaire to my brother, "Every family has a black sheep, why do you think yours should be an exception?"

and you, in Buarcos, fell asleep with your thumb between your teeth and an ankle between my ankles,

the sea swallow fell through a crevice in the rocks, we could see it agonizing in a puddle, surrounded by crabs,

after waiting for hours, sitting on the stairs without eating, my sisters finally found our director-general cousin (who hadn't after all gone to Italy to handle matters of state) in the elevator, reeking of cologne, and he said "I've been working like mad, I haven't had time to look into Jorge's case, now clear out and don't come back or I'll call the police," an ass kisser who got his first job because my father pulled strings, an incompetent who owes everything he is to my old man,

"Don't you feel ashamed," resumed the bald man, "for having troubled the commodore's wife and daughter?"

and Nicolau, "Spit out the names that the commodore doesn't know, spit out the names before I mash you to a pulp,"

"I've never been in love with him, I'm going to call it off," swore Alice with a balled-up handkerchief in her hand, "I think I'm pregnant, promise you won't leave me,"

and by late afternoon, when we went back to the rocks, the tide had carried off the sea swallow and covered the crabs with foam,

and I, stroking her neck, "Silly thing, don't be afraid, I won't leave you, how could I ever leave you?"

and Buarcos at night, Alice, and the ocean's halo, and your saliva gleaming when you smiled at me,

"I love you,"

"You mean you don't even show respect for ladies?" continued the bald man,

"My period didn't come," lamented Alice when we met at the corner of her parents' street, and she hadn't been to the hairdresser or had her nails trimmed, "What are we going to do, Jorge?"

and I, who that very morning had received word of my transfer to Chaves and was despairing at the thought of growing old in the north, "An abortion,"

"We just want to find out where he is," countered my sister Anita in a humble whisper, "We don't want to trouble you, we just want you to help us find him,"

"Commodore Capelo," I stammered with difficulty in a cloud of suffering that dissolved my voice, while Nicolau's heel pounded me

pounded me

pounded my privates, "Commodore Capelo was part of the conspiracy, we conspired to the hilt at his house in Caparica,"

and the bald man, "Commodore Capelo, acting with our knowledge and sending us monthly reports, pretended to be a democrat, he put up with your poppycock out of love for the regime, the minister has already proposed that he be promoted to admiral, and the prime minister is very receptive to the idea,"

"An abortion?" said Alice, "You want me to get an abortion, Jorge?"

It was hot, it was summertime, and you wore a straw hat with flowers and cherries,

and the director-general cousin, "You don't want to trouble me, but that's exactly what you do, I'm sick of you calling up, sending notes, talking with the housekeeper, patrolling the building,"

it was hot, it was summer, I was going north to Chaves, and I didn't want to marry you in spite of your legs, your figure, your tongue in my ear, your nineteen years of innocence, and "I met Margarida at a lotto game, the truth is that I just don't love you anymore,"

"Margarida?" asked Alice, "Who's Margarida?"

"The truth is that I got the commodore's slutty daughter pregnant," I eked out under Nicolau's shoe, "and I would have screwed his wife if she weren't a barrel of lard,"

"All families have black sheep," the legionnaire lectured, "just the other day my nephew confessed to being a Freemason, my brother-in-law made a vow to go to Fátima on foot if God makes the boy straighten out,"

Buarcos and its narrow streets, Buarcos by the sea, does Buarcos still exist, what's Buarcos like today?

Buarcos Buarcos

"From here to Fátima on foot," measured the legionnaire in his mind, "is one hell of a trek, you can imagine my poor brother-in-law's anxiety,"

"And Jorge?" asked my brother, "What about Jorge's anxiety?"

"What?" exclaimed Commodore Capelo to the bald man, "You allow this beast to insult me like that?"

"I'm in no position to be supporting children," I said while flagging a cab, "Don't worry, I'll find a midwife who'll solve the problem in a jiffy,"

"You're the only one we know who can help," sighed my sister Anita, "but don't worry, Luís Filipe, we won't be back,"

but Alice didn't go to the midwife, and she married the cadet, in Chaves I saw photos in the newspaper of the newly-weds leaving the church under raised swords, rice, and rose petals, and are there still crabs in Buarcos, what dead sea swallows float away with today's tide, what English tourists occupy the room that was ours?

the bald man got up, walked around the desk, and ordered "Let up, Nicolau," and the goiter sufferer stopped pressing with his shoe,

Margarida, I thought, when all this is over you'll take the train to Chaves, but I'm alone in Tavira, alone for centuries in Tavira, next to the beach and I can't even hear the ocean, I hear the trawlers and the bugles from the barracks, I hear the bald man yelling, "Say you're sorry, you bugger, say you're sorry or I'll kill you like a mangy mutt," I hear Alice laughing in Buarcos in Buarcos in Buarcos as the albatrosses cawed, the wind howled in the crags, and my joints were cracking, I hear the phone at Calçada do Tojal and Colonel Gomes barking "Get out of there on the double, Valadas, they're on their way to arrest you,"

Say you're sorry, you bugger, I think I'm pregnant, Every family has a black sheep, or I'll kill you right now,

or we can go to Buarcos, Margarida, I know a restaurant right on the beach, I'll bet you never saw the wagtails on the cliffs, the seaweed, the fig trees overlooking the sea, and the fragrance of the leaves, the milk of the figs, white milk, thick milk, like my blood, like happiness, like the fear I feel, white, white, You mean you allow, No I don't allow it, Commodore, this beast, We have a man waiting in Penafiel who will take you to Spain, to insult me like that?

they've already nabbed Barrela, they've nabbed Monteiro, You can put down the receiver, Major, this is no time for murmuring sweet nothings, and this absence of pain, this cloud's or bird's way of being, his slutty daughter, babies no way, I float, I hear footsteps in my head as in the attic of our house on the Calçada do Tojal, but it's a secret, says my sister Maria Teresa, we can't tell anyone, if they start beating me again, I'll tell, "Where are we going now?" I asked the corporal taking my blood pressure in the ambulance, and he lifted his eyes from the strip of mercury: "We're on our way to China, pal, didn't they tell you that you're going to China? China, that's right, and the bitch is that it takes months and months to get there."

2

It was practically impossible, when they arrested Jorge, to calm down her nervous pacing in the attic, back and forth, back and forth, so forceful that a chunk of plaster fell from the ceiling in my sister Anita's bedroom, revealing a nest of rats on a wooden beam. Teresa would go up the stairs every five minutes to quiet her down, chiding her until the pacing stopped, and then we would hear the rocking of the rocking chair or a tango on the gramophone, Teresa would come back down the stairs, and a minute later the chair and the tango would stop and the pacing resume, throwing the clocks out of kilter. The photos of the deceased also looked worried, and I remembered when we were little and I played with her and the seamstress's son in the yard by the kitchen, and I said "Why don't we ask the doctor to prescribe something for her nerves?" whereupon there was dead silence overhead, and then she began to scream.

It was Sunday, there were more storks than usual in the palm tree at the post office or else perched on the church bells and the chimneys of rooftops, Teresa interrupted her crochet to look at me, and once again I was a child, gaping at the diopters that transformed her eyes into insects and her eyelashes into insect legs.

Anita and Teresa stared at me, the caged fox whimpered with hunger, sniffing its empty bowl, and now we were about twenty years old and our bedridden father, surrounded by vaporizers that impregnated him with a eucalyptus smell, decreed "No one is to know, I don't want anyone to ever find out," while pointing at the redheaded girl sitting on the ground, diligently ripping up magazines with her fingers. "No one should be told," echoed our mother in a chair next to the bed's shadows, "No one can ever, ever be told about Julieta," insisted my father as

Jorge nodded yes, Anita nodded yes, Teresa nodded yes, and I ran my eyes over the dresser covered with pills, syrups, and ointments, out of which rose a Christ agonizing on his crucifix, and above the Christ the curtains that kept out the afternoon, enclosing the room in a mortuary atmosphere.

As the shouts in the attic shattered the crystal and cracked the vases, my sisters' indignation prolonged my father's decree, as if the old man were once again sitting on the sofa in the living room, dressed in pajamas and wrapped in a blanket, and so I added, "A doctor we know and can trust, of course, because if this hollering keeps up, not a single tureen will remain intact," and our father immediately stepped out of one of the picture frames to ask the lamps and the fireplace "What did I do to deserve such a stupid son?" It was five or six o'clock on a Sunday so hot it wilted the geraniums, my friends in the pastry shop were passing notes to the ladies with dyed hair who drank tea with their pinkies curled in the air, one of the screams from the attic broke a windowpane, it was a Sunday, just as it was when we buried our father, in autumn, on the side of the cemetery that faced the hill of Monsanto

(during a storm so heavy the priest didn't even get out of the car, he sprinkled his holy water from the window),

Anita climbed the stairs to take her a pot of herbal tea, to turn the crank on the gramophone, to beg her to quiet down, "Hush, Julieta," but the screams continued, confounding the clocks, with the cuckoos opening their doors to announce impossible hours and the pendulums swaying like a ship's hindquarters, repeating "What did I do to deserve such a stupid son?" the figures on the music boxes whirled to the jingle of frenetic minuets, it was Sunday, the storks came and went from the palm tree of the post office, the frogs croaked in the reedy swamps of the viscount's estate, our father, shrouded in the same uniform he was buried in, warned me from the silver-framed photos not to call the doctor, "No one is to know, do you hear? I don't want anyone to ever find out," and so I finally said to my sister Teresa "I'll go and look for an open pharmacy so that I can buy a bromide," one of the bromides that our mother used to make her swallow when she was pregnant (she who never once left the house) with my nephew,

(and we sent away all the maids to prevent them from sharing our shame, our revulsion, our hatred)

when her belly got so big she'd holler with fright all night long, wandering through the rooms to observe her body's changes in the mirrors, when she got pregnant and we didn't know how, since we shut her up in the pantry whenever there were visitors, nor did we want to know, since that would lend weight to her offspring's existence

(and she secretly gave birth in Guarda, in my grandmother's village, and was calm, obedient, and affable when she returned, no longer waking up in the night and skipping through the rooms),

"I'll go and look for a pharmacy that's open on Sundays," I told my sister Teresa, "I'll buy a bromide to calm her down," our mother still stared at me apprehensively from a daguerreotype in which she and her godfather, wearing tails, stood in front of a backdrop with the Sphinx and the pyramids of Egypt, but since our father didn't even budge from his row of students at the military academy, in 1899, she relaxed, my father was just ten or eleven and didn't look like any of us, he was blonder, slimmer, more handsome, and already had the quartz pupils I remember from before we moved to this house in Benfica, when we were still in Queluz and he would come home from the barracks and lock himself up with our mother, whispering, in a room at the end of the hall,

and I'd ask my sister Anita "Are they angry at each other?" and she'd answer "Shut up," I'd ask my sister Teresa "Is Dad going to hit Mom?" and she'd say "Shut up," I'd ask my brother Jorge, "What's that noise?" and he'd say "What noise?" while my sister Julieta ripped up magazines, and from where we lived we could see the ocean, or rather, we could see rooftops and balconies and beyond the rooftops and balconies the ocean,

we could see the ocean, and then we moved here and the ocean disappeared, being replaced by storks, sheep, elms, and cowbells in the late afternoon, and the men in leather breeches who drove the cows, our father stopped whispering with our mother and instead sat around in the living room to read the paper or to take apart the radio and put it back together, desperately devoting himself to useless complexities, and it occurred to me that what he was really doing was awaiting death, minute by minute, with annoyed distraction, shortening the time that separated him from death by engaging in absurd tasks that our mother observed without daring to interrupt, afraid of the shadow that was devouring his face as if he were becoming his own ancestor, in a future prior to the present in which he lived, I said

(it was Sunday and a stork was finishing its nest in the Antunes' barn)

"I'll buy a bromide, sis, to make her stop screaming, because otherwise we'll be left with no glasses or windows and the clocks will go definitively haywire, the cuckoos' springs will snap and they'll fly around the living room, eating the crumbs from lunch with their wooden beaks," our mother, wearing a hat and standing next to her godfather, whom I never met, forgot about me in the midst of the pyramids and the Sphinx, our father didn't move a tendon to jump out of his row among the academy students, my sister Teresa checked to make sure it was okay with the deceased, with our aunts and uncles who looked at us from their picnics, their donkey rides, their bicycle trips to the Sintra of yesteryear, we could hear my sister Anita talking to Julieta in the attic and could imagine their mutual expressions of panic,

it was Sunday and we'd only recently moved to Benfica, my sister Julieta, who still hadn't taken to screaming in the attic, ran behind the chicks and crushed them with a brick, and Jorge laughed, clapping his hands and egging her on, "Kill some more, there's one that's running away, kill it," but it was me the cook always scolded, it was me she always complained about to my parents, "Fernando won't keep his hands off the poultry," and so they'd send me to my room without dinner, "What did I do to deserve such a stupid son? a son without a degree, who didn't study, who works for a company doing God knows what besides earning next to nothing, a forty-year-old man who spends his Saturdays in the pastry shop with the owner of the garage and the clerk from the notions shop (because he's always been attracted to people without culture or class), winking at the prostitutes who sit around drinking tea instead of going to mass, hussies who dress like actresses and use their fingernails to pick food from between their teeth," "One of these days you'll catch a venereal disease and become impotent," predicted Jorge, "a disease that disintegrates your testicles and destroys your bladder's capacity to hold urine," and I said, "I won't catch anything, those are honest women, not whores, where would I get the money to pay whores?" and our father, wearing his lieutenant colonel's galloons in a full-length portrait, decreed "No dessert for you this week," it was Sunday, a dozen storks flew around the chimney, my sister Anita played a waltz on the gramophone, a gush of sound in three-four time descended from the attic, and the worn-out needle kept repeating the same notes with excruciating insistence, the fox squatted on its hind legs and began to bark, the forks and knives rattled in the drawers, one of the cuckoos broke away from its clock and alighted on a drapery rod, cawing out the hour as its spring dangled from its tail, the other cuckoos vehemently fluttered inside their wooden boxes, a vase with roses slid toward the edge of the table, it was Sunday, the civilian and the three soldiers arrested Jorge after ransacking the whole house, my sister Teresa, with a bunch of our parents' letters in hand, examined the photos

(a stork balanced on top of the little iron hat that crowned the chimney)

and finally consented, exasperated by the waltz and the shouts, "Buy it from a pharmacy that's far away, where they don't know you and can't guess who it's for,"

refusing to admit to knowing what she knew everybody knew, namely that we were hiding Julieta in the attic, that we'd sent her to Guarda to give birth, that our nephew lived in Ericeira with one of the maids who used to work for us, and that we acted as though the little boy didn't exist, as though he hadn't been born, refusing to accept what everybody knew since our parents' time, when Julieta would run to and fro in the yard, crushing chicks and chickens with a brick as Jorge ordered, "Kill it, hurry up, kill that one over there,"

I changed my shirt, shined my shoes, put on some cologne, combed some grease through my mustache, and left the house just as the waltz was winding down, weary of reiterating its one-two-three, and the needle scratched the record label like a knife scraping a plate or chalk scraping a blackboard, making all the blood in our veins bristle. I changed my clothes and put on cologne, because I like the ladies in the pastry shop to appreciate my taste, to distinguish me from the owner of the garage and the clerk from the notions shop, whose boots, even in summer, are always covered with mud from the neighborhoods where they live. I walked down the Calçada do Tojal to the Estrada de Benfica with the tips of my shoes glistening, I turned left at the palm tree by the post office, and proceeded to the pastry shop that was next to the church, its already lit windows full of boxes of chocolates and bottles of anise liqueur. In the bar next to the pawnshop, with three balls hanging over the doorway, delivery boys talked in Galician, with their handcarts lined up on the sidewalk. I entered the pastry shop and forgot about my sister's screams, forgot about the photographs' reproaches, and forgot about the bromides, assuming a nonchalant air as I looked for the table with blond ladies who ate cream puffs every afternoon of the week, daintily wiping their mouths, as if they were drying tears. The garage owner and the notions clerk smiled at them from behind coffee cups stuffed with cigarette butts. A little dog with an organdy ribbon wrapped around its head barked for cookies in the lap of one of the ladies, whom the waiters pampered with egg custards and dishes of strawberries with cream. Thwarting the miracle I'd been counting on for years in vain, none of the goddesses turned to wave at me with her fan, smitten with love, so I sat down in the chair that the garage owner offered me, persecuted by my father's voice,

"What did I do to deserve such a stupid son?"

the same voice that bullied me at my job, on the streetcar, and in the movie theaters that colored my dreams, my father's voice that for forty years had been making fun of me, punctuated by sighs from my mother and snickers from Jorge, who came home on weekends from officer training school,

"What did I do to deserve such a stupid son?"

the voices that persecuted me everywhere, like the screams of my sister in the attic and like the eyes in the photos,

"What did I do to deserve such a stupid grandson?"

my own voice, choked by lather during my morning shave,

"What did I do to deserve being so stupid?"

not to mention the effeminate voice, with long eyelashes, of the porcelain shepherd children on the mantel over the fireplace, the voice of the disconnected radio, the millions of voices that overlapped, vied, crisscrossed, and lashed out on the telephone, the voice of the cook, the voice of elderly cousins shrouded in the boxes of tea biscuits from my childhood, it was Sunday, the stork swooped down over the woods, and I remembered the bromides as the garage owner muttered "Get a load of that chick's legs," I remembered the pistol-waving civilian and the bromides as the streetlights came on against the silhouette of houses, and soon afterward, accompanied by the clerk from the notions shop, who claimed to be on a first-name basis with all the downtown proprietors, I took the streetcar to Restauradores, in search of a pharmacy open on Sunday.

Even today, as an eighty-one-year-old widower who occupies a couple of rented rooms in a fifth-floor walk-up on the Rua Ivens and goes to Camões Square and the top of the Rua do Alecrim to gaze at the Tagus, even today, which I spend strolling down Rua do Loreto as far as the cable car of Bica, and I see the city sloping down under the sunlight toward the warehouses of Ribeira, even today, I was saying, I don't know Lisbon. A dentist with an office at Príncipe Real gardens my jaws, pruning my ever spottier rows of teeth, the arthritis doctor of Santos uses ointments to straighten out the wilted stem of my backbone, and the heart doctor, who installed a battery in my ribs to slow down my blood, forbids me to eat fats in a ground-floor clinic at Sapadores, where the victims in the waiting room all seem to hold their hearts in their hands, with each heart squeezed by a crown of thorns like the Jesuses in the pictures decorating the cubicles of concierges. The city, for me, is an Ursa Major of doctor's offices, whose North Star is the ophthalmologist's at Rossio Square, in the building of a travel agency that promises Bermuda to the cataracts that cloud my pupils, unable to decipher the letters on the chart that gradually get smaller, like my nostalgia for you, until dissolving in the minuscule vowels of complete oblivion. The city is a constellation of sigmoidoscopes, lumbar punctures, brain exams, rubber hammers that make my knee jump, and the suction cups of EKGs in which my arteries record, on a strip of paper, their illegible signatures, a Milky Way of hospitals and diagnostic centers separated by statues of dukes and kings pointing their fingers at each other, from square to public square, in accusations I don't understand today any better than I did on that Sunday of 1950, forty-two years ago, when I got off the streetcar at Restauradores to search, with the help of the clerk from the notions shop, for an open pharmacy in a forest of tailor shops, bars, alleys full of cheap and dubious hotels, and women standing on street corners in acrylic fur coats, communicating to us through the Morse code of cigarettes. Then, as now, I missed the warnings, recommendations, and prohibitions of the dead, I missed the palm tree of the post office and the pastry shop with the blond-haired ladies, I missed the twilight falling over the trees in the woods, I missed the bougainvilleas, Conceição, their clusters of flowers hanging over the stone wall, I missed my sister Julieta running after the chicks with a brick in her arms, I missed the waltzes and the whirl of tangos from the horn of the gramophone that I sometimes think I hear today, on Rua Ivens, if I wake up in the middle of the night, racked with gout, my ankle burning. I even miss Jorge's disdain,

"You're not going to quit until your testicles fall off,"

Jorge, who wouldn't talk to you if he were alive, who would be disgusted by your varicose veins, your slippers, and your grammatical mistakes, who would say to me, "I figured you'd end up marrying a housemaid, fortunately Mom is no longer around to witness such a disgrace," I even miss my rachitic nephew, whom I never saw again, not since I moved away from the Calçada do Tojal to move in with you, I miss the kid, I wonder what happened to him, what happened to all of them, the dentist promised to fit my mouth with thirty-two plastic teeth impervious to bad breath, cavities, and periodontal disease, it was Sunday, Conceição, Sunday, Sunday like when we went to matinees at the Eden to see Mexican movies starring Cantinflas, thirty-two teeth that chew, that don't hurt, that we can hold in our hand, that we can see without a mirror, that we can take out to relieve our jawbones, the clerk from the notions shop and I crossed the avenue at Restauradores

(on top of one of the buildings a neon coach rolled on and off) and entered the Rua dos Condes, we passed by the diner carpeted with peanut shells where you and I used to have supper after the matinee or on the day we got our social security checks, we headed to Portas de Santo Antão, passing by facade after facade of crumbling carved stone, through which we could make out stairways leading to rooms of people dying alone, with a pot of beans or potatoes next to the bed, and around the Coliseum we found unemployed clowns with thinning orange hair, trapeze artists whose sciatica prevented them from flying, and the flicking of their wrists produced tiny talcum clouds, they dreamed out loud of descending to the stage to receive the ovations of an absent audience, like me when I wake up and reach for you on the half of the pillow where you're permanently missing, and Julieta appears, in a pinafore and with a ribbon falling out of her hair, and, spurred on by my brother, she drops a huge brick onto my chest, in spite of my protests, it was Sunday

Sunday

a Sunday in 1950, forty-two years ago, "What did I do to deserve such a stupid son?" and the blond ladies were going home from the pastry shop,

"I figured you'd end up marrying a housemaid," a couple of rented rooms and a kitchen we shared with a Cape Verdean family that also lived there, "Thirty-two teeth, Mr. Valadas, thirty-two teeth and you'll look twenty years younger, you'll snag a peach of a girlfriend in no time flat," and my sister running after me, raising the brick over my head, "Kill him," old age mixes up the voices from the past, but I know it was Sunday, Sunday evening,

yes, Sunday,

Sunday at Portas de Santo Antão, with the smugglers, whores, clowns, trapeze artists, and the clerk from the notions shop and I in search of bromides, passing by the Portuguese

Youth headquarters, guarded by armed legionnaires, "You've shaken hands with a deputy, Frederico, they arrested my brother, help me,"

I married a housemaid, it's true, a housemaid who bought cigarettes for her boss in the café near my job where I ate lunch, a woman who wasn't young, wasn't pretty, and didn't dye her hair, the only woman who answered my smile with a smile, who waited for me out front, pretending to be looking at the wines in the window, a housemaid, Dad, I married a housemaid, I'm stupid,

and we reached Figueira Square, a perfect square enclosed by buildings of deserted offices with balcony windows but no widows, and after Figueira Square the shapeless prairie of Martim Moniz, and there were no pharmacies, no pharmacy open on Sunday, "Kill him," and after Martim Moniz came the Rua do Benformoso, the Largo do Benformoso, the Intendente district, red lights in the windows, blind piano players, hazy and dark figures, and it was there, in the Nymph of the Tagus bar, that it all started.

3

After five or six weeks

(or ten or twelve or twenty, who can tell me how long, Margarida?)

of urinating blood in the infirmary of the Fort of Caxias, my bladder full of crushed glass

(crushed glass, Mother),

they put me into a cell on the prison's lowest floor, where I tried to guess the time by the color of the sky, scarlet, blue, pale gray, white, or pitch black,

(who could explain to me the colors, who will come to Tavira to explain the colors?)

and where the dripping from a leaky faucet on the other side of the wall resounded during the night like lead. I heard neither the waves nor the wind of the Tagus, nor even the seagulls' cawing, and on Mondays

(they always said it was Monday, not Tuesday, not Wednesday, not Saturday, but Monday, they said "Get out of bed, it's recreation time")

they forced me to hobble with a cane around the prison yard, and one day I saw the faucet, I went over to turn it off, and a voice immediately ordered "Don't stop, don't touch anything, keep moving, faster, faster," so I trudged along the walls

(the sun didn't arrive that far down, the sun didn't arrive and I was cold in summer)

dragging my ankle across gravel and moss. If I fell, a foot on my back laughingly instructed "Get up, sleepyhead, no dozing," and only when I couldn't take another step did they haul me back to my cell, making fun of me, "You've got rubber legs, Major, you've got to recharge your battery," and in the middle of the night I would wake up to a fat guy sitting on a stool next to my bed, apologizing, "I really hate to do this, Major, you have no idea how it pains me to have to interrogate you, so please just give me the list of the units you infiltrated, and I promise you can walk right out of here a free man." Sometimes the fat man was accompanied by another individual, who would immediately lose his temper, raising his hand to smack me, and the fat man would step in, protecting me with his body, "Hold on, take it easy, we're all adults here, the major is a reasonable man, he'll cooperate," and to me, "I don't know how long I can keep my colleague at bay, Major, he's a real hothead, guys like him ruin the state police's reputation, you'd better answer quickly, you'd better spit out the names of the troops before something terrible happens," and his colleague, foaming, "Get out of the way, Duarte, so that I can cream this jerk," and the fat man, "See what I mean? See what I mean? Help me, Major, I don't want to see you get killed,"

the sky, without seagulls, turned from blue to scarlet and from scarlet to pale gray before it began to get dark, and the fat man, reasoning with his colleague, "Don't pressure the major, don't you ever have lapses of memory?" the faucet from the yard kept dripping, the drops of water pounding inside my brain, and the colleague, "Baloney, Duarte, sheer baloney, let me at him, because when I see a traitor it makes me ill," and the fat man to me, "For God's sake, Major, please start talking,"

the sky was black, completely black in the tiny window, the colleague smacked me, my mouth started bleeding, a kind of paste with some small hard bits rolled over my tongue, "I'm tired," and the fat man, "What?" "I'm tired," I repeated, "I'm going to sleep some, don't wake me up,"

and I went back years and years, to when the maid raised the blinds and said "If you don't get dressed right now, you'll be late for school and your father'll get mad at me," and I, hiding my eyes in my pillow, "Let him get mad, what do I care, just shut the window, you idiot," the blinds completely raised and the maid leaning over me, smelling like cereal and the silver polish, shaking my shoulders, "Get up, young man, get up,"

and I, buried in the sheets, "Leave me alone, Amalia, go to hell and leave me alone,"

and the fat man to his colleague, "He's tired, Fonseca, the son of a bitch says he's tired, give him a little wake-up medicine,"

and I to the fat man, without feeling the punches, "I'm going to tell my mother that you called me names, Amalia, I'm going to tell my mother that you hit me,"

and the maid, "All I did was shake you, it was nothing,"

and the colleague, "That's enough, Duarte, the guy blacked out, stop it, let him go,"

and the fat man, "Who cares if he blacked out? All I care about is that he gets what he deserves,"

and I, "Yes, you did hit me, I've got a bruise on my neck, I'm not going to school because you burst my veins, I'll have to go to the hospital and my mother'll fire you, Amalia,"

the sky in the window was blue, not scarlet, not pale gray, not black, the hill of Monsanto was green, the walls were cream colored, my father bounded three steps at a time up the stairs, "Are you ready, Jorge?" and I, in my underwear, "I'm ready I'm ready I'm ready I'm ready,"

the dentist at the Fort of Caxias extracted my broken molars and stitched my lip, the medics replaced the cast on my leg with a splint and rubbed my forehead with an ointment that burned, "So you had a little tumble, eh?"

and I to the maid, "Let me go to your room, Amalia, let me sleep with you for half an hour,"

and the colleague to the fat man, "The guy's gone dotty, I swear he's gone dotty, he's not just pretending, and it's no wonder after five days without ten winks of sleep,"

the sky changed from one color to another, orange, lavender, lemon lime, brown, bright red, and the fat man, "We'll

let the shrink have a look at him and then continue, I'll be a
monkey's ass if we can't get this guy to talk,"

and the maid, who was making my bed, "My room, Jorge,
you want to go to my room?"

"Jorge," shouted my father from downstairs, "do I have to
go up there and get cross with you?"

Monsanto all green, its trees on the sunny hillside, and
the rooftop of the prison at the top, surrounded by electric
poles, the maids lived in the attic and took their baths in a
wooden tub,

and the colleague to the fat man, "I'm assuming no responsibility, Duarte, the soldier goes straight to the infirmary, and
only when they give the green light do we continue,"

Monsanto all green and my mother's parakeets in the cage
out back, dozens of parakeets brooding eggs in their little wooden
boxes, and after a disease wiped them out the cage was empty
for the longest time, until someone gave us a fox, and I pressed
my chest against the maid's chest, "Touch me, Amalia," I'll never
forget your hands, I'll never forget your knees, I heard you immigrated to France and I wonder in which city you're growing
old as a concierge, how you live, whom you live with, how many
grandchildren you have, and if your body still smells like cereal
and silver polish,

and the shrink to the fat man, "He flipped out all right, so
I'm afraid you're going to have to lay off for a while,"

at first the fox drank milk from a baby bottle, ate cookies,
and slept in the kitchen, and my sister Maria Teresa only put it
in the cage (over my sister Anita's objections) when it began to
rip up the rugs and sofas, to knock over vases, and to pee in the
corners like me in Caxias, Margarida, just like me in the infirmary of the prison at Caxias,

they gave me shots, they removed my cast, I stopped feeling crushed glass in my bladder, I could chew again and walk
without a cane, it became easier to guess the time, it was always

midday and warm, my love, always the same blue, always the seagulls, always the river, ah, and the sirens of boats, Margarida,

"Where were you last night, Jorge?" asked my father, sitting with me in his locked office and tapping his horsewhip against his thigh,

and I gained seven pounds, my scars and bruises went away, I had a haircut, changed my clothes, shaved, and the doctor asked, "How do you feel, Valadas?"

"Don't put the fox in the parakeets' cage," pleaded my sister Anita to Teresa, "I'll clip its nails, I'll teach it to pee in some sawdust,"

"In my bed, Dad, where else would I sleep?"

"You understand, of course, that no one beat you up, no one mistreated you," the doctor explained, "You fell down, it was an accident,"

"Of course it was," I said, "I'm prone to losing my balance,"

"The fox smells to high heaven," decided my sister Maria Teresa while placing a bowl of water and a dish of food in the cage, "I can't abide having the creature indoors,"

"Nor would I put up with any violence," stressed the doctor, "our police force is a model of good behavior,"

"I can only thank the agents," I said, "for having acted like perfect gentlemen,"

"In your bed, you rascal?" snorted my father with his whip in the air, "In your bed, you say?"

it's your smell, Amalia, that I've always smelled when hugging a woman, it's your gestures I've always seen in theirs, and the hands that caress me have always been your hands,

"Outside it will get cold, Teresa," said my sister Anita, "outside it will get sick, poor thing,"

"In my bed, Dad, please don't whip me,"

"Well, I think you've understood," said the doctor brightly, "Do you feel you received inhuman treatment in our infirmary?"

"Lower your arm, you rascal,"

"Poor me," answered my sister Maria Teresa, "that I have to put up with its stink,"

and Amalia, walking down to the front gate and looking younger without her uniform, "They didn't say so, but I know it was because of you that I got fired, Jorge, my godmother's husband is going to be livid,"

Monsanto all green, my brother Fernando in the yard next to the kitchen, my sister Julieta chasing the chicks, the seamstress's son was cross-eyed and almost didn't talk, and you weren't even angry, Amalia, you weren't even bitter, just sad, walking toward the gate and drying your eyes with your hankie,

"Absolutely not, doctor, do I look like I was mistreated?"

and the next day Amalia returned with her godmother, whom my mother received in the living room, and the doctor said to me, "I would appreciate it if you not cross your legs when speaking to me,"

and when I was released from the infirmary they didn't take me back to my cell, they took me to a car at the hospital's main entrance, from where one could see not just the river but Lisbon, Estoril, and Cascais, and the open fields beyond the stadium, and my father, Amalia, hit me with the horsewhip, "You little rake,"

and we drove along the shore road slowly, as if on a leisurely outing,

(fishermen on the embankment, sailboats, people in swimsuits, umbrellas, ice-cream vendors, and I thought, It's Sunday, it must be Sunday, but which month?)

and the car entered the city at Commerce Square, proceeding directly to Rua António Maria Cardoso, where I was shown ("This way, Major") to an office occupied not by a bald man or goiter sufferer, but by an inspector with varnished hair parted in the middle, various phones on his desk, and bookshelves against the wall, the godmother slapped Amalia as they went out the door, "Just wait till we get home, you little trollop, just wait and see what's in store for you," and I said "I slept in my bed, Dad, I swear I slept in my bed, stop hitting me," and then a functionary appeared with a file folder, the sticky-haired inspector looked at me, "I'll be right with you," took a pair of glasses from a case, and began to initial, without reading, the papers he was handed, murmuring "Paperwork, paperwork, the time that's frittered away on paperwork," and my sister Anita, "Stink, what stink? the poor creature doesn't stink, I'll keep him in my room, sis, you can forget about the parakeets' cage,"

Monsanto all green, Monsanto with its so green trees, Amalia, do you remember the green of Monsanto in France?

and the gentleman handed over the last paper to the functionary, saying "Thank you, Proença," carefully folded his glasses, put them back in their case, and began with a sigh, "If by chance any of my staff went a little too far, then don't hesitate to tell me, Major, because if there's one thing I hate, it's gratuitous violence,"

"You were with the maid, you little rake, don't lie," shouted my father, "I saw you leave the attic in your pajamas,"

and the inspector, "In fact, it's not only gratuitous violence that I hate, Major, the very idea of violence abhors me, at the police academy I'm forever insisting on this point, I will not tolerate torturers among us,"

and my father, "There will be no hanky-panky in this house, absolutely no hanky-panky,"

and I to the gentleman, "I've been treated with the utmost consideration, sir,"

"If you think the fox doesn't stink, then you've lost your sense of smell," concluded my sister Maria Teresa, "but it's not just the stink, it's the shredded rugs, upholstery, and curtains, what we should do is give the animal away," and so they finally asked my brother Fernando to put it in the birdcage, and for the first few days the fox refused to eat and wouldn't quit barking and shaking the wire grating, and I, in the seventh cavalry at the time, would get woken up by its whimpering,

the godmother flogged Amalia on the back with her pocketbook,

and the inspector, "Unfortunately violence is intrinsic to man, as you can see from all the cruelty in the world in spite of the pope's appeals, in spite of the church's injunctions, just look at what the Germans did to the Jews, think of those ghastly photos of skeletons, and the Inquisition, for crying out loud, just think of the Inquisition,"

my sister Julieta talked only to me, she wouldn't obey anyone else, she'd call me into a corner and whisper "I want Mommy,"

and that's who I want right now, Margarida, I want my mother to hold me in her lap here in Tavira, to explain to me the colors of the sky, and to demand, "Open up the door, because I'm taking my son home,"

and my father, dropping the whip onto a chair, "Next week you're off to a boarding school in Santo Tirso, I don't want to see you until summer vacation,"

"History, Major, is a long line of gross atrocities," lamented the inspector, "The genocide of the Russian Revolution makes my blood curdle, the czar and his family executed, thousands of people slaughtered and millions deported, not to mention the hunger and poverty, what other nation has seen so much horror?"

Santo Tirso was far away, hours and hours on a train that wound through pine trees under an invariable rain, a large and chilly building with priests in cassocks and the students in breeches, I'll bet they all slept with their maids, I thought,

and my father to the headmaster, while shaking off the rain, "He's not to have visitors, he's not allowed to leave the school grounds, and he's not authorized to receive letters or to write his family," and the headmaster, "You can rest easy, Lieutenant, we've been dealing with difficult youngsters for over seventy years,"

Deer jorji I miss you mom dissmist the cook

"And yet, Major," continued the inspector, "it surprises and saddens me that right here in Portugal certain ignorant people are trying to implant a Bolshevism founded on blood and corpses, which is assuredly not what I dreamed for my children,"

Deer jorji the pairakeats all dide

"This young man isn't difficult, he's impossible," asserted my father, "He lied to me, he dishonored me, and he dishonored one of our maids,"

Deer jorji maria tereza is bad she wont let me play with her dolls

corridors, classrooms, dormitories, the footsteps of monitors in the gym, the cypress trees during recess, a mountain range in the distance, puddles, cigarettes in the bathroom, the geography teacher indicating tributaries on a map with his pointer,

"With faith and the right pedagogy even the most recalcitrant spirit submits, Lieutenant,"

Nothing, not even the barracks here in Tavira, is as grim as Santo Tirso, Margarida,

and my father to the headmaster "Don't let this rascal fool you, he's a smooth talker, a hoodwinker if there ever was one,"

Deer jorji I askt the seemstruss to male you this postcard

"And so, Major," persisted the inspector, "when I finished law school the police seemed to me the ideal career, albeit a thankless one, for combating violence,"

"Did you also get sent here because of your maid?" I asked the kid who sat in front of me,

and at the Rua António Maria Cardoso there are no pigeons, Margarida, there's the screeching of streetcars and a theater,

and the fox pranced along the wire grating, I never saw it stop and lie down in the cage,

"With our methods," assured the headmaster, "in five months' time you won't even recognize him,"

"Valadas," commanded Father Correia, "write five hundred times on the blackboard I promise not to smoke again in the lavatory,"

Deer jorji anita sez your coming home in awgust

"And it's in the name of that struggle," concluded the inspector, "the struggle of those who want the best for our country, that as one man to another man I urge you, Major, to describe your subversive activities,"

and I to Father Correia, "I'm not writing anything," and Father Correia, "What?" and I repeated "I'm not writing anything," and Father Correia, brandishing his ruler, "Hold out your hand, Valadas,"

I didn't go home that August or the next August, I spent the whole summer in the empty building of Santo Tirso,

"I'm not a subversive and I'm not a Bolshevik, all I want is democratic due process,"

"I'll complain to my mother, and she'll call your godmother and send you away," said the democrat to Amalia,

Deer jorji I dont like fernando I dont like anita I dont like tereza the seemstruss is ok

and the inspector, "Are you daring to suggest, Major, that corporativism is not democratic, that corporativism is not the best form of government?"

and I, thinking of Amalia and Father Correia, "That's right,"

and he, holding a finger in the air and answering the phone, "One moment, what? No, I wasn't talking to you, what is it, Portas?"

and my father, offering me a cigarillo, "I hope Santo Tirso has done you some good, and if you wish to apply to officer training school, then all well and good, we have five generations of army officers in the family, and it doesn't look like Fernando will amount to much of anything,"

and the inspector to the telephone, "If he won't sign the confession willingly, then have him sign it unwillingly, I don't understand your doubt,"

and my father, pouring me some brandy, "The cavalry is our branch of the service, son, I can't think of anything more ridiculous than an officer without a horse,"

and the inspector into the receiver, "Lawyer? Who cares about lawyers, Portas? Give the bozo some electric shocks and he'll swear he killed his aunt, if necessary,"

and my father, "Don't worry about the physical fitness tests, I've got friends in the administration, and if you graduate at the top of your class, I'll buy you a car,"

Deer jorji mom crize all daylong in her rume I dont no wuts rawng

and the inspector, "Since when have we worried about lawyers, Portas? Just give him the shocks, because the judges are on our side, in case you didn't know,"

"This horsewhip belonged to your grandfather and accompanied me in the Battle of Monsanto," stressed my father, "and it's only right that you should have it"

(the monarchists in trenches and the republicans scaling the hill and shooting their rifles, smoke, cannons, breeches, Captain Ramalho wounded in the stomach, the reinforcements that still hadn't arrived, my father stumbling in the gorse as a terrified crow cawed overhead),

and the inspector, hanging up the phone and pressing a buzzer, "So you want democratic due process, so you want socialism," and I said "I was never a Socialist, sir,"

I was never a Socialist, Amalia, forgive me, but I don't even like poor people, they age so quickly, dress so badly, look so ugly,

"And because of Monsanto," sighed my father, "I went through some hard times,"

and if they move up in life, Amalia, they buy tacky furniture, hideous cars, and atrocious bibelots, they dress their kids like circus dogs, and still use toothpicks, still burp at the table,

"Didn't I tell you," gloated the headmaster, "that your son would change? Faith, pedagogy, and a few raps on the knuckles have a transforming effect,"

If I were ever fool enough to marry you, Amalia, you'd cover the walls with pictures of kittens and fill the shelves with chinaware clowns, "I was never a Socialist," I insisted,

Deer jorji the doktor sez mom is sik and neads to have shots

"Thanks for the horsewhip, Dad, the leather is fantastic," I thanked him while flagellating my leg,

and two men wheeled a contraption with various dials and a pair of electrodes into the office on Rua António Maria Cardoso, the inspector said "There's a socket behind the sofa," and I thought, What's going on?

Deer jorji mom is wurse and anita told me sheeze going to be admittid into a clinick

and one of the men plugged in the contraption, a bulb lit up, a needle started twitching, the other man came up to me with the electrodes, and the inspector ordered, "The names of the revolutionaries, Major,"

"I was never a Socialist,"

"A wonderful horsewhip," agreed my father, "if well handled, it can slice an ear off, it's a pity they don't make them like this anymore,"

the first man pressed a button and my body lurched, my teeth rattled, my head flew away from my neck, and my heart, full of helium, stopped cold before it began beating again,

"I was never," Monsanto all green, Amalia's room, "a Socialist, sir,"

"Of course you weren't," concurred the inspector, "of course you weren't, again,"

and again my body leaping, again my teeth rattling, again my head separated from my neck, again my heart drifting and my blood at a dead halt, waiting,

"Again," ordered the enemy of violence,

Monsanto all green, the parakeets' cage, my brother Fernando playing in the yard next to the kitchen, the bald man, Alice, the goiter-afflicted Indian, the shrink, the fat man, the fat man's colleague, the faucet at Caxias, no seagulls, horsewhips aren't what they used to be, Amalia, they can't slice off ears, the school building at Santo Tirso in the rain, five hundred times on the blackboard, hold out your hand, Valadas, the republicans scaling the hill, the crow above the oak trees, cigarettes in the bathroom, chinaware clowns, if I married you, Amalia, would I be happy?

Happy, Amalia, happy in France with you surrounded by children, "I was never a Socialist," cleaning their gums, "I was never a Socialist," with toothpicks, never a Socialist, never a Socialist, never a Socialist,

"Again," instructed the inspector, and my heart
(the rest of me, furrowed with veins, doesn't matter)
drifting for an eternity,
"Step up the voltage,"
Deer jorji mom dide
"Up the voltage,"
Deer jorji mom dide
"Voltage,"

and then, on the Rua António Maria Cardoso, in the office with telephones and bookshelves, I shouted in their faces what they wanted to know: that my father hid my sister Julieta out of anger and shame that he wasn't her father, he didn't want anyone to know that the mother of his four children had then given birth by another man, he didn't want anyone to ever have the slightest inkling that after my brother Fernando was born he'd become impotent, he wanted everyone to suppose that he was still a man, that he was a man until the end of his life, and I, slowly but surely, am becoming like my father, I flag, I fade, I fail, I fall, in the presence of a woman, however much I pretend, I'm a castrated dog.

4

At day's end, Conceição, when the pigeons of Camões Square depart for the cornices of Loreto and I feel lonely lonely lonely in this fifth-floor walk-up on Rua Ivens, afflicted by the weight of my childhood and the angina in my chest,

when the voices from the past, my sisters' voices, the maids' voices, surround me with their sweet chatter, with their mist of words that don't exist,

when nothing exists but the darkening rooftops, the castle sailing in the distance, and the pills I take for my gout, my rheumatism, my heart, my bladder, my liver, back, cough, and heartburn,

at day's end, Conceição, when I get the urge to scream like roosters at dawn, I sometimes wonder why my nephew, the one who was born in Guarda and lived in Ericeira, the son of my sister Julieta and the only one in the family I have left, never walks up to Chiado and up the four flights of my building to visit me, so that we can talk about the Calçada do Tojal, about Benfica, about my younger days,

such as the Sunday in 1950 (I was thirty-nine years old) when a civilian and three soldiers arrested my brother Jorge, and the howling in the attic, the rocking chair, and the tangos on the gramophone wouldn't cease,

and I went out to buy bromides, I took the streetcar to Restauradores with the clerk from the notions shop, and after walking past Portas de Santo Antão, past the retired acrobats and trapeze artists, past perfectly square and sad Figueira Square with its bronze King João shrouded by shadows and widows' garrets, and past Martim Moniz, we ended up at the Intendente district,

Rua do Benformoso, Largo do Benformoso, freight trucks in the falling night, and not a pharmacy in sight,

and we went into the Nymph of the Tagus bar to get for-
tified before continuing our trek past the shoe stores of Avenida
Almirante Reis,

and there was a blind man, nephew,

(it's too bad you weren't with me, the family dunce, on
that particular day)

playing the piano on a platform beneath a mermaid who
had red hair like your mother's and a circle of seashells setting
her off from the wall, there was a long bar, stockades of bottles,
Formica tables

and a booming clientele of former circus artists, lion tam-
ers with whips, galloons, and hip boots, contortionists holding
cigarettes between their toenails, a troupe of aging dwarfs who
made a human pyramid but kept falling off one another's shoulders, the couple on high-seated bicycles who rode on the ceiling, and especially

(listen)

clowns,

clowns,

clowns blowing clarinets and saxophones without hitting
a right note, stunt clowns preparing for the flying leap they'd
never again make, tumbler clowns doing somersaults next to the
swinging door of the bathroom that said Gents under the silhouette of a top hat, clowns with angelic white faces, toreador
slippers, and accordions on their chests,

and I remember that day as I sit here waiting for you,
nephew, in a minuscule living room on Rua Ivens where no
photograph moves its eyes to censure me and no cuckoo cheeps
heartless hours,

waiting for you after the syrup for my bowels, between the
seven o'clock capsule for my gallbladder and the pill at eight for
my blood pressure, certain that you'll come, because it isn't right,
even at age eighty-one, that a man be all alone, because some-

one will have to come visit before I'm hauled down the stairs in a flimsy freight crate announcing Fragile on the lid,

someone will have to come and listen with me to the silence of this apartment, just as the clerk from the notions shop listened with me to the two-steps of the blind piano player at the bar on the Largo do Benformoso, and the tightrope walkers rubbed resin onto the soles of their shoes while talking "about the time we did that show in Abrantes, remember? I've never been colder in my whole fucking life, I came that close to falling off the wire, just thinking about it makes a chill run down my spine,"

the clerk from the notions shop ordered a gin for himself, a gin for me, and a gin for the bearded lady who wasn't really Russian, she was from Oporto and could bend iron bars and rip dictionaries and phone books in half, and she explained that "my problem, guys, is arthritis, no doctor's been able to do anything for it, life is so unfair, I get invitations to perform in Barcelona, New York, and Paris, but I have to turn them all down, which means that I can hardly scrape up the rent money for the room in Poço do Barratém where I live with my invalid husband, who fell from the trapeze on a day when there was no net, he can't even lift his pinkie to thank the applauding audience," and the notions clerk, while ordering another round of gin, said "Poor guy," and I, distracted by the Gypsy clairvoyant, who at this point could only predict the past, accepted the gin and concurred, "Poor guy," the human pyramid accepted a drink, one of the dwarfs at the base coughed, the lion tamer gave him a slap on the back, and fifteen gnomes in loincloths tumbled down on top of us, shouting "Holy shit" while the lion tamer, as if shooing away horseflies, flicked off those that hung from his lapels, the clowns were shaking everybody's hand with their extremely long gloves, the couple that pedaled on the ceiling while tossing balls and hoops to each other regretted not being able to come down to have a drink, little dogs dressed up as Spanish dancers yelped in anguish while teetering on their hind legs, "Where can I find an open pharmacy?" I asked the maestro who once conducted the Coliseum band and still waved his baton, though none of the musicians obeyed him, each one playing a different march, "I need bromides for my sister Julieta," and the Chinaman in charge of the seals pulled a mackerel from his pocket and swallowed it whole while smiling his aurora borealic smile, my father suddenly appeared and lamented to the wizards, while pointing at me with a frown, "What did I do, gentlemen, to deserve such a stupid son?" "Bromides? Did you say bromides?" asked a magician engaged in sawing his wife in two, and he pulled an infinity of colored handkerchiefs from his pocket, "Are you sure you wouldn't rather have a bouquet of flowers, presto, or perhaps the national flag? Here, it's yours." "You're drunk, filthy drunk," said my disgusted brother Jorge, "Don't even get near me, you reek of wine." "I'm starting to get bald spots in my beard, look," said the woman who ripped up phone books while tugging at my arm, "one day I won't have a single whisker left." "Drunk my ass," I answered, "I'm trying to find a pharmacy,"

and all of this from just two dinky shots of gin, if that much, Conceição, I swear I had just two shots, I was married to you for nineteen years and you know very well that except during meals I never let so much as a glass of vermouth touch my lips, nineteen years walking every afternoon with you to the Príncipe Real park to watch the retirees play cards, nineteen years until the doctor came out of the bedroom and announced "She's dead," and I went in to find your cousin pulling your dentures out of your mouth and sticking them in a drawer,

and they're still in that drawer, Conceição, the crowns gritting with furious tenacity,

nineteen years watching twilight darken the aces and trumps, nineteen years dining on biscuits and tea without sugar at the table next to the window, thinking, forgive me, of how bored I was, thinking of how in all my life I'd never been so bored,

not even at the business school where my father enrolled me in the hope that I could at least learn enough to get a job as an office employee or as a functionary in the Finance Bureau, a school located in Benfica, Conceição, where my dazed head confused square roots with logarithms, credits with debits, forgive me, Dad,

"What did I do to deserve such a stupid son?"

you didn't do anything, I'm the one who's inept, who bungles everything up, who didn't have the brains to become a cavalry officer or an engineer and who eventually, with no money to my name and no social graces, shacked up with a housemaid just as everyone predicted, because I've always been attracted to people without culture or class,

"He's always been attracted to people without culture or class, that's the sad truth, unfortunately I see my children exactly as they are, and I can only see Fernando in a low-rent neighborhood spending Sundays in his pajamas, he has no worries, no interests, no self-will, no sense of struggle,"

you're right, Dad, I don't struggle, can you teach me how? What was your struggle like when Mom got pregnant with Julieta?

"I hate to admit it, because he's my own flesh and blood, but there's no getting around the fact that Fernando is a good-for-nothing,"

I remember the whispering around the house, doors slamming, a sulfuric air of conspiracy, I remember my father locked in the office with my grandfather, shouting "I can't stand to look at her, I'm getting a divorce, I'll put in for a transfer to Luanda," I remember the tense lunches, the phone calls made in undertones, my aunts saying "Don't abandon your children, Álvaro, they're not to blame for what happened," my grandfather announcing "Your wife will accept whatever terms you dictate, no one ever has to see the little girl, when visitors come she can be locked in a room,"

"I've given up trying to make him into a man, he'll never amount to more than a pencil pusher, case closed,"

and until his dying day my father never again spoke directly to my mother, and not only didn't he speak to her, he didn't even look at her, acting as if neither she nor my sister Julieta existed, and he slept or pretended to sleep on the couch in his office, and I say pretended, Conceição, because when I'd get home from the pastry shop or the movies, I'd find him awake, looking at the wallpaper with a book on his knees,

"What did I do, ladies and gentlemen, to deserve such a stupid son? Wasn't his disgraceful mother enough to embitter my existence, to ruin my life?"

and he went back to his bed only a few days before passing away, surrounded by medicines and pots full of boiling eucalyptus berries, the steam fogged up the windows, and he looked at us from his pillow with the envy of the sick,

"What did I do to deserve such a stupid son?"

but I liked you, Dad, I wanted you to be proud of me, I tried to please you, I enlisted in the Legion so I could have a uniform like yours, I smoked Venezuelan cigarillos like you, I used your monogram on my shirts, I imitated your expressions and mannerisms, I tried to hate Mom, I tried not to answer when she asked "Did you change jobs, Fernando?" and my sister Anita said "Mom asked you a question," and I, without looking at her, "Did she?" and my sister Teresa, "Have you lost your tongue or what?" and I, "Lay off," and my mother leaning toward me without understanding, "Are you having problems at your job, son?" and I, "Leave me alone," while my sister Julieta, who was pregnant but not yet showing, marveled at the far end of the table, above the glasses and silverware, even as the bearded lady marveled as she pointed, "Just look at all the gray hairs in my mustache, look at how white my sideburns are getting," and I, accepting another gin, "That's nonsense, you don't look a day over thirty,"

and she, fishing a handkerchief out of her sleeve, "If I went to Oporto, my cousins wouldn't recognize me, I've lost eighteen pounds in two months,"

and I thought of you, Dad, with your sunken temples and your neck reduced to tendons and wrinkles, I thought of how I begged you "Don't die," as I begged you, Conceição, "Don't die,"

"Don't die, Dad, don't die,"

"What did I do to deserve such a stupid son, who starts bawling in my presence as if I were going to die, but he's crazy, I who on the twenty-second of January, 1919, fought for the king at Monsanto with my army mates from the second group of squadrons in the fourth cavalry, I who held out in the lunette of the barracks without ammo or food or any hope of reinforcements, withstanding the fire of the artillery and the navy and civilians, I, who didn't die from the bullets of the Carbonari, am certainly not going to die now, however eager that adulteress over there is to see me bite the dust so she can call up her lover, 'He just now croaked,' and my idiotic son Fernando, who even imitates my voice, just stares at her dumbly, hundreds of soldiers amid the smoke and booming of guns, the regimental train, the breeches of the weapons we couldn't carry, and he, the ninny, checking the pockets of the wounded in search of bromides for his sister,"

I wasn't drunk, Conceição, I'm not drunk, Dad, it's not the alcohol, it's the piano music of the blind man, it's these two-steps, these people, the circus performer of the Wall of Death revving his motorcycle, that's what's got me agitated,

"When I go to Oporto, my family will gasp, 'What happened, Lucinda, is your husband beating you, did he fall off the trapeze, did he cheat on you again with the Indian woman who flings hatchets at volunteers from the distinguished audience?'"

and I felt a tingling, an urge, a force, a wave coming over me, I grabbed on to the bar, I started puking, and the circus figures were replaced by a clientele of truck drivers, shoe repairmen, junior plumbers, junior clerks, and salesmen from the grungy shops nearby,

the blind piano player, who was finishing a two-step, gazed with the look of a drowning man at the smoke coagulating next to the ceiling,

and as I turned to answer the bearded lady, who was actually a ragged seller of lottery tickets expounding to a half liter of red wine, someone tapped me on the shoulder, "Hi," and it was the seamstress's son, holding a mug of beer,

and I may be stupid, Dad, but I never told anyone that I saw him come out of Julieta's room when my mother and sisters were at mass and my brother at Costa de Caparica conspiring against the government,

I never told anyone that he walked around the house to enter through the kitchen and go up the stairs to the attic, assuming that I, since it was Sunday, would be sound asleep and impervious to any noise after a night at the pastry shop with the garage owner and the notions clerk, winking at the ladies who giggled behind their teaspoons and whipped cream pies,

assuming that only with the smell of fish for lunch, long after my mother and sisters had returned from mass, would I wake up, stumble down the stairs without taking a shower, sit down, smack my lips, and reach for the oil and vinegar,

so that he didn't even act stealthily, didn't even lower his voice, didn't even try not to make noise, he turned the crank on the old horn gramophone and inundated the Calçada do Tojal with an aria, indifferent to the photos' indignation,

and I heard his footsteps and the echo of their talking and the sound of something that fell and broke, as years before I'd heard my mother talking with the man who visited on the afternoons when my father stayed at the barracks, talking softly and close together, in the living room, and from behind the curtain I saw them kiss, I saw my mother lean toward the red-haired man and kiss him,

red-haired like my sister Julieta, who had freckles all over her face, even on her lips and eyebrows, on her neck and ears,

and as the church bell rang communion the seamstress's son walked past my bedroom, whistling the aria of the gramophone in spite of the fox's moans, his mother used to bring him along on the days she came and hunched over the sewing machine, sewing buttons and mending hems, and he played with me in the backyard, rolling around in the dirt, "Heavens, how filthy, just look at you,"

rolling around in the dirt and my mother in the living room, running her fingers through the red hair of her visitor, whose arm clasped her waist, I never opened my mouth, I never told a soul, not even when my father called me into his office and asked, in the presence of his father, "What did you see, Fernando?"

and after October, when it began to rain, and that autumn it rained a lot, the parakeets had died long ago, the seamstress's son stopped coming over on Sunday and the rocking chair danced in the attic, making the floorboards creak and creak and creak,

the rain battered the windows, the rocking chair groaned, and during mass, after the bells, an aria blared in the attic,

"I didn't see anything, Dad," I said, "I didn't see anyone,"

my sister Anita would set down her dripping umbrella and run up to the attic to silence the gramophone, and it rained all day, at two o'clock we'd turn on the lights, and my sister Julieta would pace around over our heads, "What's with her today?" and so it went every Sunday of that winter, every rainy Sunday of that winter,

"What's with her, Fernando?"

"How should I know, Mom, the usual,"

the seamstress came on Tuesdays and Thursdays, and as she ate her lunch on a tray next to the basket of clothes my sister Julieta, with swollen ankles and hands on her belly, paced around her, sniffing, a winter that grayed the grass, deplumed the bushes, and spread mildew over the walls, my mother called the doctor, and I heard him explain "She's already in her third month, Mrs. Valadas, an abortion's out of the question," and my mother "But how on earth did it happen?" And the doctor, putting on his raincoat, "It happens to the best of families, that's life, give her these iron capsules and vitamins fifteen minutes before each meal," and my mother to me, "Did you see who it was, Fernando?"

"Let him be, Álvaro, calm down, stop tormenting him," counseled my grandfather, "If the kid had seen anything, he'd talk, children spit out everything, just one look at him and it's obvious that the boy's in outer space,"

"He's always been in outer space," answered my father, "and he'll die in outer space and married to a housemaid, even with my heirs I've been unlucky, get out of here, Fernando,"

and my mother, as the rain pattered the windows, "I can't imagine who it might have been, to avoid problems and temptations not even my children's friends are allowed over, to avoid problems and temptations we simply don't have visitors,"

and the doctor, "When misfortune decides to strike, it strikes, what I find miraculous is that I still haven't come down with the flu in this lousy weather,"

"Get out of here, Fernando," my father ordered, "what I should do is grab a pistol, say to hell with the family, and kill that bitch,"

and in 1950, seven years later, there he was, Conceição, the seamstress's son, father to my nephew, saying "Hi" across the foam of his beer without knowing that I knew, without ever imagining that I might suspect him since he was the only person who came over on Sunday mornings, without ever thinking that I might have woken up and listened to their voices, that I might have noticed him entering or leaving through the gate, and I, still dizzy from when I'd puked, wiping my mouth on my sleeve and remembering all the rain that winter, said "Hi,"

"I'll send her to Guarda," decided my mother, "and after the baby's born we'll wait a month or two and then bring her back,"

and my sister Julieta, who never talked, who refused to talk except with Jorge, said "No,"

she still wasn't showing, but she looked haggard, pallid, with circles under her eyes, and she'd shut herself up in the attic, wearing a new skirt and with her hair all brushed, as if she were waiting for someone,

she'd shut herself in the attic, put an aria on the gramophone, and rock back and forth, back and forth, while the mildew of November spread across the walls and my sister Teresa sighed "One of these days we'll have to get the ceiling replastered, just look at those cracks,"

and in spite of all her protests and refusals, they put her on a train to Guarda, and when she came back many weeks later, Conceição, she wouldn't talk with anyone, not even Jorge, she floated through the living room like a ghost,

she never again brushed her hair and never again put on a new skirt, she turned the crank on the gramophone and listened to the same aria until the record emitted nothing but a series of screeches and isolated violin notes, and my mother implored "Do something about that music before I go stark raving mad,"

my sister Teresa would climb up the stairs to talk with her, the aria would stop, my mother would drink lime-blossom tea, "Are you all trying to kill me? Bring her downstairs and let her be with us," and she, "No," which was the only word she would still say, "No," anything we asked her, no matter what it was, "No,"

and in 1950, on the day they arrested my brother Jorge, the seamstress's son wasn't much different from how I remembered him, the same sparrowy fingers held on to the mug of beer, the same stuttering voice greeted me, "H-h-h-hi," and I, the family dunce,

("What did I do to deserve such a stupid son?")

moving toward him, stepping on the ragged seller of lottery tickets, said "Hi,"

the mermaid moved back and forth, "Hi," the clerk from the notions shop offered a shot of gin to an old man with a scarf who wasn't as old as I am today, surrounded by this chatter of the past, by your housemaidish absence, by a mist of words that no longer exist,

"Hi," I said, I the family dunce, the one with no brains, the one who never struggled, "Hi,"

the aria started up again in the attic, my sister Teresa, "Stop it, Julieta," and Julieta, "No," my sister Anita, "How about a waltz?" and Julieta, "No," my brother Jorge, "I won't ever talk to you again," and Julieta, "No no no no no,"

"What brings you around here, Fernando?" asked the seamstress's son, who had just come out of the attic, buckling his belt and straightening his tie, and now placed his beer on the zinc bar as the blind piano player leaned into the keys and my sister Julieta screamed in the attic "No," and my mother, "What's with her, Fernando?" and my father, "What did you see, Fernando?" and I, the dunce, taking a step forward, bumping against the seller of lottery tickets and picking up a bottle, "What I should have done eight years ago, buddy, namely smash your face in. Nothing much, as you can see."

5

I must have said what they hoped I'd say, because as soon as I'd recovered my wits and the notion of time I was transferred from Rua António Maria Cardoso to the prison at Peniche, which was almost as somber as the Catholic boarding school in Santo Tirso, where daylight emanated from the carved gold that wrapped the chapel's saintly statues in a doomed luminosity suggestive of shipwrecks. In Peniche it was likewise always winter, but under an evenly stone-colored, cloudless sky. The waves broke against the prison walls, covering the sentries with foam, the clerk who signed me in warned, "Don't try anything smart, Valadas, we don't like guests who misbehave," and I could tell by looking at him that he felt as forlorn as me in that huge cube of wind-thrashed walls, with weeds growing between the flagstones. Forlorn, Margarida, and it wasn't just he and I who were forlorn, it was the prisoners I ate lunch with and slept next to who were forlorn, it was the guards who oversaw us at lunch and recreation who were forlorn, it was the warden who lectured to us in the refectory on Sundays who was forlorn, and next to him sat the priest who blessed the soup and the medic who drilled teeth without anesthesia to facilitate confessions. But there didn't seem to be any problem with my confession, because I was never once summoned for interrogation until one morning, after three months had gone by, I was led into the room where prisoners talked to visitors, a room with a partition in the middle, a picture of the prime minister on the wall, and a man who announced, while pulling papers from his briefcase, "I'm your lawyer, Major Valadas, and I need a few bits of information to complete your defense." "Defense against what?" I asked, and he, "Against the charge of conspiring to deliver the nation over to the Communists, Major, since as far as I know you haven't aggravated your crime by kidnapping children, or have you?" and I, "I don't know what you're talking about, sir," and he, separating a file folder, "Excuse me, but I have here a copy of the confession you signed, and don't try to tell me that the signature was forged."

The sea crashed against the walls, the lifeboat's siren emitted its wail from the far end of the beach, I heard the voices of fishermen on the pontoon, I heard the whistle of the cannery summoning workers, and the lawyer, thumbing through my dossier, "You provided the police with a very thorough report, Major, including the names and ranks of conspiring officials, passwords, keys to secret codes, meeting times and places, a list of the units contacted, and a preliminary plan of military insurrection that would have neutralized dozens of the regime's key figures," the lifeboat's siren passed by us howling, and I, "What kind of a joke is this?" and he, "What do you mean, joke?" and I, "It can only be a joke, because I never told anything to anyone and especially not to the police," and he, "If you were playing a joke, it was in very bad taste, since based on your affidavit over a dozen officials were given the ax," and I, "What?" and he, "I've got the list right here, want to see it? Their photos were published in the papers," and I, "Hold on, hold on," trying to remember what had happened in the inspector's office with telephones and bookshelves where I'd been given electric shocks, and what I remembered, as if it were a dream, was that I'd said something about my father, and the lawyer, "What is it, Major?" and I, "Forget it, it's nothing."

The cannery's whistle continued to summon workers after I'd returned to recreation, and from the voices of the fishermen on the pontoon I deduced that a trawler was trying to dock without success, and I envisioned the captain flailing his arms toward land, one or two crew members throwing cargo overboard, and the lifeboat rocking on the crest of a wave, and after three days I sat once more in the visitors' room, and the lawyer,

"In view of the fact you cooperated, the judge is willing to lighten your sentence," and I, "What do you mean, cooperated? I didn't cooperate with anyone," and the lawyer, "Save the twaddle for your fellow inmates, who must be seething with rage against you, I'm going to accept the judge's offer," and I, interrupting him, "What's that about my fellow inmates?" and he, "People don't like informers, which is understandable, I'd be careful if I were you, because you never know," and I, "Careful?" and he, "Careful, it wouldn't be the first time that an unpleasant accident happens to a prisoner," and I, "What the fuck's going on, I never opened my mouth," and he, "Sure you didn't, because if you say you didn't open your mouth, then you didn't open it, go and explain it to the other inmates, and while you're explaining and not explaining, I'll concentrate on your defense, all I ask is that you don't dash it all to hell at trial," and I, "Dash it all to hell at trial?" and he, "I expect you to be polite, repentant, willing to give more details to the judge," and I, "You're off your rocker," and he, "You cracked under pressure and ratted, Major, don't take it so hard, you're not the first," and I, "I forbid you to be my lawyer," and he, "If you think I like defending you, you're wrong, thanks to you the jerks who run the police nabbed various individuals I happen to respect," and I, "Something's wrong here, there's a dreadful mistake, it can only be a mistake," and he, "And I'm the queen of England, just sit tight and keep a stiff upper lip, Major, it's a little late now to be shitting in your pants, and as for being your lawyer, I wish they'd let me off the case, I wish I'd refused it in the first place, because it disgusts me to help a weasel," and I, "What day is it today?" and he, "Tuesday," and I, "Well, let me tell you that this is the worst Tuesday of my entire life."

When I arrived at the prison yard, recreation was just ending, and recreation, Margarida, meant walking around for an hour under the vigilance of armed guards, the same ones who watched us in the refectory, who inspected our cells, "Get out," and who escorted us after breakfast to the workshops, ordering us to keep in step with the inmate ahead of us. Recreation was ending, the sky was retreating to make way for nightfall, the sea moved beneath us, thrusting up the rocks of the cliff, and the prisoners stared at me with indignant censure, blaming me for the police interrogations, blaming me for the fact they were there in that prison, coughing from the cold, defecating in buckets, eating scraps, getting sick in their lungs and bowels, the prisoners stared at me, Margarida, and I shouted, "It's a lie, I swear it's a lie, I went an entire year getting beaten and sleep deprived and I never squealed on anyone."

But they didn't believe me, because from that day on I felt them lurking around me like those birds whose name I don't remember that lie in wait to rip open our guts with their claws, to devour our livers with violent thrusts, I felt them all around me, during lineup, in the workshops, at recreation, in the cells, and in the john, observing me, talking about me, poisoning my cabbage and potatoes in the kitchen, until I finally asked to see the warden and announced, "They want to kill me, sir," and he, "They want to kill you, Valadas?" and I, "Give me a cell to myself," and he, "With private bath and maid service?" and I, "Give me a cell to myself, get me away from them, put me in solitary confinement," and he, "You're nuts, Valadas, and I've got more important things to do," and it dawned on me that he was on their side, it dawned on me that he was also a bird, one of those birds whose name I don't remember, and he, "What's wrong, Valadas, are you paralyzed, didn't you hear me?" and I, "If you want to shoot me, then shoot me, but don't make me put up with this farce," and he, "That's enough, Valadas," the lifeboat's siren emitted a shout that was a message, and I, "Shoot me, you fiend," and he, "Get out of here, goddammit," and a guard came and shoved me out into the hall, and I, "Kill me right now, you bastards," and the lawyer, "What's this I hear about them sucking your blood out with syringes?" and I, exhibiting my arm, "Just look at the needle marks," and he, deliberately ignoring the five or six marks on my arm, "You're imagining things, there aren't any needle marks," and I, showing him a pink spot, "If I'm imagining, then what's this?" and he, rubbing it with his finger, "A birthmark, what else?" and I, "You've all ganged up on me, I'm going to write to the papers," and he, "Don't get hysterical, Major, let's see if they can't bring you a tranquilizer," and I, grabbing the briefcase from his lap and hurling it against the wall, "Like fuck! If you think you're going to do me in with cyanide, then think again," and as I ripped up his papers he ran to the door, "Guard, guard, hurry up," and they whacked me in the kidneys, I fell down flat on my face, and the coldness of the stone floor was sweet in my mouth, calm and sweet, and the sea flowed over my body before sinking into the sand where my feet lay, white and naked like the feet of dead pigeons.

Even today I hear the waves of Peniche, Margarida, even today I hear the whistle of the cannery (was it a cannery, was it really a cannery?) summoning the workers, I hear the water beneath the flagstones, not the water of Tavira, not the sea of the Algarve, but the waves that tore through the fortress walls like a knife, even today I hear the waves of Peniche and the lawyer explaining to the warden, "It was hysteria, Lieutenant, he had a fit of hysteria," I feel the hands that rubbed my face into the stone, and the lawyer, "No, he didn't hurt me, he tore up a few of my papers, that's all," and the warden, "He came into my office the other day with a strange song and dance demanding to be put in solitary confinement," and one of the guards, "He keeps to himself, suspects his food has been doctored, and doesn't want anybody to touch him," and the warden, "It's probably all a ruse, Azevedo, you know how sly these guys can be," and the lawyer, "That may well be, Lieutenant, I don't deny it, but I still say that he's got a few loose screws," the lifeboat sounded its siren and hushed, "Don't make me get up," I begged,

"let me go, I don't have any blood in my veins," and the warden, "Hysterical or not, I'm not about to indulge the prisoner
in his whims, if he's asking for solitary, then it's for a good reason, there's a tunnel that leads out to the cliff," and the guard,
"Come on, Valadas, let's get up, slow and easy, up on your feet
like a good little boy," and the lawyer, "A tunnel, Lieutenant, I
had no idea," and the warden, "I can spot these hoodwinkers
from a mile away, I've been at this job for fifteen years, and no
one asks to go into solitary just for the fun of it," and the lawyer, "I guess you have a point, Lieutenant, the guy is more of a
rascal than I'd imagined," and the warden, "Yes, but I'm no
pushover, I'm understanding and do what I can to accommo-
date, but no prisoner's going to fool me," and the guard, "Good
boy, Valadas, now stand at attention," and the warden, after
dislocating my jaw with a slap, "Pick up the papers you threw
all over the floor, Valadas, and learn not to mistreat the people
who are trying to help you."

Even today, here in Tavira, I hear the waves of Peniche,
Margarida, the waves of that winter, even today I hear the whistle
of the cannery summoning the workers, I hear the foam under
the flagstones, and I remember how the prisoners tried to weaken
me by putting barbiturates in my soup, how when I was alone
they would call me, imitating the voice of the headmaster at
Santo Tirso, the voice of Alice, the voice of my father, forcing
me to return to the past so as to eliminate me from the present,
and it wasn't just the prisoners but the guards, the warden, and
the lawyer who spread his papers across the table in the visitors'
room, "You look better today, Major, let's try to make a little
progress on your case," and it wasn't just them but my family,
and you, Margarida, I heard you talking with them, and I, who
hadn't been sleeping at night for fear they'd riddle my heart with
bullets, agreed with the lawyer, "Yes, I'm not looking bad, because try as you all might, you're not able to break me," and he,
"Before you start talking nonsense, Major, I'd like to know if

you'll agree to meet with Colonel Gomes and his lawyer," and I, "Colonel Gomes?" and he, "He was admitted into the prison yesterday, the warden has given the go-ahead for us to meet and talk," and I, putting together the pieces of the puzzle, "Is Colonel Gomes the mastermind behind the conspiracy against me?" and the lifeboat was quiet, the whistle was quiet, and even the waves that lapped the walls of the fort were quiet, and Colonel Gomes, wearing serge trousers and shivering in a worn-out overcoat, held out his hand to me, "Hello, Valadas, won't you shake hands with an old friend?" and I, "With a friend, yes, but the problem, Colonel, is that you're not a friend," and his lawyer, "For heaven's sake, Major, Colonel Gomes holds you in the highest regard," and Colonel Gomes, "I was the one who called to warn you that the police were on your tail," and I, "You mean you sent them to my house, you mean you contacted them and sent them straight to my house," and Colonel Gomes, "I won't stand for such insinuations, I won't tolerate being insulted," and my lawyer, "I beg your pardon, Colonel, Major Valadas didn't mean to offend you, it's just that his nerves have gotten frazzled from nearly a year spent in jail," and Colonel Gomes, less huffy, "If he takes back what he said, then I'll forget it," and his lawyer to me, "What we'd like to do is forge a common strategy, decide what to say and what not to say, because the public prosecutor is one tough cookie," and I, "I'm not saying boo at the trial," and I didn't say boo, Colonel Gomes was dismissed from the army and sentenced to eleven years, with Commodore Capelo, now promoted to admiral, testifying against him, I thought I saw Alice in one of the back rows of the courtroom, sitting between her mother and husband, but when I looked closely I saw other spectators or just empty seats, the judge postponed my sentencing on the doctors' advice, we returned to Peniche in an armored wagon, and Colonel Gomes to me, "Eleven years, Valadas, I won't last eleven years," on leaving the courthouse I'd noticed his wife, who was crying, and I, "I certainly hope you don't, Colonel, I've got too many enemies as it is," and when we arrived at Peniche it was thundering, the sky was lacerated by streaks of lightning that shredded the town, that shredded the sea, momentarily possessing the phosphorescent shadows before they withdrew into their folds of darkness, a boat almost on the horizon floated over clouds that oozed red tears, houses crumbled, the fishermen's sheds and the anchored trawlers slid out toward sea, the amputated cliff, exhibiting its bowels of slate, released swarms of terrified birds, and the next morning Colonel Gomes hung himself in his cell, and when I saw him, before they'd covered him with his overcoat and a burlap bag, he wasn't purple and his tongue didn't hang out, he wore a friendly expression, eyes peacefully shut, so that I thought, He's asleep, he didn't hang himself, he's just sleeping, and in spite of his disjointed shoulders and the red streak on his neck I thought, He's asleep, he pretended to hang himself to fool me, and then I bent over him, put my thumb on his forehead, which was cold, saw wine-colored splotches on his scalp, and the boots at the end of his legs, Margarida, looked as empty to me as the shoes of beggars.

6

When the weather improved, Conceição, and we went to the doctor, or out for lunch on Sunday, at that diner on the Calçada do Combro, you'd put on the only dress you owned, the one you took to the grave, and around your neck you'd hang a little enamel heart that had my picture inside, and instead of slippers you'd wear the shoes I'd stopped using because they pinched my toes,

and since you didn't tie the laces you walked through the living room like a diver on a ship deck, with the heels making a thundering sound against the floorboards,

and I half expected to see little air bubbles rising from your mouth with each breath, and squid floating around us between the curtains and the furniture.

That's how it was right from the start, when I left the Calçada do Tojal and my sisters to live with you, grateful to you for being the first and last woman who took an interest in me, who found me handsome, who held my hand and accompanied me to matinees at the Eden, who agreed to go to bed with me in a flophouse on the Rua dos Douradores, cheerfully climbing up three flights of stairs and then depleting me of my remaining energy with kisses that smelled of bleach and stew, not cereal and silver polish but bleach and stew,

a windowless room on the Rua dos Douradores, fifty cents an hour, where I promised to liberate you from your boss, to buy you a ring and take you to the justice of the peace, you who until your dying day called me Mr. Valadas, as you'd called the other man Mr. Esteves,

you who'd stopped sleeping with Mr. Esteves after the stroke that left him immobile on the sofa, unable to talk,

Mr. Esteves, the man who, after his wife died, brought you to Lisbon from Beja

(the cold of Beja in winter, the wheat fields scorched by frost, the wind rushing across the plain like a roaring train)

to work for him, to warm up his dinner, to clean his apartment on the Rua Conde de Valbom, and to occupy the side of the mattress that the departed wife had exchanged for a plot and tombstone at Prazeres Cemetery,

Mr. Esteves, whom I met when I went with you to fetch your things from his ground-floor apartment, where the departed wife smiled from out of a crocheted oval frame,

Mr. Esteves, unshaven, who had no one but you, clutching with his fists the fringes of his blanket,

a man who was older than I am now, and whose neck was formed by plaits of skin that shrunk into his jacket like a tortoise into its shell,

Mr. Esteves with the two badly fitting halves of his face, like puzzle pieces that don't really go together,

and we filled a trunk with sugar bowls, salvers, and silver spoons, with towels, earrings, necklaces, and bracelets, with ivory figurines and tureens, with papers from the safe, with a picture of you and him at a sidewalk café in Badajoz,

we plundered his apartment and Mr. Esteves just sat there, enormous in his statuesque quietude, exuding a urinary stench, and I almost tripped over him while carrying a trophy to the trunk, I shoved against him while fondling you on the sofa, I gave him a friendly slap on the cheek as we got up to leave,

and he didn't react, Conceição, he with his legs wrapped by the blanket, from under which the tips of his plaid slippers poked out, making no sound except a rumble from his stomach when I took my leave, "Thanks for the dowry, Mr. Esteves,"

and you, with moist eyelids, "In spite of everything he's a good person, Mr. Valadas, don't make fun of him, in spite of everything I do like him a little bit," but the pawnbroker in Alverca, a smooth talker, offered us almost nothing, "This is all junk nobody uses anymore," he argued, "there's not a piece of silver here that isn't scratched, not one bibelot that's worth anything,"

so that with all that we'd filched, including even the invalid's radio, which you used to play at high volume to entertain the widower lost in his limbos without memory, we got barely enough to buy a set of cheap furniture for this attic on Rua Ivens, where you eventually died, Conceição, and where this year or next year I'll die too, like Mr. Esteves in his apartment on the Rua Conde de Valbom, with the photo of his wife in a crocheted oval frame,

Mr. Esteves without spoons, without sugar bowls, without crystal, without music, staring at the darkness and the daylight with his disjointed features,

Mr. Esteves, who perhaps still lives there, amid the console tables left by some businessman uncle who died centuries ago,

Mr. Esteves still alive but without relatives, without anyone to take care of him, waking up at dawn and nodding off at dusk in the tortoiseshell of his jacket,

Mr. Esteves, of whom I'm jealous even now, jealous of that human wreck, of that cadaver, of that tortoise who uprooted you from Beja

(the cold of Beja in winter, the wheat fields scorched by frost, the wind rushing across the plain like a roaring train)

to work for him, to heat up his supper, to clean and wax and vacuum his ground-floor apartment, to shake his rugs, to iron his sheets, to mend his shirts, and to occupy the side of the mattress that the departed wife vacated,

it makes me jealous that he touched you, jealous that he hugged you, that he put you on his lap, ran his hand over your body, undressed you,

so that when you happened to mention his name I'd say "Button your lip," so that whenever you said "I wonder what's become of poor Mr. Esteves?" I'd say "You want to get slapped?" so that whenever you asked "Let me go see how he's doing, Mr. Valadas," I'd warn "You can go, but if you do, I'll smash your body to a pulp, it's your choice,"

and you never again mentioned him, you never went to see him, and if you became very quiet, I'd get suspicious, "Are you thinking about the widower?" and you, answering quickly while moving your chair away from mine, "No, Mr. Valadas, I was thinking that we could go to the Politeama this Sunday,"

and on Sunday, instead of slippers, you'd wear the shoes that pinched my toes and walk with me through Chiado, my smile hanging around your neck, to a darkened theater where after five minutes you were sniffling into your handkerchief, full of sympathy for the actress beset by adversity, releasing with each breath a cloud of bubbles that danced for a moment before dissipating in the projector's beam, emitted from a tiny window in the back, the only flame of the Holy Spirit I believe in.

And after we'd installed half a dozen pieces of rickety furniture (a bed, a table, a stove, two chairs, and a mirror) in our garret on Rua Ivens, after we'd paid the engineer who sighed with grave doubts about renting us the place, and after I'd transferred my unmatching socks to Mr. Esteves's trunk, I announced, "Tomorrow I'm going to present you to my family, Conceição," and you, "Present me, Mr. Valadas?" and I, "Comb your hair, buy a dress at the five-and-ten, and don't talk too much or you'll make me look bad,"

and after examining your hair bun and your clothes, I called to the house in Benfica on the Calçada do Tojal and said to my sister Teresa, "I'm bringing my fiancée over for lunch," and she, "Your fiancée?" and I, "Yes, my fiancée, what's so odd about that?" and she, after a silence in which I discerned my parents' silence and heard the clocks' cuckoos, "Is it someone I know, Fernando?" and I, looking at your dress and thinking, How ugly, "Don't ask questions, sis, let yourself be surprised,"

and I opened the gate on the Calçada do Tojal, instruct-
ing "Chew with your mouth closed and don't prop your elbows
on the table," and it was March, I remember, because the bad
weather and thunderstorms of April hadn't yet arrived, the fox
pranced around its cage, and tiny flowers were blooming in the
backyard

(the same flowers I knew in my childhood, Conceição,
the same ones I'd known ever since we moved from Queluz to
Benfica, the gardener would water the beds and the smell of earth
was sweet in my nose),

and instead of using my key I rang the bell, and my sister
Anita opened the door, saw you, and looked surprised, "We
didn't expect the new maid until tomorrow, come in, come in,
did you have a good trip, where's your suitcase?"

and I emerged from behind your shoulder, and Anita,
putting on and taking off her glasses as she did whenever she
got flustered, "Oh, I'm sorry, how embarrassing, I'd completely
forgotten, I don't know where my head went,"

and we entered the living room, where the sun shone
through the curtains and cast a circle of light on the rug that
the fox had ruined, and I gazed at the pictures, at the end tables
with vases, candlesticks, and ashtrays,

I gazed like a stranger in the house where I'd grown up,
among its silences, its smells, its echoes,

I heard the footsteps of my sister Julieta and wondered,
Who could that be? I heard the creaking of the rocking chair
and wondered, What's that? I heard the tangos of the gramophone and asked myself, Where's that fanfare coming from?

and my sister Teresa arrived, wiping her hands with her
apron, and I said, "This is Conceição, Teresa, say hello to your
future sister-in-law," and you didn't know what to do as she sized
you up and speechlessly shook her head,

and I, who may be stupid but not as stupid as my family
supposes, knew exactly what my sister was thinking, namely, A

housemaid just like our father predicted, if Mom were alive, she'd never be able to endure this, first Jorge in prison and now Fernando with a fiancée who could pass for a vendor of suckling pigs at the fair in Viseu, and then the son of my sister Julieta came down the stairs, and I, "Say hello to your aunt,"

and you standing akimbo in the foyer, and my sister Anita, showing you a chair, "Won't you sit down, can I get you something to drink?" and you "Some schnapps, if you please, because my throat's bone-dry," and my sister Anita, rummaging through bottles, "I don't know if we have any schnapps, but I can give you some orange juice with ice," and you, sitting on the edge of a chair and looking in my direction for me to guide you in the strange world of upper-class decorum and politesse, you, completely lost in a labyrinth of social procedures that overwhelmed you, "Orange juice gives me dysentery, ma'am, do you have any red wine?"

but you held your fork correctly, you remembered to spread your napkin, you chewed with your mouth closed and without propping your elbows on the table,

answering my sister Anita's questions with "Yes, ma'am, No, ma'am, Is that so, ma'am?" while sucking air through your teeth,

feeling troubled by the silence of my sister Teresa, who examined you from head to toe, troubled by the silence of my already stocky and balding nephew, who never lifted his nose from his plate, troubled by the photographs, the pendulums, and the cuckoos' bows, startling you every time the clocks struck their hours, and you longed for the coffee to arrive so we could go home, and you regretted having left Mr. Esteves, who brought you to Lisbon from Beja after a long talk with your godfather in the cottage where you lived outside town, amid olive trees dotting the rolling fields,

and your godfather, "Pack your bags, honey,"

and you, "My bags?"

and Mr. Esteves in the car, squeezing your knee with his hand, "I need someone to take care of my apartment, Conceição. Have you ever been anywhere except among these wheat fields scorched by frost, with the wind rushing across the plain like a roaring train?"

and you, withdrawing your thigh, "No sir,"

and that night Mr. Esteves went into your room without turning on the light, whispering "Don't be afraid, girl, don't be afraid, take off your gown, I won't hurt you,"

and he lay on top of me coughing, he grabbed my breast, and I spread out my arms in a cross and it hurt me and I gritted my teeth so as not to cry but I didn't feel like crying I felt like returning to Beja,

and Mr. Esteves, lighting a cigarette, "Pretty good, lass, pretty good, if you can cook, then I'll keep you on,"

and for Christmas that year he gave me a ring that fit only after I wrapped some thread through it, and he moved me to his bed, "From now on you sleep here with me,"

and I got used to the old man's snoring, I got used to his cigarettes, I got used to hearing him talk in his sleep, I got used to the alarm clock that pierced my ears like a burning wire,

Mr. Esteves, who had no friends and no relatives, who never received visitors, never talked with anyone and never read the paper, who turned the radio dial to the opera station and explained, "This is Verdi, Conceição, listen,"

but to me it was just a lot of shouting, to me it was a man and woman having a loud argument, like my godmother and godfather at the cottage in Beja,

and one Thursday he turned the radio up louder than usual, "*Tosca,* Conceição, just listen to this tenor," so loud that the neighbor from the basement apartment, a skin doctor, started banging on the ceiling with a stick, and I, frightened by the doctor's fury, went to turn down the volume, at which point I found Mr. Esteves slumped on the floor, shaking and drooling,

"He had a stroke," said the skin doctor, tapping Mr. Esteves's joints with a hammer while still holding, under his armpit, the broom he'd banged against the ceiling, "at least I won't have to put up with any more opera,"

and my boss wanted to say something, I stuck my face in front of his, I shook him by his lapels, "What is it, Mr. Esteves, what is it?"

and he, "*Tosca,* Conceição, that glorious music," and eleven months later I met Mr. Valadas at the restaurant and liked his double chin, he wasn't as handsome as the skin doctor who hated Verdi, but I felt sorry for him, always by himself, eating lunch all alone,

and my sister Teresa, who kept looking at you and shaking her head as if she'd been hit by the world's worst tragedy, "When is the wedding, Fernando?"

and my sister Anita to you, as she cleared the dishes, "When is the wedding, Conceição?"

and you, depositing an olive pit on your knife, "Mr. Valadas knows the date, Mr. Valadas is handling it all, because I can't read or write,"

and so in the afternoon I'd find the opera station for Mr. Esteves, and as the man and woman jumped around screaming inside the radio, he didn't budge, and the skin doctor banged his broom on the ceiling, and only my nephew made no comment, he just peeled a pear with his nose to his plate, seeming not even to hear the gramophone of my sister Julieta, the gramophone of his mother, whining tangos in the attic, and as soon as we were out on the street you asked, "Did I do okay, Mr. Valadas?" and I, "You were great, Conceição,"

thinking of my sister Teresa, who when lunch was over didn't even come out to say good-bye but remained in the kitchen, pulling her hankie from her sleeve and repeating, "Blessed Mother Mary, how Dad would feel if he ever knew," thinking of my sister Anita, who extended her hand, let it hover, then withdrew it, tracing a difficult gesture of farewell, "It was a pleasure,"

and so I couldn't tell whether he still appreciated opera, so perfectly still did he sit on the sofa, stinking of urine, Mr. Esteves, who was born in Beja and had no children, no cousins, no friends or co-workers who took an interest in his life, my godmother would send some sausage and write me at Easter, the concierge would read me the letters, "We all have a cross to bear, Conceição,"

thinking of my nephew, who left abruptly, "So long," running late for his job at the National Tourist Office, my nephew, who was almost as stupid as me, almost as passive as me,

thinking of the rage of the dead, of the useless rage of the dead,

and on Saturday I took the streetcar to the Calçada do Tojal to fetch some things I'd forgotten: my three suits, a pinstripe, a blue suit, and a brown suit with a mysterious stain on the vest that the dry cleaners couldn't get out, my sweaters, my shaving kit, and my leather strop that had become shiny from the using,

and the tiny flowers in the yard were blossoming in the sun, the bushes sprouted new leaves in the sun, the footpath's milk-colored gravel sparkled in the sun, the green downspout stood out from the wall in the sun, two chimney sweeps crawled around on the roof, and the fox barked in the cage,

and I went through the gate, with its engraving of Pontius Pilate on the terrace of the temple, condemning Jesus before a multitude of tunics, and as I stepped into the living room I noticed that they'd removed the photos of me from the walls and the furniture, and in the pictures where I appeared with other family members they'd covered my face with circles of tissue paper, so that I was only I, Conceição, from the neck down, like those painted figures in photographers' studios to which we supply the head,

with everything, in other words, as it always was except that I no longer existed for them, and my sister Teresa came into the living room with a tin full of kidney beans that read Rice on the outside and said "Go away, Fernando, we don't want you here," and I, attacked by the cuckoos' hiccups, "This house is as much mine as yours," and I, "Who covered my face in the pictures?" and she, "You've insulted the memory of our parents, you've insulted the family, you're insensitive, Fernando, get out of here, Dad was right about you," and I, " I was going to ask you to be the ring bearer, Conceição absolutely insists on it," and she, "Go away, Fernando, if Jorge were here, he'd kick you out like that," and I, "Jorge can't kick anyone anymore, Jorge committed suicide in Tavira," and my sister Julieta stopped rocking and began to scream in the attic,

and I went up to my room to collect my suits and sweaters and shaving kit and leather strop, Monsanto Hill shone in the window with its electric poles and the prison on top, and without feeling sad I thought, This is the last time I'll ever look out this window, I'm sixty-one years old and this is the last time I'll ever look out this window, until the skin doctor complained to the police, and from then on I kept the volume on the radio down, and my sister Teresa, "Don't talk about Jorge, don't you dare talk about Jorge,"

Jorge, who had drowned himself in the ocean, who had escaped from the prison in Tavira to drown himself in the ocean, according to what the commander of the barracks told us, they'd found his body on a crag, bloated with water, and we brought him to Lisbon in a lead coffin, sweating in the hearse amid daisies, Jorge,

the chimney sweeps, holding on to the gables, were gathering up their brushes, and my sister Anita, "If Jorge were here, you wouldn't be getting married, Fernando," and I, with suitcase in hand, "I'll send you invitations, and if you want to come, then come,"

but the only people who came, Conceição, were you and I, and the clerk from the notions shop who acted as our witness, and I never returned to the Calçada do Tojal and don't know what became of my sister Teresa, my sister Anita, my sister Julieta, and my nephew,

and our wedding reception consisted of draft beers and hot dogs at the counter of a snack bar off Camões Square, where the muffins and croquettes were covered with flies, like the ones that rubbed their legs against your cheeks when you died and stopped hearing the wind of Beja rush across the plain like a roaring train, and Mr. Esteves and I continue in our separate parts of town, both of us sedentary, both aged, both quiet, both without music, he waiting for you, Conceição, while I wait for my nephew, who will never arrive,

and after we'd finished our beers and hot dogs in the snack bar with muffins, croquettes, and blowflies, you with your dress from the five-and-ten and I with my pinstripe suit, we wiped the mustard off our fingers and walked home in the dusk to our garret on Rua Ivens, with four flights of stairs protesting under our soles,

and we stopped at each landing to calm our blood and catch our breath, as perhaps Jorge stopped, at the water's edge, before advancing into the sea, "What did I do to deserve such a stupid brother, a brother who married a housemaid?"

and when we reached the top I looked at the cheap furniture we'd bought and your slippers under the bed, and thought about going back, about returning to the Calçada do Tojal and my sisters, and to the fox and the tangos, and to my days of sitting in the pastry shop, smiling at the blond ladies who whispered to each other without paying me any heed, and you, worried by my silence, "Are you feeling all right, Mr. Valadas?"

I shook him by his shoulders the way I'd shaken Mr. Esteves, during the opera on the radio, afraid he'd had an attack, afraid of ending up with another boss who would drool on himself, sitting on the sofa with a blanket over his legs,

and I far from Beja, far from the cold of Beja in winter, far from the wheat fields scorched by frost, far from the wind rushing across the plain like a roaring train, taking care of him, feeding him, wiping up his feces, dressing him and undressing him, tucking him in bed,

"Do you feel all right, Mr. Valadas?"

and I, homesick for Benfica, "It's nothing, Conceição, don't worry, it's a lot of stairs for me to climb,"

and you, relieved, "Whew, Mr. Valadas, you gave me a scare,"

and I looked out the window at the Lisbon night as when, in my childhood, I'd wake up before morning, lean out the windowsill, and feel frightened by the trees that grew toward the sky.

7

After they stuck me into the ambulance for the first time and I asked where we were going, they said "We're on our way to China, pal, and it takes a long time to get there," and I journeyed all over the place until I finally dropped anchor in the Algarve, at Tavira, in the barracks next to the sea where I can't see the sea, where I hear the waves and can't see the waves, where I hear birds and can't see the birds, and so I realized that they'd lied to me, that I'm not in Tavira, or in a barracks, or in the Algarve, I realized that they must have taken me across all sorts of rivers and countries and continents before dropping me here, not in Portugal but near the Chinese border, in a country reminiscent of my grandmother's Oriental dishware, with women holding fans, with pagodas resembling newspaper kiosks, and with bushes hanging over hibiscus-flanked lakes whose shores are joined by bridges as dainty as eyebrows arched in surprise. I realized that I inhabit not a prison but a porcelain tureen, kept in the cupboard next to the porcelain spoons with dragons whose tongues extend up the handles. My sister Anita stared wide-eyed at the mandarins that smiled on the teacups, my sister Maria Teresa was frightened by the terra-cotta Buddhas whose heads bounced back and forth, and we'd hear the old maid plod down the hallway with her cane, like a gondolier, to forbid us from touching the teapots and saucers emblazoned with dwarf almond trees on whose branches slithered snakes that had wings, like angels in missals.

I realized that they'd purposely left me at the border of China so that I'd have to cross it alone, just as at night, when I was a child and had to pee, I had to cross through dark rooms to reach the toilet, tormented by shadows that conspired with faint sounds (the furniture's whispers, the clocks' sighs, mice scampering behind the walls, the refrigerator's breathing when it changed position in its sleep). I realized that one morning they'd suddenly order me, "Go," and I'd leave what they call the barracks for what they call Tavira, hearing the waves without seeing the waves, hearing the seagulls without seeing the seagulls, hearing people's voices without noticing the people, heading toward the painted figures that silently waited for me in the porcelain landscapes, even as the deceased wait for us behind a final door, which we realize is final only when it's too late, when it closes on top of us like the lid of a tomb.

And so I stopped worrying about being pursued, since no one could pursue me but I myself, I stopped worrying about being spied on, since no one could spy on me but myself, I stopped fearing I might get killed, because I was the only one who could do it, and I accepted their food, and their water, and their glass of wine on Sundays, and the visits of the phony commander who pretended to be concerned about me, "Has your appetite picked up, Major?" and I, as if I knew nothing, "I'm feeling great, Lieutenant Colonel," and he, "Have you gotten those strange ideas out of your head?" and I, "Yes, Lieutenant Colonel, completely out," and he, already turning the doorknob, "Sit down, sit down, Valadas, I'm delighted to see you're better," and I, placing the napkin around my neck and starting in on my soup as the bugle summoned the officers, "I appreciate your concern, Lieutenant Colonel, care for some soup?" and he, already outside, "Enjoy your meal, Valadas, if you keep on like this, I'll call your family and tell them they can contact you," and that afternoon, Margarida, they allowed me to walk freely around the barracks until suppertime, and I passed by brick buildings that imitated barracks with men who pretended to be soldiers, complete with rifles, and a phony captain bought me a whiskey in the mess hall, where phony lieutenants and second lieutenants played cards or paced around a pool table.

But it wasn't until the following week that I stood before the waves and saw ships and fishermen mending their nets, it wasn't until the following week that I walked down through the town, on my way to China, and found the sea, after first talking with the phony commander, who came up to me near the sergeants' bathrooms, pulled a case from his pocket, and asked, "A cigarette, Valadas?" and as he struck the match in his cupped hands and I leaned toward the flickering flame, he said "I wrote your sisters and told them you're here in the Algarve, so I expect they'll get the train and come visit," and I thought, What about Julieta? and he "What's that, Major?" and I thought, Will they take Julieta out of the attic, will they pull her away from the tangos to bring her down here? and he, "Did you say something, Valadas?" and I, inhaling the smoke and thinking he'd given me the order I'd been expecting ("Go"), said, "Thanks for remembering them, Lieutenant Colonel," and the commander, closing the cigarette case, "I'm not a jailer, Valadas, I'm a military man, I don't give a hoot about politics," and I thought, They'll bring Julieta to display our shame before one and all, they'll bring Julieta to humiliate me with my impotence, to humiliate us with the impotence of my father, to make fun of us, "They're not men, they're not men, they're not real men, they're a disgrace," Julieta, who had never before left the Calçada do Tojal, bawling at the Lisbon train station while clutching on to the gramophone, and the commander, "I don't approve of your having conspired, Valadas, but a military post, at least while I'm in charge, is not a dungeon," and my sister Maria Teresa, "Hush, Julieta," and my sister Anita, "Maybe we should go back to Benfica," and my sister Maria Teresa, "If they wrote us to go and see Jorge, then we're going to see Jorge," and my sister Julieta, "No no no no no," and the porters staring at the three lost creatures next to the platform, one with a wind-up gramophone in her lap and the other two pulling at its horn, and as soon as the commander went away, complaining about the orderly who gallivanted with Tavira's housemaids instead of watering the flower beds, I prevented my sisters from leaving Benfica by calmly walking, without hurrying my steps, to the main gate of the barracks, and then toward the town, at the same time that the sentry straightened up with the jerky motions of a mechanical doll.

What the men dressed up as soldiers designated as Tavira looked very much like the real Tavira: it had the same sun, the same layout of streets and houses, the same old buildings around the square, the same Roman bridge I'd always liked, the same outdoor cafés with the same widowers seated in the same chairs before the same untouched fruit drinks, the same dogs, the same fish smell, the same seagulls, and even the same tiny hotel above a garage, the Rabat Inn, remember? a whitewashed hallway with rooms on either side and a shower at the end, and the two of us, after lunch, counted the mosquitoes on the ceiling that at night, as soon as we turned off the lights, would drone like airplanes around our ears, and you, "The first thing I'm going to do to-morrow is buy some insecticide," and I, turning on the light and slapping at my own face, "I'm putting on my swimsuit and sleep-ing on the beach, because I can't put up with these little beasts anymore."

It wasn't the real Tavira because it was a different maid who washed the floor at the hotel entrance with a mop and bucket, it wasn't the real Tavira because the hardware shop where we bought the insecticide for the mosquitoes had given way to a shop that sells wedding dresses, with mannequins in the win-dow decked out in satin and gauze and accompanied by grooms wearing double-breasted suits and gloves, frozen in embraces that would never be completed. I remember that when I got back from Santo Tirso and before I entered the military academy, I once saw a bunch of these dummies arrive, still naked, at a cloth-ing boutique, carried in by employees from a van parked on the sidewalk and chock full of other mannequins, like a crowd of sexless people. I remember how they struck me as androgynous beings from outer space, strategically placed on the avenues of Lisbon to spy on unsuspecting humans with their tenebrous smiles. But I realized that it was me they were keeping tabs on only when it was already too late, when at the tailor's I found a jacket I'd ordered marked up with chalk and worn by a mannequin whose limbs and head had been amputated.

It wasn't the real Tavira, and the fact that the mannequins had followed me (but how, using what means of transportation, obeying whose orders?) to the border of China prompted me to enter the shop with wedding gowns in search of clues that would help me discern the intentions of the creatures in the window, who continued to look at the street with simulated indifference, offering lace veils to the notary and deeds office just opposite (where ants carrying rolls of official-looking paper went to obtain the blessing of a raised seal), and I was greeted by dozens of shiny cheeks that looked at me in a deceptively friendly way, all of them supplied with felt spikenards that pervaded the store with fake corollas. Statues dressed in tails looked ready to take flight in their patent-leather shoes, maids of honor with oakum tufts were being choked by their phony hair, best men with striped trousers presided over groups of tuxedos that assumed various postures, protecting and defending themselves between the counter and a door that announced Office, behind which there were no doubt more shiny cheeks, more spikenards, and more satin dresses swelling, in the store's basement, with the din of wedding marches. I ran out of the establishment when one of the mannequins asked "Can I help you, Officer?" and trotted down lanes and alleys that took me to the square next to the Roman bridge, and from the square I walked on the same streets we once took to go to the sea, fleeing from the mosquitoes that hummed in the darkness at the Rabat Inn, and we stretched out on the August sand, counting stars that blended with the boats' lanterns, as if we were between two parallel skies, with bats swooping above and below us, and Tavira sliding toward Africa with its outdoor cafés and its widowers seated before untouched fruit drinks.

From the public square of Tavira, which wasn't really Tavira since the mannequins were watching me, and if the mannequins were watching me, that meant it was the Chinese border, I arrived at the beach, Margarida, not the beach we went to but a beach exactly like it and yet different, with fewer seagulls and a more transparent sea, a beach where the fishermen mended their nets with lizardly languor, and the same dogs, smelling of figs and lemons, had come down from the Algarve's inland hills, attracted by the odor of the fish being auctioned, the same blind man, sitting on a canvas stool, observed the surf with his black mica glasses, the same June waves moved like enormous, gently breathing gills, and right beyond the sea lay China, just like on my grandmother's plates and tureens, China, which was closely guarded by the old maid, who plodded down the hallway with her cane, like a gondolier, to lock up in the cupboard the dragons, the snakes, and the terra-cotta Buddhas that nodded yes, my sister Anita stared wide-eyed at the mandarins that smiled on the teacups, Fernando picked up a porcelain spoon and the maid, furious, "Put that down, Fernando," China, where it takes a long time to get to, with its strange flowers and bridges like eyebrows, and as we drove home I asked my mother "Is China very far away?" and my sister Maria Teresa, who still had braids in her hair, "It's in Grandma's house, we were just there," so that for me, Margarida, the Orient was located in a third-floor apartment on the Rua Braamcamp and consisted of room after small room of ornately carved beds, upright pianos, and leather armchairs covered by sheets, with my grandmother, who looked so tiny in her huge stuffed chair, giving us anise-flavored candies until she died and they sold China to the Peruvian consulate, so that the Rua Braamcamp, without going anywhere, suddenly became South America, with poncho-clad diplomats playing guitar in the depths of the tureens. "China is nowhere," decided my father, who was driving the car, "China doesn't exist," and I, with my chin propped on the front seat, confused because I'd just seen China on the shelves of the cupboard, "But what about the pagodas and the ladies with fans?" and my brother Fernando, who years later would get married to a homely housemaid, "It does too exist, Dad, I even broke one of its saucers," "I'm going to tell your grandmother," bleated the maid with a cane, "I'm going to tell your grandmother that you're destroying her dishes," and my grandmother to me, from the depths of her stuffed chair, "Are you Fernando or Jorge?" and I, insulted that she could confuse me with that nincompoop, "I'm Jorge, Grandma," and she, "Then I was right, you always have cleaner fingernails," and my sister Maria Teresa, not noticing that the old woman was asleep, "Fernando broke one of your saucers, Grandma," "That's precisely why China no longer exists," said my father while passing a streetcar, "because you broke a saucer," and my mother, "Honestly, Álvaro," and my brother Fernando, "It does too exist, there's still a whole stack of saucers," and my father to my mother, while honking at a wagon for going slow, "Honestly, Álvaro, what?" and my sister Maria Teresa, "Fernando broke one of your saucers, Grandma," and she perfectly still, and my mother to my father, "If you think it's cute and you encourage him, then the boy will smash the whole kit and caboodle," and my sister Maria Teresa, shouting, "Grandma, Fernando broke one of your saucers, do you hear?" "So what if he does?" replied my father while making an obscene gesture at the wagon, "I don't want any of that junk," and my grandmother didn't budge, didn't talk, she just snored with her mouth opened and her dentures coming unglued, and I, frightened, "Grandma, what's wrong, Grandma?" and my father to my mother, "You won't understand what I'm going to say, but ever since I was a kid I've dreamed of taking a stick to that cupboard and everything in it," and my mother, "Wonderful,

Álvaro, what a wonderful example you're setting for your children," and I imagined my father in breeches, dressed up as a sailor just as I was, shattering all the porcelain with a stick, and the very next time we went to the third-floor apartment on the Rua Braamcamp, I immediately threw a pitcher on the floor, and my uncle Eduardo smacked my bottom, and my mother, "Is that what you wanted, Álvaro?" and my father to my uncle, "If you touch Jorge again, I'll cream you," and my grandmother, with a fistful of candies in her hand, "Did someone ask for more candies, children?" and my uncle, who wasn't in the army, he was a lawyer, "Just try it," and my father, "I'll try it, I'll try it, let me go, Madalena," and my sister Anita, grabbing on to his trousers, "Dad Dad Dad Dad Dad Dad Dad," and my father, "Show what stuff you're made of, show what you can do," and my uncle Eduardo, sticking out his chest, "I'll show you, I'll show you right now, do you think I'm afraid of you?" and there was an old photo, the color of tincture for scratches, that showed the two of them holding a bicycle without tires, and my uncle José, who was a bachelor and worked for a shipping firm, suddenly appeared, "Get over here fast, Mom just had a seizure," and we reached the bedroom just as my grandmother's hand opened up, and anise-flavored candies rained down from her fingers.

It must have been ten or eleven A.M. when I arrived at the beach on the Chinese border, and the blind man, sitting on his canvas stool with a visored cap, turned his mica lenses toward me, and it wasn't the same blind man we saw, Margarida, because in spite of many similar features, this one was thinner and had a face plowed by furrows and hollows like an eroded boulder, it wasn't the same blind man, it was a creature worn down by the wind and by the waves going back and forth like gently breathing gills, a blind man without shoes and with the ankles of a seagull, observing me with a statue's severity and snarling "Can you spare some change, pal?" The blind man, the dogs smelling of figs and lemons that had come down from the

Algarve's hills, attracted by the odor of fish being auctioned, the fishermen mending their nets with lizardly languor, and the boats with keels in the air that waited for night, and I waited for night with them, crouched in a crate, ready to set sail for China.

At sundown the bugle from the barracks signaled that it was suppertime, and I thought, I'm hungry. I thought, Maybe it would do me good to eat before crossing the border, but then I thought, It doesn't matter, it'll just take a few minutes, I'll eat as soon as I reach the other side. There were no longer any fishermen, nor any seagulls sheltered by the arch of the bridge, just the blind man and the dogs barking with nostalgia for octopus guts, and the streetlights of Tavira (but it wasn't Tavira, I assure you it was an invented town) digging into the facades, like when a kerosene lamp is brought up close to a face, and we detect its ridges and valleys, the rivers of its arteries, its pores that open and close, the placement of its whiskers. Just the dogs, the blind man, and me, the moon rising out of the sea, and the sound of the waves, until the blackness swallowed the blind man and the dogs, and when I couldn't even see the crate where I was crouched, I got up, straightened my army jacket, and walked toward the waves. I thought about taking off my shoes, since they would make it harder to walk on water, but I decided it would look bad to arrive at an unknown country in my socks: I'm sure you'll agree, Margarida, that my parents wouldn't have liked it.

BOOK FOUR

Life with You

I

I don't like living in Alcântara, because it's too far away from school. Even when it's not raining it takes me at least an hour to get there—two buses plus the time spent waiting between them—and when I come home in the evening it's even worse, with all the people who've just gotten off work pushing and shoving at the bus stops. The other thing I don't like about Alcântara is that there's no movie theater, just houses, apartments, seedy bars, garages, and vagrants milling around the abandoned warehouses. Not one movie theater, not one café, and not one pool hall for our leisure hours, nothing. Just squalor and crumbling walls: a wasteland. Maybe we should have stayed in Lourenço Marques, where my mother lived with her father on an island with monkeys and coconut trees on the beach, and when I get bored I picture the monkeys sitting on the sand and staring at the sea. In the Lisbon Zoo the monkeys, instead of staring at the sea, stare at us with a hurt sadness, just like the man who sleeps with me and whimpers for kisses instead of peanuts. At the dinner table his skinny fingers remove the fish bones with the delicacy of a mandrill removing lice from her children, and after dinner he crosses his knife and fork on his plate and disappears into the backyard to weep in silence the way animals do. I don't see him, but I can feel him there, on the stone bench, sweating tears underneath the walnut tree. Or laughing. Or listening to the trains that run along the river, and to the lighthouse lowing in the fog. Shortly after we met he told me that when he was little he'd hear the lighthouse low all day long, crying out for help, and a beam continuously swept his bedroom in search of him, and he cowered under his covers lest the light find him and take him away. Then his godmother died, he was taken to Lisbon, and the lighthouse became silent.

Our apartment at Hyacinth Park consists of my room, my aunt's room, my father's room, the kitchen, and the room with the TV and the dining table. We wash our hands in the shed, where there's a mirror, toothbrushes, and a tub for taking baths. I hate that mirror, because my face doesn't smile in the tin. It reminds me of those photo-booth pictures, whose contracted expressions give me the creeps. As Colgate drips off my chin, my face calmly gazes, examining me: not judging or condemning me, just examining me, waiting for me to wilt and reach its age, as the plane trees wait for the October wind to make them look like their true selves, reduced to the verdigris of their limbs.

From our apartment on Rua #8 I can see down to the Tagus and beyond, to the ships and the bridge, and when my father isn't watching television, the upstairs neighbors aren't making noise, and no pan is sizzling on the stove, I can hear the seashell echo of the bridge traffic, which causes the ceiling lamp to sway, and the trains answer with their urgent roaring. Since I prefer silence, I'd rather live in a part of Lisbon where there are cinemas, snack bars, and pool halls instead of the river, and where the man who sleeps with me wouldn't have a stone bench under a walnut tree. In Alvalade, for example, like my cousins, who weren't born in Africa and aren't obsessed with digging through the floor to fly under the earth, my cousins, who call my father and my aunt by their first names, and to whom my father and aunt show deference, not daring to sit down until asked. Or if not in Alvalade, then in Campo de Ourique, where Laura's grandmother lives, next to the theater, and from the window you can peek at the actors going in for rehearsal. But since we can't afford an apartment that keeps out the winter rains, we live here, chattering our teeth in December and January, when the ramp leading to Hyacinth Park becomes a mire and the dogs stop scampering down the streets. We live here, where I fry in August and spend an eternity, the rest of the year, going back and forth between Alcântara and my school, an eternity in the

morning and an eternity in the evening. We live here, and before the man who sleeps with me started to take care of the landlord, the grocer, and the butcher, there were months when we
couldn't pay the electric bill, and my father would switch on
his helmet's light and say, "It seems like we're back in Johannesburg, hand me my pickax, Orquidea, because I smell gold in the
walls," and my aunt, "There's no gold in the walls, Domingos,
sit tight or the landlord will kick us out," and my father, stimu-
lated by his beer, "What do you mean there's no gold, Orquidea,
just listen to the approaching mine cars," and I, worried he might
destroy one of the walls, "Those aren't mine cars, it's the train
from Cascais," the train's rumbling swelled, exploded, and receded, and my disappointed father, setting down his pickax and
sitting in the chair where he passed his days, "Those good-for-
nothing blacks took off without a word, I'm going to tell the
foreman first thing in the morning." My aunt, forgetting about
her ailing kidneys, would borrow money from a neighbor to pay
the electric bill, and my father, disgruntled because the lights
were working again, would sink into his chair and promise, "The
next time I go down in the mine elevator, I'll bring back a cart-
load of sand and stones, and we'll be rich." And it was around
this time, in the snack bar across from the high school, that I
met the man who sleeps with me.

To be honest, I didn't even notice him at first, it was Laura
who nudged me as soon as we found a free table, "An older man,
over there, is in love with you," and Ana and I began to laugh,
because Laura, from so much peeking out her window at the
actors from the theater, had gotten drama happy, inventing ar-
dent passions left and right, when what boys really want is to
pet us, feel us up, and see you later, and after they found out I
was diabetic and couldn't drink milkshakes or chew bubble gum
because of my blood sugar, they avoided me altogether, and I
realized they were afraid they might catch my disease, even as I
supposedly caught it from my mother, who also took insulin

shots and whom I never met, I don't know if she's alive or dead in Mozambique, I just know she refused to take the boat back to Portugal, and I don't blame her, because she lived on an island with monkeys and coconut trees on the beach, and I'd no doubt do the same thing if I knew that the alternative was Hyacinth Park. There's no worse place in the world to live.

I ignored Laura's nudges and comments, but I remember that it was raining, people shook their umbrellas like ducks coming out of the water, and Ana suddenly pulled on my sleeve, "Don't look, but the older man has left the counter and is walking straight toward us," and Laura, "It's just like I said, but you wouldn't believe me," and I, "It's probably the grandfather of one of our classmates, they were supposed to meet but missed each other, and now he's going to ask if we know where she is," and I felt the weight of a shadow on me, I felt a smile seeking me, I heard a timid voice ask, "May I?" Laura and Ana moved aside, giggling uncontrollably, while a lemon tea slid toward my club soda

(the doctor said nix on juice, Coca-cola, chocolate milk, and flavored yogurt)

and there sat a short, bald, and ugly gentleman as old as my father, shaking a sugar packet and saying, "Sorry for butting in, I hope you don't mind if I join you," the women at the next table glared at him indignantly, two fellows reading the newspaper cast pitying glances at him, and he, unaware of how ridiculous he looked, poured the sugar outside his cup and onto the table, where the sticky granules gleamed, then excused himself, pulling his handkerchief from his pocket, "Don't get the wrong idea, it's just that whenever I get a cold I feel like talking to someone," and Ana, "And you get a cold every week, right?" and one of the women at the next table, "Talk about lechers," and he, "As a matter of fact, no, and it's a good thing, because I have bronchial congestion, this is the second cold I've had this winter," and although it was only four o'clock the manager of

the snack bar turned on the overhead lights, which hesitated before spouting out their full fluorescence, stripping the skin off
features and gestures, and the older man, stirring his lemon tea
with a spoon, "May I take you home? You live in Alcântara, don't
you?" and Laura, "He's fallen in love, poor guy," and Ana, "Let
him take you home, maybe he has a car," and I, "Take me
home?" and the older man, "It's an excuse for me to see that
part of Lisbon, to see the trains and the river, I love the Tagus
River," and the woman from the next table, "Why, I never, if I
weren't a woman, I'd have already slugged him," and one of the
men reading the paper, "Be nice to Grandpa, little girl," and
Laura, "Let him take you home, stupid, he might have a car,"
and the waiter, eyeing the suit and the manners of the man who
sleeps with me, "Is this gentleman bothering you ladies?" and
Laura, "How everyone will laugh when this gets around school,"
and I, "No, he's not bothering us, he's a friend of my father,
they worked together in South Africa, how much is the club
soda?"

When we arrived at Alcântara it was still pouring down rain,
a rain as gray as the warehouses, garages, and stone walls of
Avenida de Ceuta, as gray as the vacant lot where the Gypsies
anchored their trailers and pitched their patched and repatched
tents, and I thought, I'll bet it's already raining in the apartment,
I'll bet there are at least ten pots with water rat-a-tatting against
the aluminum as my aunt skips around with a mop and bucket
and my father, with a bottle of beer in his lap and a helmet on
his head, exclaims "This is nothing compared to Johannesburg,
this isn't even rain, just drizzle, there's no lightning and no thunder, I remember one day when we came up on the mine elevator to discover that the workers' neighborhood had been washed
away by a storm, all that was left standing were a few walls, and
the black women in front of their shipwrecked furniture," and
my aunt, "This isn't Johannesburg, Domingos, it's Lisbon, I
couldn't care less about Johannesburg," and when we got off the

bus we couldn't see the Tagus, we couldn't see any boats, and the man who sleeps with me invited me for a lemon tea at the bar and grill on the traffic circle, where the truckers bound for the Alentejo region wolfed down steaks and wine to gain courage for the endless cork trees, and since I didn't feel like helping to distribute pots and pans over the carpet while my father expounded on typhoons in the tropics, I decided to accept, skating along with him in the gutters, and he, dripping water from his coat and sneezing, "Isn't it a beautiful evening? What wonderful weather," and I thought, The guy has flipped, I guess that's what happens with age, the water was gushing down the canal of my back, I thought, Tomorrow I'll wake up with pneumonia and a one-hundred-and-four-degree fever, and this guy tells me it's a beautiful evening and the weather just wonderful, the sign of the bar and grill was reflected in the sidewalk, a stream was now rushing down the slope of Hyacinth Park and there wasn't a silhouette on the street or even any Gypsies, who are protected from the rain by their bell jars of mystery, just building facades all in a row, the branches of the trees, and the tiny drops dotting the halos of the streetlights, none of the truckers turned to look at us, the owner stopped shouting orders at the kitchen, where someone was grumbling, and walked toward our table while wiping his hands on a cloth, and the older man, while dumping a packet of sugar into his cup and brushing away granules with his sleeve, "You won't get mad, I hope, if I ask you to marry me."

There are times when I think I'd be happy if my father hadn't brought me to Lisbon, and by happy I mean not so alone with my disease as here, secretly probing and measuring it in my body, monitoring its progress in my liver, in my heart, in my kidneys, and injecting myself with insulin in the bathroom at school, so that my classmates won't suspect anything, because those I told imagine I'm carrying around a contagious death, and I don't even talk about it with my aunt, I return from the doctor's and she, acting as though she doesn't know where I've been, "Hi, dear," my aunt, who never approved of my father getting married in Africa to a strange woman, perhaps even a mulatto woman, without advising the family, without first bringing her to Portugal to get my grandparents' blessing, and the only time they came from Africa for a visit they didn't forewarn anyone, they docked in Oporto and continued by bus up to Esposende, with my mother looking out the window in search of Mozambique, and they showed up at my grandparents' house at lunchtime, with a trunk full of statuettes and wooden masks, and my grandfather, who sold fabrics in a shop called Dacron Unlimited, "What's going on?" and my grandmother, crossing herself, "Get this face of the devil out of here, Domingos, it smells as if hell itself just walked in the door," and it was the smell of diabetes, and my mother, ignoring them, not talking to them, leaned against the windowsill to search for the trawlers of her island, and intrigued by the sea swallows, she asked my father, "What birds are these, Domingos?" and my grandfather, picking up an ivory giraffe, "Look at this critter, Orquidea," and to my parents, "Are there elephants where you live?" and my father to my mother, "Those are sea swallows, they swallow up ships until there's not even any foam trailing behind the propellers," and my grandmother, clutching her rosary, "I smell the fumes of hell, do you hear? it smells exactly like hell, like the flowers of the dead, hand me my shawl, I'm going to fetch the priest," and my grandfather, while pouring himself some brandy, "I'd give ten yards of flannel to see elephants galloping in the jungle," and my aunt, "And what about hippos, Domingos, can they even swallow hippos?" and my father, "Not even fog or wind escapes the sea swallows, they devour whatever's in sight, they even gobbled up a traveling cinema that was here one summer, isn't that right, Orquidea, isn't it true that the guy who worked the projector was never again seen?" and my aunt, "The cinema went to Póvoa, Domingos, since when do sea swallows peck at films?" and my grandfather, refilling his shot glass, "The only elephant I've ever seen is on the calendar at the bar," and my father, "They don't peck films but they pecked your friend who worked the projector and sold tickets and never returned to make love to you anymore," and my grandfather, "What?" and my father, "Ask Orquidea, have Orquidea tell you about the weeping willows," and my aunt, "You liar, may God make you crippled, you liar," and my grandfather, "What's this, you slut? Under the weeping willows?" and my mother, "Sea swallows, Domingos, did you say they're called sea swallows?" and my aunt, "He's making it up, Dad, the air in Mozambique made his brain go batty," and my father to my grandfather, "Why don't you come visit so we can fly under the earth together?" and the priest, after blessing the trunk and the four corners of the shop, held a huge crucifix in front of my mother, saying "It really does smell like brimstone and the flowers of Satan, but it's not from the statuettes, it's from that sinner right there," and my grandfather to my father, "You fly under the earth, son?" and my grandmother to my father, "Oh my God, Domingos, you've brought the devil into our home," and the priest, sprinkling holy water on my mother, "In the name of Jesus Christ *vade retro,* emperor of darkness, I command you to free your servant and go hither to your kingdom," and my grandmother, "What if she gives birth to a werewolf?" and my father to my grandfather, "I flew in the Johannesburg mines, Dad, if you have a pickax and want to try it out, I'll teach you, we can dig a hole right here," and the priest, *"Vade retro,"* and my mother, "They devour ships, but right now they're flying over us and cawing, maybe they'll come gobble us up," and my grandmother, tossing wooden macaws and crocodiles out the window, "A dark furry baby, how hideous, a baby that will jump out of its crib and trot around the house, years ago, riding on the train from Lamego, I spotted two of them in the distance, laughing in a pine forest," the priest held my mother by the arm, *"Vade retro,"* and my father,

"Hold it, you jerk, let go of my wife's hand," and my grandfather, "I don't have a pickax, son, will a rake do?" and my aunt, "I didn't sleep with anyone next to the canvas wall after the movies were over, I didn't want to lose what you only realize you have after you lose it, what only matters when it stops existing because when you had it it didn't exist, and what I had remains in the sand of Esposende and is part of the tides and the shrubs on the beach," and my mother, "I have no desire to end up shrieking like them above the house," and my father to the priest, "If you touch her again, I'll punch your face in, go and rain your water somewhere else," and my grandmother, "How about some incense, Reverend? if you brought your censer, then just swing a little smoke around her and we'll leave it at that," and my grandfather, "A rake, a shovel, a stake, some scissors, it just needs to be able to dig holes, right?" and my aunt, "I never saw him without his hat, I never saw him naked, but I miss his breath in my ear, I miss his fingers, I miss the peace that followed and the sea that beat my bones on the rocks, and I didn't want it, Dad, I didn't want it, I wanted it and didn't want it, I wanted it, I didn't want to want it and I wanted it, I went to Póvoa to visit him, and his employee said, 'There's a girl here to see you, Claudino,' and he said to his employee, 'I've never seen her in my life, tell her it's a mistake,' and the employee said to me, 'He's never seen you in his life,' and I without the courage to speak, I fiddling with my hair clips without realizing I was fiddling with my hair clips," and the priest, sprinkling holy water on my father, "I didn't touch your wife, sir, I came to exorcise the Prince of Darkness," and my grandfather, hammering at the floor, "Do we need to go down very far to fly, Domingos?" and my aunt, "But I stayed till the end of the film, and when everyone had left and the employee turned off the lights, shut and locked the doors, closed up the ticket booth, and disappeared on the streets of the town, then the cinema owner skipped down the steps of the projection booth, and there

I was, the girl who was a mistake, the girl he'd never seen in his life, staring at him, not reproaching him or slapping him or crying, just staring at him, and he asked, 'What do you want?' and I said, 'Just give back what you took from me in Esposende, and then I'll go away,'" and my mother, used to seeing coconut trees all along the beach, "The sea swallows have eaten the trawlers, how sad," and my father to my grandfather, "Forty or fifty feet are enough, from there we can hop on the mine elevator," and the older man, blowing his nose and ordering another lemon tea in the bar and grill where truckers gained heart for the Alentejo, placing his hand on mine, removing it, placing it there again, the older man running his free hand through his hair, "You still haven't answered my question: Will you or won't you marry me?"

And so I took him to Rua #8, thinking that our apartment in Hyacinth Park would disillusion him, thinking that the neighborhood, the wilted dahlias, and the muddy sidewalks would scare him off, thinking he would think, as I imagined everyone thought, that it was horrible to live in a subdivision traversed by screaming trains that ravaged the walls, but the older man, steeping his zeal and becoming ever more immersed in it, ever more like a drowning man hoisted out of the water by a hook, "Not bad, not bad, this is a nifty little residential neighborhood you have, peaceful streets, pleasant gardens, the Tagus," and I, "Do you think so? Did you say it's a residential neighborhood?" and the streetlights weren't even working, so that we had to grope in the dark as if trying out steps in an unfamiliar hallway, and in the foyer, without power like the rest of our building, the rest of the Park, and the part of Alcântara stretching from Avenida de Ceuta to the grade crossing, in the foyer, which was about the size of a closet, the light on my father's helmet blinded us with its green glow, like sunlight filtered through vines, and my aunt, "Who did you bring home, Yolanda?" and the older man, sneezing and tripping on the hat stand, "You must be the young lady's aunt, pleased to meet you, ma'am, forgive me for invading your privacy like this," and I thinking, When I tell this at school, Ana will keel over, and my aunt, oblivious of the older man's courtesies, "Who did you bring home, Yolanda?" and the electricity returned, revealing the living room's shabby furniture, the chairs, the table with a phone directory propping up one of the legs, the beer bottles, the peeling wallpaper, the floor that the pickax had torn up, and the man who sleeps with me, "Allow me to introduce myself, ma'am, I've come to ask for this girl's hand," the TV came back on, blaring, and my aunt, twisting the mop in spite of the kidney doctor having warned her not to exert herself, "Marriage? Am I hearing right? Do you want to get married to this kook, Yolanda?" and I, dazed by the noise from the TV and feeling the lack of insulin in my system, thinking, I need to give myself an injection, answered, "I don't know," because I didn't know, because I hadn't thought about it, because my body was weak and ready to pass out, because beneath the cold I felt warm, because the hyacinths in my breath proliferated on my tongue, because I was going to die, to die while that older man informed my aunt of his marriage to me, because I was fading, fainting, holding on to a chest of drawers while the living room went out of focus, and I saw my father turn off the light on his forehead, I saw him open the tenth, or hundredth, or thousandth, or millionth bottle of beer of the evening, I saw him hold up the pickax and ask, as if he were offering precious information about a fortune, a prize, or a present, "Do you know how to fly under the earth, my friend?"

2

I never would have gone to Hyacinth Park if she hadn't insisted: "Come." It's out of the way, there's no night bus, and there's not even a taxi stand at the traffic circle, so that for public transportation you have to hike to the Cais do Sodré train station, where the vending machines buzz in the deserted lobby. When I arrived at Rua #8 and got a whiff of the funerary smell, a smell of musk and tombs, I realized that the perfume that lingered on our fingers whenever we shook her hand came not from inside her, but from the wilted dahlias at the building entrances, rows of stems falling over each other like eels that the Tagus, when it receded, had left behind but would come back to claim as soon as it noticed they were missing from the seaweed pockets of its coat. And so whenever I visited her I was afraid I'd find the river in search of dahlias on the lanes and in the backyards of Alcântara, pawing through the chicken coops the way beggars paw through garbage cans, and when I confessed to her my fear, she answered, plucking the petals from a corolla that peeked out of the iron gate:

"The river doesn't need to trouble itself, because the locomotives take the dahlias down to its shore."

In fact, as soon as we started to study geography or math or English and I felt the smell leaning on my shoulder like those people on the streetcar who lean into our newspaper, breathing down our neck, a locomotive would cut through Hyacinth Park, transporting armfuls of flailing flowers with water-famished petals that dilated and shrank.

And so I finally understood trains. I grew up behind the Santa Apolónia train station, in a building whose walls were blackened by locomotive smoke and cracked by the vibrations of the wheels. The whistles of departures plowed my sleep and

caused feathers to fly out of our mattresses, so that when we
traveled to Castelo Branco or Santarém or Águeda, Lisbon went
with us through the mountains and pine forests, across bridges,
and through villages at the foot of hills. I grew up behind Santa
Apolónia, looking out the window at the farewells and suitcases
of emigrants, so that for me the trains were an aquarium of tears
with baskets and eyes swimming inside them, eyes lost in basement apartments of France and Germany, watching the snow
fall in the frame of the window. Only in Alcântara did I finally understand that the trains don't carry people, they carry
the wilted dahlias back to the Tagus, they return the eels to
the river's coat pockets, so when I came home for dinner I told
my parents,
    "I discovered that the occupants of train cars come from
the flower beds of Alcântara,"
    and my mother, setting the table,
    "I'll bet you've been with those lunatics who fly, I don't
know how many times your father has forbidden you from hanging out with people who've come back from Africa."
    I never would have gone to Hyacinth Park if you hadn't
insisted: "Come." Where I live is smaller than your garden apartment in Alcântara, there's just my parents' room, my uncle's
room, and the living room, where I sleep on the couch after
everyone shuts their door and leaves me alone with the leftovers
from dinner still on the table and with the saint on the wall who
keeps me from playing with myself in the dark, and where, as
soon as I turn out the ceiling light, the tablecloth and napkins
float all around me like crumpled birds whose cotton wings are
buoyed up by the night. My father, who can't work because of
his stomach ulcer, sits around drinking milk, eating cooked cereal, and popping heartburn pills, while my mother, who's a
cleaning woman at Arroios Hospital, complains about the pro-
lapsus of her uterus, and my uncle, from nine in the morning
till six at night, goes from doorstep to doorstep with Bible in

hand, preaching the word of God to the neighbors, having given up his job as an insurance agent to offer eternal life to the neighborhood, recommending temperance and chastity to the streets' indifference. My mother, my father, and my uncle ensconced in their plastered burrows, and I with the saint and the whiteness of the doilies all night long, listening to the train for Paris rumbling in my body. Night after night with my legs hanging off the couch and the pillow slipping out from under my head, with my uncle periodically breaking into the living room to proclaim the end of the world and the resurrection of the flesh, ordering me to get on my knees and ask St. Stephen to have mercy on me, until my mother threatens to have him committed, and the apostle locks himself in his room, blessing the world with his haggard palm.

I never would have gone to Rua #8 in Hyacinth Park, at the other end of town, because the dahlias unnerve me almost as much as the older man who sleeps with you, waiting for me to go away before he pries himself off the stone bench to come back in, and when I lift my eyes from the geography book, the math book, or the English book, I see him swelling among the cabbages like a vegetable staring at me, the same way the ocean stares at us, and I feel like leaving your room and going around to the back of the building to assure him that I don't have a crush on you any more than you have a crush on me, that I don't love you as you don't love me, that I've never hugged you, never fondled you, and never even kissed you, that I just feel sorry for you, reduced to the company of two idiotic girls who dress like Spanish dolls because the other students are afraid of your disease, afraid of your caramel custard odor, afraid of a classmate who eats only white fish and mustard greens, who gets the shakes and injects herself in the bathroom at school, a classmate who at least once a year is placed on a stretcher and rushed in an ambulance to São José Hospital, as

if she were going to die. I would sit down on the stone bench
next to the old man and say,

"Why don't you go back inside, sir?"

and perhaps he'd hear me between the cabbages' sighing
and the walnuts' castanets, perhaps he'd straighten up, smile,
and say

"Thanks, young man,"

and I'd occupy his place, observing the bridge that crosses
the Tagus to go nowhere, like the bramble-lined paths that wind
among the corrals in my mother's village in Trás-os-Montes. I'd
tell him

"I'm not her boyfriend, sir,"

I'd tell him

"No one's her boyfriend, and no one wants to be her boyfriend, because of her diabetes and her smell and her fainting
spells and the medicines she takes,"

I'd tell him

"Don't worry, Yolanda needs you,"

I'd tell him

"She's cranky, but don't take it personally, it's because of
the disease she got in Africa that's rotting her insides,"

and the old man, without opening his mouth, would grab
his briefcase and stand up, look at her bedroom window, then
sit back down, and I,

"So aren't you going back in?"

and he, poking at the cabbages with his umbrella,

"Yolanda doesn't need me, she's not interested in what
I say,"

and my mother,

"Keep away from those lunatics, Alfredo,"

and my uncle, consulting the Bible while having a second
helping of soup,

"Jesus Christ was the only man to walk on water,"

and I to the old man,

"And what do you talk to her about, sir?"

and the trains traveling from Hyacinth Park to the river, loaded with dahlias from the flower beds, and the night that doesn't descend from the sky but rises to it from the water, and the old man, in a glycerine voice, with the briefcase on his knees,

"About my childhood, about my aunts, about Ericeira, the Calçada do Tojal, the footsteps in the attic, whatever,"

whereas in my mother's village the night begins in the sky and in the willow trees next to the laundry tanks near the square, and it drifts across the cemetery and the mayor's house toward us, a night that strangles insects, voices, and the bells of the cattle in the stable, and my grandmother hunched before the fireplace with a glass of muscatel, and my uncle,

"Ite missa est,"

the night descends from the willows, where by day it's reduced to a few seeds of shade, as if it were a child being incubated by the trees in their slate-colored wombs, and the old man, in a soft and intrigued voice,

"They never told me whose footsteps I heard in the attic, they never told me what happened to Uncle Jorge in Tavira, my aunt Teresa just told me to keep quiet, 'Hush up,' and in my bedroom I listened, trembling, to the footsteps and the opera music,"

like me, in Santa Apolónia, listening to my uncle, who's so fanatical he made my mother rip down a curtain to sew him a tunic, which he wore when yelling at the neighbors "Save your souls, sinners," and I've nearly forgotten about the village and the finches in the redbuds all morning, about diving into the laundry tank and the women complaining to my father, and my father

"That's not what we sent you to school for"

didn't hit me or scold me or raise his voice, my father kneeling in the orchard and setting the traps for the robins, "Exactly like you, sir," I'd say to the old man, "because even in your gestures you resemble each other," and Yolanda,

"You got that problem wrong, dummy, it's not eleven point three, it's twelve point seven,"

and I without hearing her, I in the village laundry tank, under the redbuds, and she,

"What are you looking at, Alfredo?"

and a train zoomed by carrying armfuls of dahlias, like an offering, back to the river as your father swung his pickax at the floor, and I,

"At the old man sitting on the bench under the walnut tree out back, waiting for me to go home to Santa Apolónia before he comes back inside,"

and as my mother still says today, I should never have gone to Alcântara, even if Yolanda did insist and plead and order me, "Come," even if she had no friends except for that pair of Spanish dolls, even if she was sick and always passing out in a cold sweat and getting rushed to the hospital, even if she was, as she seemed, the saddest person in the world, even sadder than my grandmother, who wore a coat at the height of summer, hunched before the fireplace with her glass of muscatel, I should have done like the other students, who keep their distance and avoid you, who go to a different snack bar so as not to risk drinking from your glass, and you,

"I wish the old man wouldn't come back inside, he spends the night wide awake whispering idiotic stories into my ears,"

and I thought, Like my uncle, whom people laughed at when they saw him on the street, wrapped in his curtain and warning everyone about the Flood, and when my mother complained "Take a bath, Artur, you smell like a badger," my uncle, fleeing from the faucets, answered, "Only in the Jordan River,

Ausenda, next week I'll catch a cab and go there," so I know for a fact that Hyacinth Park isn't the only place with lunatics, and my family never even lived in Africa, and my uncle, being near-sighted, never had to fight in the war, and my mother, "Pretend that the Jordan River is here, Artur, I bought some wonderful soap and will draw you a nice hot bath," and I, correcting my answer to twelve point seven,

"Do you know any story that's not idiotic, Yolanda?"

and my uncle,

"I'll only take a bath in the Jordan, Ausenda,"

since in my opinion stories are as silly as life is, as silly as studying math and English and geography, and once I've learned the right answers to all the problems, the tenses of all verbs and the capitals of all countries, I'll lie down like my grandmother did, I'll ask for a glass of muscatel in a feeble voice, and drop dead, and after the funeral my mother never wanted to go back to the village, so that I gradually forgot about the laundry tanks, the redbuds, and the finches,

"Stories are always silly,"

I told her, and then,

"Why don't you open the window and call him, so that he'll get up from the bench and come in, why leave him out there in the dark, propping his chin on his hand?"

and my mother,

"If this isn't Palestine, then what is it, Artur? Now take off that tunic, because you stink,"

and he was finally admitted into a clinic run by monks, where he recited the Gospel to his fellow patients, who recited it back to him, and the monks shooed them like chickens into a species of blockhouse where their sleeves continued to gesticulate salvation, and when we visited him there, my uncle, wearing slippers, exclaimed

"*Deo gratias,* brothers,"

and my mother, handing him a little bag of almonds,

"How do you feel, Artur?"

and I, to Yolanda,

"Call him,"

and my uncle and I walked past the infirmaries and sat down among some bushes near the fence, eating almonds as women in blue smocks and caps appeared at the gate of the cookie factory and cars passed by on the road leading to the church of Luz, next to the tiny square that has a school and a barracks and a poor people's market in July, and I to my uncle,

"Do you like being here, Uncle?"

and he, crunching almonds and looking straight ahead,

"Deo gratias,"

but he didn't look like a prophet, he looked like a beggar taken in by charity, or like one of the bums who ply the Avenida and sleep in cardboard boxes, with newspapers for blankets. And I thought, This isn't my uncle, because where's his Bible, where's his zeal for saving the planet, now he's calm, paying attention only to the factory workers and the cars on the road, eating almonds and mumbling *"Deo gratias,"* and I to Yolanda,

"Call him, because I feel sorry for him out there in the dark,"

and I don't know if I was asking her to call the man who sleeps with her, or if I was asking her to call my uncle, who, oblivious of me, repeated *"Deo gratias,"* or if I was asking her to call us, to call my mother, to call my father, to call her father, to call me, who would never have gone to Hyacinth Park if she hadn't insisted, "Come," Hyacinth Park, where for public transportation you have to trudge under the plane trees to Cais do Sodré because there's not even a taxi stand in the traffic circle, to call me, who should have gone to see detective films with my friends rather than risk catching the disease of her building's wilted dahlias and their smell of musk and corruption, and then gone along, after the film, to that joint full of women in Graça where everyone drinks beer and dances in a room plastered with mirrors, so that you see yourself in all the walls, from every angle and position, as if you were no longer one person but a brood of yourself holding on to a brood of women, who charge fifty cents per tango and twenty-five cents per waltz, and my father, sniffing me,

"Did you buy a gallon jug of perfume for whores, Alfredo?" and I,

"That's crazy, Dad, I hate perfume, it's probably a reagent from chem lab,"

and my mother, drying the dishes,

"My brother smells like a badger and my son like a prostitute, something's up,"

and then, after my friends lent me money for one last beer and another tango, I should have gone home to Santa Apolónia like dogs that return to their old haunts to sniff out their absence, home to occupy my uncle's now empty bed as a train definitively departs, and my mother,

"Your sheets reek of perfume, Alfredo, where have you been going?"

because I no longer sleep in the living room with the picture of the Virgin, who kept me from playing with myself in secret, I have a tiny room with a balcony overlooking Alfama, a tiny room like my parents', with a mattress, a night table, a chest of drawers stuffed with gospels, and a picture of my uncle with his buddies, before he became an apostle, before God chose him to warn people about the Apocalypse, and before the monks shaved his hair and beard and allowed him to sit with me near the fence, crunching almonds and praying

"Deo gratias,"

I have a bedroom, and my family doesn't want me to get close to you lest I also rot from the diabetes you brought from Mozambique, lest I marry you and your father shows up in our neighborhood with his sister and a pickax on his shoulder, blind-

ing people with the lamp on his forehead, and Yolanda, opening up the window,

"I'll call him, but it's you who's going to put up with his
stories, Alfredo,"

but he didn't seem to hear when she shouted "Come inside," since nothing, not even a shadow, moved in the backyard,
he didn't seem to hear when she shouted louder, "Come back
inside," and only a dog barked back, with no waving in the
walnut tree (whose branches I could distinguish) and no rustling in the cabbages, so that I thought, He died, and I stood up
from the desk and left her room, I walked past the TV to the
front door, then around the building, which was embalmed with
the breath of dahlias or eels from the river that the trains carried
back to the water where they'd originated, and I groped my way
toward the stone bench, trampling on vegetables as I went, the
window appeared as a mangled diamond of light, a second dog
howled in the distance of Alcântara, or Ajuda, or Santo Amaro,
and my knee bumped against a corner of the bench, I sat down
as I'd sat down with my uncle, crunching almonds before the
road to Luz's church and the women who worked at the cookie
factory, Yolanda's silhouette, with a pencil in hand, leaned out
at us from the windowsill to ask, "What are you doing?" and
the old man stirred, like a pigeon in its nest, and with his mouth
against my nape, as if he were talking to you, in a murmur just
like the dahlias' rustling, he said,

"Do you know whose footsteps I heard in the attic, my
love?"

3

It was on a Sunday after lunch, Ana, while my father was watering the dahlias and using his pickax for a cane on account of his
bad knee, that a taxi stopped in front of our building, and the
man who sleeps with me

(I warned him from the start that I wouldn't make love
with him, that I wouldn't kiss him or let him touch me, and
when he tried to take my arm I said "Not on your life")

stepped out of the backseat with a suitcase bound by straps,
a Tyrolean hat on the crown of his head, and an umbrella, even
though it was a clear day in August, and my aunt told me to
help him find a place for his things in my room

(and I, "Don't think you're going to see me naked, if I catch
you spying on me, I'll clobber you")

which meant pushing his luggage underneath the bed,
because there was no more room in the closet or on the hangers
that dangled from a rope stretched between two nails. I forbade
him from snooping in the drawers, from opening my books,
from reading my diary, from taking down the pictures of singers and movie stars that I cut out of magazines, I gave him the
pillow that's coming unstitched and causes asthma, the one
whose stuffing leaks onto the sheet, I told him to turn off the
light, I shut my eyes, and I heard him take off his shoes and
clothes in the darkness as softly as silkworms breaking the tissue of their cocoons. The bedsprings creaked, a sigh drowned
in the pillowcase, my father railed at the foremen of Johannesburg, and I heard the man who sleeps with me go on about a
house that no longer exists, a house where opera arias descended
from the attic like the drizzle in October. The neighbors downstairs (the retirees who hate each other, who stab each other with
scaling knives and screwdrivers) saw him on the porch, with his

hat in his hand, talking to my aunt and giving her the envelope with his paycheck, and they heard the soft coughing of my father in his chair, then noticed him waiting for the last train to take him across the kitchen, and he bumped into the sink, the chairs, and the cupboards before beaching on his mattress, as at an erroneous port.

At first he struck me as having the celestial temperament of a distracted cherub, incapable of lighting the burners on the stove, of peeling an orange, of squeezing toothpaste onto his toothbrush rather than off it, and I imagined that if he removed his coat and unbuttoned his shirt, a pair of winglets would start flapping on his shoulder blades, lifting him off the ground with difficulty, like a museum airplane, before he ascended through the blue afternoon into the clouds. An angel in Alcântara, trying out the breeze and jerking upward until he'd vanish over the river, where he would be awaited by a band of seraphim, all with Tyrolean hats and suitcases bound by straps, fluttering just like in church paintings, around the sufferings of martyrs. The downstairs neighbors, who were so intrigued by his birdish movements they forgot they hated each other, found him amid the cabbages on a Saturday during Pentecost, talking with invisible creatures in a lunar language, and my aunt sometimes spotted him hopping about at the traffic circle, near the bar and grill with snails and octopus salad, oblivious of the traffic and smashing against the facades like a partridge unable to fly, until he would come back home, apply iodine and Band-Aids to his wounds, and plop down on the bench in the backyard with the resignation of a failed angel, and Monday morning, armed with briefcase, umbrella, and Tyrolean hat, he would again take the bus to the National Tourist Office, as he took the train in that fateful July of last year, when my aunt decided we would go to Esposende to visit my grandparents. We rode for hours and hours across a landscape of pine trees and dunes, and not until the next morning, Ana, did we get off at a coastal town with weeping willows and rockroses on the seashore and the clouds grazing the waves, and we came to my grandfather's fabric shop, with the blinds still shut, at one end of the long square,

("Rockroses" repeated my aunt in the kitchen for some strange reason while over a plastic tub she disrobed the chicken for lunch, "rockroses rockroses rockroses rockroses")

the fabric shop, the bus station, the cafés still asleep, and I thought how if my father hadn't immigrated to Africa I would have been born in that gray, seagull-colored place called Esposende, I would have been born by another mother and wouldn't have diabetes, or flowers on my breath, or insulin injections, or the shame of my disease that ostracizes me from others, that prohibits me from milkshakes, strawberry candies, and chocolate milk, that prohibits me from apple pie, lollipops, and having children, no one had woken up in the town except the albatrosses that cried on the beach

(that perhaps cried in their sleep on the beach)

and my father knocked on the door with his miner's pickax, the man who sleeps with me approached with his briefcase, and a siren started howling

(shrill and hoarse, shrill and hoarse, shrill and hoarse)

from down by the water, a lock sprang open with a bang, my grandfather appeared on the threshold with a double-barreled shotgun that was bigger than a cannon, my father said "Hi, Dad," and my grandfather, over his shoulder, "Get me my glasses Isaltina, I think it's Domingos," the old geezer pointed his gun at us with precautionary wrath, and I said "Hi, Granddad," and he, "Who's with you, Domingos?" and the man who sleeps with me

(but who doesn't make love with me, but who never saw me naked, but who never touched me, Ana),

"How do you do, Mr. Oliveira? Let me introduce myself," and my grandfather, taking aim at him with his blunderbuss, "Who's that with the funny hat, Domingos?" and my aunt, "It's

Domingos's son-in-law," and my grandmother, "Come in," and
the sun got caught on the cock of the church's weather vane,
which groaned with effort each time it moved, and I looked
around at the shelves with flannels and wools and cottons and
velvets and satins, at a cash register that jingled its conversation
of coins in a corner, and at a room off the shop furnished with
a bed, a table, a kerosene stove, a sideboard, and bottles of wine,
my grandfather put on his glasses, sat down, and followed our
movements with his shotgun, as if we'd come to rob him, and
his dentures suddenly came loose, he coughed, his finger inad-
vertently pulled on the trigger, and the room rocked with the
blast, a windowpane disintegrated, the wooden blinds flew into
splinters, and as the smell of gunpowder abated, the shopkeeper
smiled, and said "Sorry," pulled a cartridge from his pocket,
inserted it into the gun, and my aunt, "Dad, if you don't put
down that shotgun, you'll kill us all," and he, "I have to be pre-
pared for burglars, how do I know you're really my children?"
and my grandmother, "I've been after you for years to get new
glasses, the only thing you can make out are wine bottles," and
my grandfather, "That's not true, just the day before yesterday
I shot down the kite that was circling above the chickens," and
my grandmother, "That wasn't a kite, it was one of those characters with turbans who've been hovering over the town, the
poor fellow bled to death in the backyard while you called the
pharmacist to come yank his guts out and have him stuffed,"
and the man who sleeps with me, "And did the pharmacist stuff
him?" and my aunt, "Rockroses," and my grandfather, "It had
to be a kite, because yes, it did get stuffed, it was given two glass
eyes and placed on a pedestal, poised to attack, in the Town Hall
lobby," and I imagined the medium falling into the tomato
patch, I imagined his fellow mediums looking for him, cawing
overhead, hitting their sleeves against the windows and seeing
him lying there, with open arms, like a stiff prey, and my grandfather, "They even asked us to send the bird to Lisbon, with some

crazy story about it being an endangered species, when there are dozens and dozens of them stealing our chickens, hand me that bottle, Orquidea," and I thought, If he discovers that the man who sleeps with me spends his evenings perched in the walnut tree, he's sure to pick him off, and my aunt, "Rockroses," and my grandmother, "What does your son-in-law do, Domingos?" and the sun broke loose from the weather vane, I heard the waves of the incoming tide hitting the crags and the flanks of the trawlers, I heard the seagulls

(on my mother's island there weren't any seagulls, Ana, there were monkeys sitting on the sand and my mother gazing at the horizon to count the boats with her finger),

I heard crabs hiccuping on the rocks and voices talking on the street, and I thought, So this is Esposende, and as my grandfather, with the shotgun lying on his lap, observed us with his myopic pupils, I felt homesick for Hyacinth Park, the trains and the seashell echo of the bridge, and the man who sleeps with me

(but who doesn't make love with me, but who never saw me naked, but who doesn't touch me because no man will ever touch me, they kiss us and the next day forget who we are, the next day we never existed),

"I work for the government, ma'am," and my grandfather, "Are you the one who wrote from Lisbon asking for the bird?" and in the afternoon we went to the Town Hall and saw the fellow with the turban staring at the waves with glass eyes, and my father, "I know him," and my aunt, "Rockroses," and my grandmother, "What?" and my grandfather, "Since when have you had kites for friends, Domingos?" and a fissure with cawing gulls opened up in the clouds, and my father, "He was a professor of hypnotism by mail, he used to come to Alcântara to drink beer and to ask questions about the man who sleeps with my daughter," and my grandfather, "These creatures are

a damn nuisance, you go in the yard to shoot one and find two
or three," and my father, "He lived in a rooming house on the
Praça da Alegria and was in love with a mulatto hooker," and
my aunt, "Rockroses," and I, thinking only about returning
to Lisbon, proposed, "Now that we've visited my grandparents, we can get the night train to Lisbon," but we didn't get
the night train, Ana, we stayed in Esposende, my aunt walked
toward the beach

(and I know where to, I know exactly where to, but I didn't
say anything, it was to the place where years ago they pitched a
traveling cinema, it was to the place where she met with the cinema owner),

my grandfather and my father, hoping for kites, took
the blunderbuss into the backyard, and the man who sleeps
with me

(but who has never seen me naked, Ana)

watched them while leaning against an acacia tree, as quiet
and innocuous as ever, as quiet as I am in my bedroom day after
long day, as quiet as I am in the flower smell of my diabetes,
leaning against the acacia and blowing his nose, looking at me
and sniffing the breezes, and I suddenly realized he would go
away, I realized he wouldn't remain with me in Hyacinth Park,
in our apartment pulverized by the roaring trains, I realized I'd
stop hearing him talk during the night about childhood events
in a house that no longer exists but where opera arias once descended from the attic like the drizzle in October, I wanted to
call out his name, to say "Wait," my aunt searched for her blood
in the dunes, the pine trees murmured in the wind, the man who
sleeps with me abandoned the acacia tree and ran a few steps,
flapping his sleeves up and down

("What happened to my uncle Jorge in Tavira, what happened to Uncle Fernando, to Aunt Anita and Aunt Teresa, to
the seamstress and the seamstress's son, and that other woman

whom they think I never saw but I did, that woman who turned the crank on the gramophone and who might be my mother?")

and tripped on an irrigation channel, and fell, and got up, and began running again

(and I said to him, "Don't go," because I'd gotten used to his silence, because I'd gotten used to him liking me and sitting on the bench under the walnut tree, because perhaps I liked him, Ana, even if I wouldn't let him fondle me)

and he rose a few inches, in his Tyrolean hat, above the onions and the clover, the celery and potatoes, and I said "Stay," and my aunt, walking among the weeping willows, "Rockroses," and I smelled fish, and the seagulls came and went from the square to the ocean and from the ocean to the square

(and I said, "Kiss me," and I invited him, "Touch me, I'm here, touch me")

and he rose higher, still higher, up to the top of the acacia tree, while I remembered the snack bar, his lemon teas to fight colds, and his smile, mostly I remembered his smile, "Don't leave me, tell me about Ericeira, tell me about Benfica, hold me and tell me about your life before you met me," and my father and grandfather in the tomato patch looking for kites, and my grandmother frying fish in the kitchen, and my aunt looking for herself in the dunes

(Rockroses)

and he rose beyond the tree, higher and higher, until I could hardly make out his features, until I could hardly make out his Tyrolean hat, until I could hardly make out his raincoat, and the siren quieted, then started back up, and he was a dot above the town, above Esposende, which I hate, I hate Esposende, "Come back," I pleaded, "Come back," I pleaded, "I don't mind that you all make fun of me," "Come back, talk to me, come back, I promise you won't sit on the stone bench anymore, surrounded by glistening cabbages, forgive me," and at that moment my grandfather pointed with his finger, "Look, Domingos, there's one taking flight," my father raised his shotgun, and in the wake of the blast the vegetables, the acacia, the chickens, the buildings on the square, and the seagulls all froze stock-still, and I ran into the house so as not to see him fall, bleeding, into the backyard.

4

And one Friday, Yolanda, about three months after the man who sleeps with you had disappeared in the fog of Esposende

(but you claim there's a stuffed angel with a Tyrolean hat and glass eyes in the lobby of the Esposende Town Hall, next to a kite with a turban),

I didn't go to Rua #8 in Hyacinth Park to study English or math or geography, because the monks let us take my uncle on an outing to Cruz Quebrada, to soothe his nerves with the bromide of the waves. We found him not among the bushes behind the blockhouse and near the fence, talking Latin and observing the women at the cookie factory and the cars heading toward the church by the square in Luz where there was a poor people's fair in July, but at the entrance to the clinic, clean shaven and wearing a suit and tie, and accompanied by a male nurse. My mother, wearing a floral-patterned dress with a coral broach on her chest, said

"You've gained weight, Artur"

in that voice used for policemen, sick people, and children, and my uncle, utterly normal, kissing her as in the old days, before he donned a tunic made of curtains and prophesied the Flood,

"I feel splendid, Ausenda,"

(and you, distracted from the math equations, "It kind of spooks me that they stuffed his belly with straw and varnished his face")

and while I was noticing how the monks had shined the prophet's shoes, greased down his disheveled apostle's hair, and covered his shins with pressed trousers, the nurse called aside my father and handed him a little box of pills,

"Two of these after lunch and two more in midafternoon, because to be God is stronger than any medicine, and your brother-in-law can't handle it,"

and monks with clacking sandals passed by in a hallway, leading patients by the sleeve as by a halter, and my mother, fondling her coral broach,

"Would you like to see the seals at the aquarium, Artur? You always liked seals,"

one of those cheap broaches set in chrome, depicting a woman's profile from a Greek vase, and I, Yolanda, thought of how I hate the aquarium, how I hate those rooms of thick-lipped fish, how I'd rather go see the sea at Caxias or at Algés, where the sewers vomit the city into the river, regurgitating entire alleys, houses, outdoor cafés, women at their windows, coal depots, bars, until there's nothing left of Lisbon but the cry of peacocks on barren hills. Propping my elbows on the wall, Yolanda,

(and you, "He'll never again talk about Benfica, he'll never again perch in the walnut tree at night")

I wait for our building at Santa Apolónia to slide downriver, I wait to hear the locomotives' whistles among the groupers, confusing the rowboats and frightening the seagulls, and the nurse to my father,

"If he takes less than four pills, he'll start preaching the Gospel,"

and my uncle, walking arm in arm with my mother down the steps,

"I'm not in the mood for seals, Ausenda, I feel like a steak with a fried egg at a restaurant in Cruz Quebrada,"

and I, correcting a verb for you,

"There's no lack of older men in the world, now let's study"

and my father, clutching the box with the medicine,

"Two at lunchtime and two in midafternoon, don't worry, I'll make sure he takes them,"

with returned emigrants swimming in the sand of the river-
bed, mixed up with the turbots, and my uncle to me, patting
me on the shoulder,

"Getting good grades at school, Alfredo?"

and we walked across the courtyard toward the gate, passing by laurels, mulberries, and a plane tree supported by the iron
grating, and my mother to my uncle, with a cheeriness for en-
couraging cancer victims,

"We'll catch the streetcar at Cais do Sodré, so that you can
enjoy the scenery on the way,"

and the nurse to my father,

"All I ask is no complications, no having to traipse out to
Timbuktu with a straitjacket for the poor lunatic,"

and my uncle to my mother, while blessing the laurels so
discreetly that only I noticed,

"Sounds great, Ausenda, it's been a long time since I've seen
the derricks on the river,"

and so we got on the bus to downtown Lisbon as the gold-
finches mistakenly alighted on the patients' shoulders and the
nurse waved from the sidewalk, insisting on the tablets,

"Don't forget, or your brother-in-law will go back on the
blink,"

and you,

"I can't memorize anything, Alfredo, I feel sorry for him,
reduced to a stuffed creature in Esposende on a plywood column with an inscription in Latin,"

and I,

"Forget the old man, Yolanda, what's the capital of Norway?"

and she, glancing at the cabbages in the backyard,

"Paris,"

and we rode past Santos, past Alcântara, past Belém, and
my uncle to my mother, pointing to the blue sky with his chin,

"Too bad about the rain,"

and my mother,

"What rain, Artur?"

and my father, butting in,

"The rain, yes, of course, you never notice the rain, Ausenda,"

and I to Yolanda,

"Paris?"

and you eyeing the cabbages, your words embalmed in sugary petals,

"Paris or Budapest, who cares, but tell me: How would you feel if the pharmacist of Esposende stuffed you?"

and we passed Algés and Pedrouços and the aquarium with seals where our science teacher took us during second semester to see a sperm whale fetus in a glass coffin, and it disappointed me that there were no mermaids, as it disappoints me when night falls in Santa Apolónia and my mother switches on the living room light, causing the furniture, the curtains, and my life to become sad, everything seems as incurable as leukemia, and I suddenly feel like crying, I lock myself in my bedroom without saying anything, Yolanda, and my father,

"What's wrong, Alfredo?"

and I,

"I have a stomachache, Dad,"

because I can't explain that it's the night that makes me ache, and my uncle to my father, sardonically,

"Do you really think it's raining, Teodoro?"

and it's even worse in winter, with all the clouds, the wet asphalt, and I shivering under the sheets, and the hopeless faces underneath the streetlights, I think growing up would be easier if there weren't any night, and my father,

"You're the one who talked about rain, Artur,"

and Cruz Quebrada was a hillock from the stadium to the sewers that extended into the river's slime and seaweed, and I refuse to be like them, Yolanda, but I will be like them, one day I'll look at my face in the mirror and live off the past as off a retirement pension, feeling sorry for myself, and my uncle asked my mother's opinion,

"Did I talk about rain, Ausenda?"

and you, chewing the tip of your pencil while glancing at the cabbages,

"Do you know Benfica, Alfredo?"

and my mother, glaring at my father,

"Of course not, Artur, you know how spacey Teodoro can be,"

and I don't know Benfica, but I'll bet it's just like Santa Apolónia or Hyacinth Park, because there are trains and locomotives all over this country, I'll bet it's like Algés or Pedrouços or Cruz Quebrada, with the same streets, the same stone walls, and the same sun over the same gloomy interiors, even if Benfica has more photos of army officers and more clocks and footsteps in the attic, and my father, regretting that we'd taken my uncle out of the monks' clinic for the afternoon,

"Spacey, am I? I had no idea. I'm glad you know more about me than I do,"

and as I noticed his torn shirt collar, I wondered why it is we never had a car and why we never had any money, I wondered how your family will pay the rent and the electric bill without the man who sleeps with you, I imagined your father, with helmet and pickax, digging into the floor in search of gold, a thousand feet below ground, to pay off the gas bill and the refrigerator installments, and we got off at the last stop, and before climbing down the steps of the train car, my uncle stuck out his hand and announced,

"You're right after all, Teodoro, it's raining,"

and it was a hot day, not a cloud in the sky, the beach at Cruz Quebrada full of people and sailboats, and my father desperately opened his hands to my mother, who answered in silence, What do you want me to do? and my father, with more hand motions, Call the nurse and tell him to rush out here, but my mother gestured no, and my uncle, hands in his pockets and nose in the air, sniffing,

"What a downpour, brethren, this is undoubtedly the Flood,"

and my father pulled out the box of pills, worried about the people who were beginning to look at us,

"How about a couple of these yummy vitamins, Artur?"

and my uncle, shaking off the proposal with a disdainful gesture,

"What we need to do is quickly build an ark and put two of every kind of animal in the hold,"

and I,

"Why don't we have the steak first?"

and my mother, hopefully taking up my suggestion,

"After a juicy steak you'll build the ark in no time, Artur,"

while Lisbon puked itself into the Tagus, with birds planing over the debris, the rubble, the table scraps and dead animal guts, perhaps the birds will swallow the locomotives' whistles and the sadness of our living room's curtains and flounced lamp shade, perhaps they'll swallow Santa Apolónia, the dahlias of Hyacinth Park, Benfica, the halos of the streetlights, and my urge to cry, perhaps they'll swallow our voices and our memory, and my parents coaxed my uncle into a workers' diner overlooking the beach, with a radio at full blast, and you, breathing out corollas, sought the man who sleeps with you on the empty bench under the walnut tree, and the bay of Cascais was visible in the distance, and my uncle, pushing away the menu, declared to the aproned waiter,

"All I eat are locusts and wild honey,"

and my father, almost kneeling on the floor,

"Do it for me, Artur, take your medicine,"

and a woman's voice rattled out news on the radio while a

mutt slept in the kitchen, its back curled like a cutlass, and my mother to my father, getting up from the table,

"Do you have the clinic's phone number, Teodoro?"

and I imagined monks stepping out of a screaming ambulance to snap up my uncle and take him back to the clinic near the church of Luz and the poor people's fair in July, and the waiter,

"Excuse me?"

and my uncle,

"Locusts and wild honey, like my disciple John the Baptist, who cleansed you in the Jordan River,"

and my father,

"He's joking, sir, don't pay any attention, bring us four steaks medium rare and topped with a fried egg,"

the Timorese immigrants from the shanties of Vale do Jamor, homesick for the monsoons, had come to the embankment to gaze at the Tagus, and their ragged sweaters reminded me of my grandmother from Trás-os-Montes lying in her coffin, dressed in her wedding gown, which had been stored in lavender since her marriage sixty years previous, when the night and the trains and Santa Apolónia still didn't exist, and it was December, it was snowing in her village, and our feet left long black prints on the floor, we ate cookies and drank small glasses of muscatel, the shepherd's dogs howled her death, my uncle walked around the bed anointing the deceased with an olive branch soaked in brandy, and the cold and darkness came not from winter but from the mouth of my dead grandmother, with a solitary tooth sticking out from her lips like an asparagus, even as the Timorese immigrants came not from the shanties of Jamor but from the sewers' sludge, and as your odor, Yolanda, came not from you but from the dahlias of Hyacinth Park, the dahlias of Rua #2, Rua #4, Rua #6, Rua #8, impregnating all of Hyacinth Park with their musky perfume, and my uncle, eyeing his steak and egg,

"I don't see locusts on this plate,"
and the waiter,
"Excuse me?"
and my mother, fondling her coral broach,
"Do you by chance have a phone directory?"
and my father,
"Take the pills, Artur,"
and you, closing the textbook,
"I miss seeing him under the walnut tree,"
and it was as if the cabbages, the stone bench, the shadows, and the sun on the stone wall had disappeared from the backyard, leaving nothing but your nostalgia for him, a seagull perching on the embankment stared at us with its scarlet eyes

(One day, I thought as I soaked some bread in the egg, I'll go away to a place without any night, a place without trains where the streetlights won't scare me)

and even in Cruz Quebrada the locomotives hissed like sea parrots, and the immigrants from Timor stood there, waiting for their island to approach like a ship, and my uncle to the workers at the other tables,

"Who will help me build the ark?"

as the seagull stared at him, and stared at us, and the owner of the diner turned off the radio and asked from behind the counter,

"Is something wrong with the meat, pal?"

and my mother hunted in the phone directory for the number of the clinic, and my father,

"Sit down, Artur, sit down and at least try your steak,"

and now there were five seagulls lined up on the embankment, three females and two males, and the village priest, covered with snow, opened the door and announced,

"The Lord's peace be with you,"

but there is no peace, Yolanda, there's this constant worry, this anxiety, how does anybody get through life? and my uncle, to the owner of the diner,

"As far as I'm concerned you can stick the meat up your rear end,"

and I counted twelve seagulls besides the ones that flew over the rowboats, twelve seagulls staring at us, and the workers at the surrounding tables also stared at us, and the Timorese from Jamor, and the train cars, and the waves, and my grandmother in her coffin, dressed as a bride and laughing at the priest with her solitary tooth, my mother couldn't find the number in the phone directory, and the proprietor walked out from behind the counter with a carving knife in his hand,

"Do you care to repeat that?"

and my uncle, unflappable,

"As far as I'm concerned you can stick the meat up your rear end,"

and the waiter grabbed him from behind while my father, trying to separate them, explained,

"He's sick, gentlemen, he doesn't have all his marbles, he's been in a nuthouse for over a year,"

and your father to you, looking at the street from the railroad platform,

"Where the hell is the man who sleeps with you? Esposende isn't big enough to get lost in,"

and your aunt,

"He told us to wait while he went to drink a lemon tea at that café over there,"

and your father,

"If he misses the train, he'll have to wait until tomorrow for the freight train,"

and the lifeboat droned and hushed, droned and hushed, and your father,

"Of all the damn fool times to have to drink a lemon tea,"

but the man who sleeps with you didn't show up in Hyacinth Park, he never again crossed the traffic circle with his briefcase, never again climbed the slope with his moribund gait, and while pulling the insulin syringe from your purse you asked your father,

"Are you sure Granddad didn't pick him off with his shotgun, are you sure Granddad didn't shoot him down in the tomato patch of Esposende like he did to the man with the turban, now stuffed and on display in the Town Hall?"

and your father,

"What turban, honey?"

and you,

"The professor of hypnotism by mail who could fly, the one who worked for the state police before the Revolution and who came to Alcântara to ask questions about us,"

and your father,

"Your mind's not working right, dear, since when do people fly?"

and your aunt,

"Turbans?"

and the owner of the diner to my mother,

"Illness is no excuse, ma'am, my liver's shot to hell, but that doesn't mean I insult people,"

and you, in a voice the color of the dahlias out front,

"The turbans that pass by here on their way to Morocco,"

and my uncle, whom the waiter was strangling,

"Let go of me, Beelzebub,"

and the male nurse, tying him with the straps of the straitjacket,

"Didn't I tell you to give him the medicine, for Christ's sake, didn't I warn you he'd go berserk without the pills?"

such that on the following Saturday, when we visited him at the clinic, I again found him beyond the blockhouse, sitting among the bushes near the fence, observing the women who worked at the cookie factory and the road to the church of Luz, and I asked,

"How are you feeling, Uncle?"

and he,

"Deo gratias,"

and I felt relieved, thinking, Since he hasn't gotten better, he won't be released and I can keep his bedroom and play with myself without being censured by the saint on the living room wall as I think about the women who cost fifty cents per tango and thirty cents per waltz plus the ginger ales and beers, a bedroom with a balcony looking out onto Alfama's pigeons and staircases and garrets and downspouts, a balcony without trains or a river flowing by, and it occurred to me that having a room to myself might help me get through the night, and I thought, Perhaps if I open the doors to the balcony, the smell of dahlias will reach me from Hyacinth Park, where I know you must be glancing at the bench under the walnuts that chatter like teeth, in hopes that the man who sleeps with you will be perched on a branch, waiting for you to fall asleep so that he can come into your room and talk to you about Benfica, opera arias, and echoes in an attic, but I can assure you that he won't come, because on that same afternoon, after we left the clinic

(and my mother,

"See you next Saturday, Artur,"

and my father,

"See you next Saturday,"

and my uncle,

"Deo gratias")

we stopped in a snack bar in Luz, next to the high school, so that my mother could get an espresso to perk up her blood pressure,

(and the doctor to my parents,

"We'll have to monitor him closely for a month or two, because the river air worsened his condition,"

and my mother, fondling the coral broach that was set in chrome and depicted a profile from a Greek vase,

"He started preaching the Flood in a restaurant, doctor, you can't imagine the scare he gave us")

it was five or six o'clock, and the tables were packed with students our age or close to it, all of whom were talking, smoking, looking at magazines, and sucking on vanilla milkshakes, except for a girl near us, who was taking notes in a spiral notebook, next to which lay a history book, a muffin, and a mineral water,

(and the doctor,

"I think it's better if he doesn't leave the premises, ma'am, just think what might have happened if the nurse hadn't arrived in time,"

and my father,

"You're absolutely right, doctor, I very nearly got punched," while I thought,

Oh goody, I won't have to sleep in the living room anymore)

and I can assure you it's a waste of time to pretend you're asleep, waiting for him, because when the waiter brought my mother her espresso, a coffee with milk for my father, and a pineapple juice for me, I saw the girl who was taking notes in a spiral notebook look up at a man with a Tyrolean hat who had a briefcase in one hand and a tea in the other and who leaned toward her and asked, with an embarrassed smile,

(and the doctor to my father,

"There you go")

"May I introduce myself? Don't get the wrong idea. I just want to talk with you."

BOOK FIVE

The Hallucinatory

Representation

of Desire

I

All of this happened a long time ago, because everything happened a long time ago, including what just now happened, which was that I turned the crank on the gramophone to listen to an aria of *La Bohème* and sat down in the rocking chair before the hill of Monsanto and the greenness of its trees, tinged blue by the refraction of the distance, as when my father fought there in 1919, during the monarchist revolution. My sister Maria Teresa and my sister Anita say they remember that year because the telephone rang incessantly, and they went to the penitentiary to visit my father, and they told me that our mother, pregnant with me, looked pale and was forever throwing up, but my oldest memories go back here, to the Calçada do Tojal, and not to Queluz, where my brothers and sisters were born in a ground-floor apartment near a park with beech trees, wooden benches, and grass littered with paper and cigarette butts. Perhaps I would have liked to live in that house, which they describe to me as somber and eerie, though any house is somber and eerie when we're children and haven't lived there long enough to realize that the somberness and eerieness are in us and not in things, and after we realize this we gradually become disenchanted with the dull and static ordinariness of objects. My memories begin in Benfica, and when I heard my sisters talk about places I'd never known, it was like entering a movie theater in the middle of the film: I had to ask what happened before I got there in order to understand the plot and the characters, who seemed to act for everyone but me, as if they were offended because I'd walked in late. My memories begin in Benfica, not here in the attic but down below, in the yard next to the kitchen, on the side of the house that didn't face the palm tree of the post office, and I'm crouched on a step in my pinafore, watching the chickens that pecked in what must have been a vegetable garden, because there were roots peeking out of the grass, and my brother Jorge points at the chickens and orders me, "Kill them," and I grab a brick and run after the animals, and my brother Fernando, who was playing near me, starts bawling at the maid, my brother Jorge shakes him by the arm, and from the window over the laundry tank our mother asks, "What are you doing, Julieta?" She has brown hair and looks at me without smiling, and I stop not because she's angry but because I sense fear behind her anger, and nothing troubled me more than the grown-ups' fear, which made me naked and vulnerable. In this I think I'm different from my sisters, as I'm likewise different for never having felt any house to be somber and eerie, which goes to prove that I didn't have a childhood like theirs, in part because my father never talked to me, as if he didn't like me or I made him feel uneasy, and once, on a Sunday morning, when he was already sick and bedridden, I entered his room and walked up to his frail body in which his pupils glowed like a stove's embers, and he glanced at me in that noisy silence of someone who's about to speak but then turned his chin to the wall without opening his mouth, and for the first time I felt like an orphan, so that on the day he died, since I was already fatherless, instead of feeling sad I went up to the attic, opened the window that looked out onto Monsanto Park, and observed the trees in the distance, different from the trees in the nearby woods that echoed with the shrieks of peacocks. I heard the visitors on the second floor, talking as if they were in church, I heard footsteps here, footsteps there, my brother Jorge letting people in and showing them to the door, but I didn't hear the chiming of the pendulums or the cheeping of the cuckoos, because my sisters, besides covering all the photos with strips of crepe paper, had immobilized the clocks to heighten the silence and solemnity of my father's absence, and everything seemed vacuous like after a fire. Then the doorbell started to ring every minute, more people arrived, and the watch began, chairs were dragged to the bedroom and placed around the corpse, the men went into the yard to smoke cigarettes, the maid tiptoed around with platters and bottles, Monsanto faded to nothing but the electric poles that surrounded the prison, an owl or a bat passed by the buildings under construction across the street, and I shut the window, placed a waltz on the turntable, and turned the volume up as high as it could go, until the walls shook and the whole house hummed with the music, and my brother Jorge, in his lieutenant's uniform, rushed into the attic with his hands over his ears and switched off the gramophone. I went back to the window, and the figures smoking cigarettes in the backyard looked at me with surprise.

But this, like everything else, also happened a long time ago, or everything happened at the same time, in I don't know what year or month or minute of my life, before and after which everything has the same, identical texture that excludes me, like all that occurred before my birth and that will continue to occur when I go away, on a winter day, like the day my father was buried, and after the funeral they called me down to the dining room instead of bringing my lunch to the attic, my sister Maria Teresa took the crepe paper off the photographs, my brother Fernando reset the clocks, dozens of cuckoos burst out of their little doors, and I thought, Next it will be my mother's turn, and then my brothers' and sisters', and then my turn, and when my turn comes I'll be the only one living here, there'll be no one to gather chairs around my corpse, no one who goes in the yard to smoke, and since no one will know I exist, they'll level the house with bulldozers, and a final, lingering cuckoo will sing from out of the rubble. After dessert I went to the yard by the kitchen to throw bricks at the chickens, but I remembered that we no longer had any chickens, my brother Fernando asked, "Where were you, Julieta?" and I ran up the stairs to the attic, shut the blinds, and sat there for the longest time, listening to the rain and thinking about nothing.

When I was a child I liked the month of February. I liked the sweet melancholy of its flus and fevers. My mother would have one of the maids come up here to sleep with me, and her breathing kept me awake, as if I had to defend myself from her slumber. Early in the morning she would get dressed and vanish, but the warmth in the mattress kept me from relaxing, my fever increased, the noises in the house (the faucets, the milk on the stove, the pantry cupboards' hinges) sounded like loud booms, and I feared she would return, the next night, to attack me with her bovine breaths. It's all so vivid yet all from so long ago, including what just happened (turning the crank on the gramophone to hear an aria from *La Bohème*), and I still like February and its flus, and there's no longer any maid to sleep with me, because at a certain point my mother, or father, or siblings, or the entire family, decided to keep my existence a secret from others, for reasons I never understood and perhaps didn't want to understand, for I never asked why. They pushed the things in the attic to one side, brought my bed up here, and only on Sundays did they call me to eat with them in the dining room below, in an atmosphere so tense I felt like screaming or running outside, convinced that their hatred had to do with me. No matter what time the conflicting clock dials said it was, it seemed to me that we lived all of the day's moments simultaneously, or that all of the day's moments were one moment, my brother Jorge ordered "Kill," and I got up, went to the yard by the kitchen to get a brick, and hurled it into the middle of the table, between the cruet stand and the platter with boiled onions and beans surrounding the fish, whose black eye reflected in miniature the six arms of the ceiling lamp. The next moment I found myself up here in the attic, rocking in the rocking chair, and the floor's creaking was like a bone being driven into the silence of the house. I think that even my footsteps and the gramophone's arias are a form of silence, and that noise begins when people stop talking and we hear thoughts stirring in them like the pieces of a broken motor trying to fix itself. A brick fragment hit the china cabinet, causing the crystal to shatter in a roaring cascade of clinks. My father came upstairs, whipped me with his belt, and went away, but I didn't care, because he was already dead. One or a few years later, when our mother started to complain of a blade that sliced through her temples, the parakeets quit flying, they languished with bristling feathers on their unmoving perches, and dropped dead onto the cement with soft thuds. After the last dead bird was extracted from a dish of birdseed, my sister Anita took down the perches, removed the boxes for laying eggs, and washed the cage with a disinfectant that tickled my nose. The cage remained empty until the arrival of the fox, which began prancing in a circle on the very first day, whining like a teething baby as it searched for a hole in the wire grating. Even during the night I'm woken up by its howls that assail the bougainvillea, posing questions that no one answers, just as no one answered my screams when Jorge was taken to Tavira, next to the sea. My sister Maria Teresa only said that Tavira was a city without storks, with seagulls on the bridge's arches and the boats' keels, and with old men in the outdoor cafés, drinking up the sun in their glasses of anise liqueur. I don't remember if our mother died then or a little while earlier, since everything happened a long time ago and the episodes have gotten all jumbled, but I remember that a nurse gave her oxygen every afternoon as she slowly wasted away, and Fernando locked himself in his room or else spent his evenings at the pastry shop opposite the church, smiling at the veterinarian's wife, who drank tea with her girlfriends. On the day of the funeral, shortly before the burial, I was looking out the window and saw a red-haired man arrive with some flowers, place the flowers on the doormat, and then leave without even ringing the doorbell, and I thought he must have left a message or else had the wrong address. That night I dreamed that my mother was walking hand in hand with a red-haired man through the garden, and once again my father died, like on the day he turned his face away from me and I felt as if I'd been orphaned, as I also felt when they took my child from me in Guarda, and how I fretted as the whining creature came out in jerks from between my buttocks. I remember lying in bed, I remember the pine trees that waved beyond my grandmother's house and the wooden fence whose boards were coming loose, and I remember the birds chirping in the foam of the rocks. Since there was no attic where they could hide me and no rocking chair for me to sit in, I meandered from room to room, looking out at the pine trees and the street that ended in an abandoned warehouse, which spewed darkness out into the rain. My grandmother stitched shoes next to the embers in the brazier, and I stopped hearing the trees when a picture of a bald man with a mustache looked at me with a strange severity. Then the contractions became continuous, the birds vanished, and I lost interest in myself.

When our mother died and my brother Fernando moved out, only my two sisters and I remained at the Calçada do Tojal, with its view of Monsanto Park, and we saw the farms all around us turn into apartment buildings as trucks hauled away the ivy to the city dump. With us lived the fox, and a boy I never saw except from behind, when he went down the gravel path on his way to school. He was as quiet as the seamstress's son, who used to play with me in the yard next to the kitchen, and I hated his timid gestures and the way he meekly put up with my whims, so one day I grabbed the brick I threw at the chickens to bash him in the head, but the fact he didn't flee and didn't even budge caused my raised arms to freeze above his head and to remain there, as in a photograph, while I glanced at the storks in the palm tree at the post office, with their wings spread wide over its green blades. The boy went away a long time ago, because everything in my life happened a long time ago, like other people's childhoods and like what just happened to me, even if the past doesn't seem somber or strange to me like the houses my sisters told me about but where I never lived or like the house where I've lived alone since they died, this house, where the clocks downstairs tell different times, like differently positioned corpses of a train wreck, where the cuckoos hang out of their wooden doors, where dust has overrun the photos, where spiderwebs join the volutes of the ceiling lamp in the dining room to the silverware that's waiting for the deceased, and where the windowpanes fall out like sheets of silk, making the fox's whines seem as close to me as if my own throat had uttered them. I get up from my rocking chair, lean against the windowsill, and the storks of Monsanto Park flying over the prison are the same ones that flew over the lunette of the barracks in 1919, ripping with their beaks the soldiers' uniforms. I seemed to hear distant shots, horses' hoofs, the wheels of artillery rolling over the bumpy hill, neighs, shouts, voices, and when all had quieted and the house had plunged back into its habitual silence, I started to hear steps on the stairs, hesitant like those of a child who didn't dare utter my name. At first I felt confused, which has always been my way of feeling scared, but then I thought, It can't be, it's an illusion, it's impossible, those who know me have all disappeared, and yet the child went from room to room, almost without a sound, calling me softly, like the March grass, in a secret register. Night was falling, the dusk swallowed the sparrows in the cypress trees, one of the steps up to the attic creaked, but I didn't put a record on the gramophone turntable, nor did I turn on the light: I preferred not to see my hands side by side on my lap like crab claws at rest, I preferred to forget my own countenance, to become a surprise to myself, like one who looks intently in the mirror for the first time as an adult. Sitting in the rocking chair, with the light from Monsanto illuminating the poplars, I waited for the child (whom I knew was getting closer by the stairs' creaking) to come and tap me on the shoulder. Sooner or later it would happen, and then I could abandon this house, like the others had done before me. And if from the front gate at the end of the gravel path I turned around and look up at the attic window, I would find on the white windowsill (made even whiter by the night's reflections) a child's hand waving at me like someone on a wharf who, without friendship or regret, waves farewell to a companion whom they will never again see.

2

For some months I hadn't felt well, but it never occurred to me that I might have cancer. It began with a kind of sadness, a lassitude, a vague anxiety that kept me from sleeping, and I'd toss in bed until the dawn grayly lit the blinds, shapes emerged from the shadows, and the glass plates covering the photos and the clock on the night table became hard like disdainful stares. During the day I'd sit in the TV room, and events so remote I thought they'd been forever forgotten would suddenly come back to me: a stray bullet that hit my sister's wardrobe when I was two or three years old and we lived on Rua Ernesto da Silva, the smell of the fish cannery in Algiers, the month of August building little walls of sand against the sea at São Martinho do Porto, adult arms that carried me upstairs to bed, and also the summer when I met my husband, early evening dances in Estoril, bicycle rides, picnics, card games, lazy afternoons in Mortágua, Mardi Gras. And the wind in the farm's beech trees disheveling my hair.

Even when I woke up in the hospital I didn't think it was cancer. My head hurt, teacups rattled in the corridor, unfamiliar faces leaned over me like solicitous corollas, a finger moved up my forearm as if it were following the Mondego River's meanders on a map, a needle plunged into my skin, and I saw my blood in the syringe, dark like the blood of the animals that the cook decapitated for our family lunches. I thought, I'm a dead rabbit, and my guts falling into the tin pan made me scream in aversion and horror. Gray hairs shone on a step between the cook's slippers, spring maples danced above the stone wall, it was day and night among the ceramic tiles, the fräulein who took care of us said to the other doctors, "We're going to do an EEG," leaves rustled over my head, and I found myself screaming with dread in the arbor by the pond, where the water's reflections glided across the chipped cement. My father called for me in the backyard, I heard his breathing and his footsteps without being able to answer, but since the EEG was normal, they sent me home to rest up for a week, saying I should seek out a neurologist if the walls continued to spin around me and my nausea didn't disappear.

Since I didn't have any children for the first ten years of my marriage, I became rather attached to my nephews. They ate dinner with us on Thursdays, went up to the attic to listen to records on the old horn gramophone, and helped me water the shrubs. When it was hot I showered them with the hose and they wriggled and laughed, clapping their hands, covered with drops that glistened in the sun, as on a small flock surprised by the dew, or I'd open up the piano and play for them so that they could watch the hammers hit the strings, while sheep bells jingled on the way up the Calçada do Tojal to the abandoned cemetery. At seven o'clock my husband wound up the clocks that hung on the wall next to two engravings, whose captions, which were in Spanish, read "William Tell Sends Out His Boat" (a man pushing on a galliot with his foot) and "William Tell Threatens the Governor" (the same man shaking his fist at an older man with a bright red cap), and during dessert the doorbell would ring and a neighbor called Fernando, who worked at Vacuum Oil Company and lived with his unmarried sisters in the house next door, would ask my husband if he could give him a lift downtown when he went in for his night shift at the phone company. After the Revolution we sold the house at the Calçada do Tojal and moved into a seventh-floor condo in the newer part of Benfica, near the new market, one of the engravings of William Tell broke, my nephews stopped getting showered by a hose and grew up, and one of them went away to London and came back from London, he became a surgeon, so that the second time I passed out from a seizure and my father's voice sought me in the arbor out back, it was my nephew who X-rayed my skull, repeated the X-ray, and diagnosed a stroke, and as he talked, fiddling with a chrome tool that had a rubber tip, it dawned on me how the years had flown by us. Returning to Benfica by taxi, through a forever changing city that was now strange to me, I realized I was the same age as my husband and father had been when they passed away, and when I looked in the rearview mirror for the cabdriver's face, seeking his help, I found a pair of astonished doll-like eyes, with fluttering nylon eyelashes. There was no more backyard, the house of the Calçada do Tojal had disappeared, a bank had taken the place of the palm tree by the post office, my parents' garden had been transformed into facades, as I paid the driver I wondered if my coffin would fit in the elevator or have to be lugged down the stairs, and while I inserted the key in the door my legs gave way, I fell to my knees, crawled across the rug to the telephone that kept ringing, lifted my arm to the receiver, knocked the phone to the floor, a whisper asked if this was the butcher's, skinned animals hung from hooks, blood-spattered men in aprons hacked chunks of meat, my Cape Verdean maid came out of the kitchen with the iron in her hand, the meat piled up on the scale, I tried to say "Call the doctor" and uttered "William Tell Threatens the Governor," a wind rustled the birch trees inside my chest, my dead husband came out of the bathroom with shaving cream on one of his cheeks and a razor in his hand, I started to cry because I was positive he would cut my carotids, the maid dialed a number above my sobs, the meat on the scale dripped down my shoulders, from the unit below I heard banging that turned out to be an artery throbbing in my neck, my nephew said I'd probably had a sudden drop in my blood pressure but that I should do the exams all over, and since it was July I sprayed him and his brothers with the garden hose, and they jumped and giggled, I was admitted into the hospital for analyses, and that night I was woken up by a woman's shouts, I turned on the light, asked the nurse to bring me a mirror, and noticed that my nostrils had tapered like those of corpses in caskets.

When I was released from the hospital, where from my window I could see the river, my daughter drove me home, and I tried to brush my teeth but ended up brushing my lips, my tongue, my gums, and my chin, the bristles hurt me, and I lay down on the bed, exhausted, discovering cracks in the ceiling below what must have been the toilet on the eighth floor, inhabited by a TAP pilot who had a bunch of stepdaughters and poodles and whom I sometimes saw on the elevator, impatiently smoking a cigarette. It had also become difficult for me to eat, because the rice fell off my fork, and one of my sisters, who was born in Algiers when my father worked at the cannery and I was learning to read French, sat next to me, tucked the napkin under my chin, removed the bones from my fish, pushing them to the edge of the plate, and made a little game of forking the lunch into my mouth, though I could see the panic behind her smile. In the photo next to the bed my mother, who had died twelve years earlier, also looked worried, and as soon as my nephew came by (I was sitting in front of the disconnected TV, remembering North Africa) I asked him to explain what disease I had (Arabs were arguing in the street, my littlest sister wasn't yet born, my father, still with black hair, read the paper in his easy chair, and my childhood unrolled before me as if it were occurring at that very instant). My nephew, his back to me, was looking out the window at the new Benfica market, and I remembered the summer when he fell down on the sidewalk of the Calçada do Tojal and broke his arm, I remembered the doctor at the hospital who put the arm in a cast, I remembered us skipping in the darkness down the gravel path as the parakeets of our neighbors (two spinsters, the Vacuum Oil employee, and an army officer imprisoned in Tavira for some sort of infraction) sang to the moon in their huge cage. The palm tree at the post office shook, and my nephew answered in a single breath:

"It's a brain tumor that can't be operated, next week we'll start cobalt treatments," and I patted his wrist, sorry to see him so grieved.

I'm a quiet woman who has never appreciated gushiness or tears. I've never been a talker, since most words seem useless to me, and I think that others see my life as one of calm sobriety, with no room for sadness or despair. No one saw me shed tears when my parents and my husband died, and rarely has anyone heard me burst out laughing in the seventy years I have endured. I'm a quiet woman who inhabits silence, hearing it inside sounds, inside phrases and music, the silence of the waves in Ericeira, the silence of the crickets in the Algarve, the silence of arguments when voices are raised and the walls howl, echoing people's petty hatred. My nephew abandoned the window, straightened a picture on the wall, rearranged the bibelots on the shelf, repeated "It's a brain tumor, Aunt Antonia, that can't be operated," a glimmer of sweat appeared on his forehead, I asked "How much time?" as if I were talking about a stranger, and he, lying badly, said, "With luck the cobalt will take care of the problem, let's think of this as a bad dream that will go away," I heard a stork pecking in the woods and thought that I didn't want to die in this condominium, that I'd rather die in my parents' house, where Senhor José cleaned the algae from the water tank, that I'd rather die on the Calçada do Tojal, in plain view of Monsanto Park, so I pretended to believe what my nephew said, remembering when he was sick in bed with the flu, and I tucked in the sheets and read him stories until he fell asleep. After my nephew left, the phone rang but stopped ringing before I could answer, for I moved with great difficulty, as if my joints had been rusted together, and as I walked past one of the wall clocks whose long pendulum no longer swung, I wondered why my husband hadn't wound it up, and I suddenly realized that I lived alone in this condo above the market and that by the natural order of things someone (my daughter, a relative, a stranger, the TAP pilot) would occupy it as soon as I vacated. Since I didn't feel like reading or watching TV, I took one of my late husband's sleeping pills, lay down, and instantly returned to when I was twenty years old, playing tennis with my cousins in Sintra, on a tennis court surrounded by cactuses and fir trees and crowned by a September morning. The ocean was visible in the distance, one of the balls sailed over the fence and into the fir trees, a friend of my cousins went to look for it, and I got married a few weeks later without feeling happy or unhappy, just strange, my fiancé caressed my hand, and I wished I were in Algiers, sitting in my father's lap.

Since I couldn't go out, my girlfriends visited me after lunch, sitting on the sofas and bringing chairs from the hallway or the dining room, and they talked in a livelier voice than usual, suddenly optimistic and cheery and full of plans for the future that included me, and I imagined them taking a deep breath before ringing my doorbell, like actors about to go on stage to perform a comedy of happiness and hope that none of us had, they being worried about their own suffering, their own lives, wondering (for they were close to me in age) what form death would choose to haul them away, imploring "Not cancer, for God's sake," as if God took the trouble to fashion personal, tailor-made agonies instead of merely swatting us like bothersome insects with a thoughtless gesture. Whenever my eyelids fell shut, they would hurriedly whisper about how pale I was, how thin I'd become, how my hair was falling from my temples and my nape, how I would soon plunge into a coma, how in no time I'd wear a cadaver's cross on my chest. My sisters and my sister-in-law knitted at my side, and there was a picture of the five of us, young women dressed for a ball, so different from how we are now, sinking under the weight of resignation and bitterness.

No mulberry trees waved in the window as at our house on the Calçada do Tojal, where the twilight lingered in the ivy, alarming the spinsters' parakeets. Here there was just a potted rubber plant whose leaves drooped, in spite of the attentive sprinkles of my Cape Verdean maid, who leaned over the plant as over a despondent convalescent. No mulberry trees waved in the window, but the June beetles raged in the panes, and I woke up in the morning with wings crashing into the mirror in the illusion that a second bedroom existed on the other side of the glass, with another old woman lying in a bed, other curtains, other vases. I imagined that the June beetles, knowing I was going to die, wanted to escape from my body's odor, which had acquired the smell of old linens in a trunk. I hated that smell, which soap only accentuated, and I wanted to be rid of that caricature of myself, to go back in time and walk through the pine trees to Ericeira, when my daughter and nephews were young, and the equinox made the waters shoot up the cliffs, and bathers carrying beach tents walked with the wind. The youngsters from a summer camp hunted for tadpoles in the pond, and at the Maritime Life-Saving Institute a drowned man fermented on a table. A hunchbacked boy with a straw hat, whose mother had fled the country with a Swiss lawyer, hobbled on spindly legs behind his friends, and on Saturdays my parents came from Lisbon to kiss their grandchildren and to sit at the outdoor café drinking soft drinks and eating mussels until twilight, when their car disappeared around the gas station, an enormous void swept over the beach and spread to the mimosas on the cliff, the sea resembled a giant that rubbed its hands back and forth on its knees, and I, buttoning up my knitted coat, was so alone that I felt like phoning them just to hear their breathing on the other end of the line. Now, when people come to comfort me in my sickness, full of optimism and plans for the future that include me, it almost seems that it's a Saturday thirty or forty years ago, that I'm in Ericeira, that my parents' car is driving away, with the headlights on, and I feel as forsaken and afraid as I did back then, and as soon as the headlights vanished around the gas station and I decided to call to Benfica, my nephew squatted on a stool the way he used to do in the hotel on the square by the garage, twenty or thirty yards from the beach, when his brothers went to the skating rink and he came to me to shake off his fear of being alone in the hotel, where the only other child was a little redhead named Julieta who played in the yard out back, running after the housekeeper's chickens and trying to pelt them with pieces of brick. I asked him how much time I had left, and he suddenly grew up to his present age, stopped giggling under the hose, leaned out the window to look at the market and away from me, and said, "I don't know, maybe two or three weeks," Julieta, the goddaughter of the hotel owner, was running behind the chickens in Ericeira, my nephew kept gazing at the market, and I remembered a year long ago when I prolonged summer into late October, I remembered the downpours in the deserted hotel, the albino mechanic who walked around in the storms, the albatrosses in the cellar with the boilers and on the gables of the chalets amid wild fig trees, I remembered the three gentlemen dressed in black who were ensconced in a room on the second floor, and the crow that dragged its wings around the kitchen while uttering sailor's swear words. In spite of the faulty heating, the cracks around the windows, and the shower faucet that refused to work, I felt at peace during that autumn when the high tides covered the sand and it was impossible to distinguish between sky and sea, both teeming with a kind of sulfurous froth. I amused myself by imagining that the redheaded girl was the sister of my neighbors at the Calçada do Tojal, I moved her to the house of the Vacuum Oil employee and the imprisoned army officer, and as my nephew once more straightened pictures and rearranged my bibelots the housekeeper of the hotel was struck by a heart attack, the squawking crow pulled at her apron with its claws, and the rain drenched her skirt and hair, my nephew announced with a smile, "You're going to live forever, Aunt Antonia," and I nodded so as not to upset him, I stuck a Tyrolean hat on his head and placed him in Hyacinth Park of Alcântara, married to the daughter of my parents' seamstress, a diabetic girl born in Mozambique or in Guinea Bissau or in Cape Town who was being devoured, just like me, from an incurable disease that gnawed away at her insides, and then I heard once more the sea of October and the albatrosses that squawked in the cellar with the boilers, I fell asleep in front of the disconnected TV and woke up walking around in my bedroom as under the chestnut trees of Mortágua, where my sister-in-law's father, wearing a linen jacket, solved the newspaper puzzles on the porch facing the mountains, surrounded by wasps and crickets and the silence of the sun in the olive trees.

That afternoon, after the cobalt treatment, my teeth started to fall out, coming loose from my gums while my face puckered and green roots surfaced in my mouth, so that I thought it must be spring. The rubber plant twisted toward the window, the call of the storks in the woods drew nearer, advancing across the soccer field, and the sound of the elevator took on a vitreous quality, as if it carried stacks of gleefully rattling dishes. The voices of my visitors blended with the parakeets of the Calçada do Tojal, and they talked to me from perches or on boxes for eggs, smoothing their feathers with their lipsticked beaks. My father waved good-bye, in Ericeira, with his shirtsleeve hanging out the car window, a train from Damaia whistled my name at the railway stop, and I remembered that when I went to Alcântara to the seamstress's apartment, which was overrun by wilted dahlias, I was startled by the whistles of the locomotives that rushed by along the Tagus River, whose shore bristled with derricks. The seamstress's boarder, who never stopped drinking beer, entered the cubicle where she was fixing a hem for me, knocked over the ironing board, and declared "If I wanted to, ma'am, I could fly like a wild duck to Tunisia." The seamstress sent him to his room, threatening him with her scissors, my husband wound the clocks on the wall, my sister who was born in Algiers wiped my chin with her hankie, the drunk shouted, "I feel like flying, Dona Orquidea, let me fly, Dona Orquidea," the seamstress, poking pins into the hem of my dress, told me she would have to send the drunk back to Esposende, since the people in Alcântara (who all had wilted dahlias in their flower beds) complained that he rang their doorbells and swore he was a kite, but what I remembered from Esposende were the drones of the lifeboat lost in the fog, the rails by which the boat slid into the sea, a collapsible cinema on top of the rockroses in the dunes by the beach, and the loudspeakers that mangled the actors' words, making them resemble the seagulls' screeches. I sat outside the canvas wall, behind the window of the projector, and I saw a man who inserted and removed reels, with a hand-rolled cigarette hanging from his lower lip. Between me and the waves there was a girl with a shawl who stood in the sand as if waiting for someone, and as I got ready to go over and address her I heard my youngest sister say to her "Now she nods off at the drop of a hat, it must be the first stage of coma," my cousins' friend popped out of the bushes in Sintra with the tennis ball in his hand, my husband came home from work smelling of perfume, but the cook yanked me out of bed, grabbing me by my gray ears like a rabbit, sat on a stool in the yard next to the kitchen, where the maples danced above the stone wall, it was day and night among the ceramic tiles, she slit me open with the knife, and my bleeding guts spilled into the tin pan.

3

I've never seen the sea except in pictures and photographs. In the living room downstairs there are several snapshots of my sisters at the beach, sitting in the sand with people I don't know, and in the background I can make out the advancing waves. In the bedroom that was my parents' there's a painted landscape of crags and cliffs where you can't actually see water, but you can sense the waves from some weeping willows in a corner and from the pine trees' distress. And so I imagine the sea to be a meadow with ladies wearing hats and smiling in the wind. My sister Maria Teresa told me that they could see the Tagus from the house in Queluz and that our mother sometimes took her to Guincho Beach, where a lighthouse pulsed on the rocks, streaking the night blue and illuminating the trees, the dunes, and a slowly shifting band of shadows dotted with glittering scales. Perhaps it's because I've never seen the sea that I stopped ordering around the seamstress's son when he came back from Peniche after the summer holidays and told me that the trawlers' engines woke him up when they set out in the morning, leaving a trail of oil in their wake. He woke up with the engine sound, got out of bed, and went down to the port, the moon faded in the branches of the oaks, and the departing boats formed a fan as their keels plowed the foam. From his pocket he pulled out the eyeball of a drowned cabin boy, and I was so awed by that blind eye staring at me with its milky indifference that I forgot about the chickens in the yard and the brick to kill them. That afternoon I asked my brother Jorge, who was feeding the parakeets, to take me to Queluz to look at the river, and while he brushed out the feed boxes and checked the eggs he explained that I was forbidden by our father to leave the attic, I asked why and he silently wagged his head as his outstretched arm shook a little bag of fresh seed. Three storks circled over the woods, and on the kitchen step, while the maid shucked pea pods over a bowl, the seamstress's son told me about the trawlers' return, when baskets of turbot and grouper were salted by the sailors and auctioned off to dealers who backed up their trucks to the dockside. Since his sea was different from the sea without sea of the pictures and photographs, he made me a drawing of Peniche with colored pencils on a sheet of paper, and it took a long time for him to fill in his sea, and when he handed me the drawing, what I saw were crooked porches, a butterfly larger than the chimneys of the rooftops, a smiling sunflower, and the eyeball of the drowned cabin boy. Everyone kept hiding the waves from me, and so I got mad, I grabbed a piece of brick to smash in the head of the seamstress's son, who, bawling with fear, took off running through the chickens, tripped, and fell into the lettuce, and before he could get up to keep running I hurled the brick, which almost hit him in the neck. My brother Jorge pulled me by the wrist into the house, and when they brought the tray with my dinner up to the attic, they put a record on the gramophone to calm me down, but I was so angry at them for not showing me the sea that I refused to eat.

I saw no more of the seamstress's son until years later, when the parakeets in the enormous cage had been replaced by the fox that paced around, sniffing and urinating on the wire grating. The climbing plant, with clusters of blooms, had reached the top of the stone wall, my brother Jorge still hadn't returned to the Calçada do Tojal, and my sisters still phoned in search of him, bent forward in anxious expectation, as if someone might suddenly ring the doorbell to announce that he'd been arrested by mistake, that the police were deeply sorry, and that he would arrive that evening like the trawlers of Peniche arriving from the offing, with the sunset's transparency illuminating him as it illuminated the boats. Building after building was going up on the Calçada do Tojal and the neighboring streets, the flocks of sheep gave way to bulldozers, rock crushers, scaffolds, and African construction workers with picks over their shoulders, dogs stopped barking from behind the gates of farms, being replaced by the whistles of foremen, the palm tree of the post office was chopped into logs, and the storks circled round and round the tree's remains without knowing what to do, until they finally migrated to Buraca's decaying mansions, with stone lions at the bottom of the staircases. Our mother dismissed the cook and the maids, the cuckoos in the clocks bowed incessantly, telling the wrong time, and I almost never came down from the attic, enclosed in myself like tears inside an onion. The dust that coated the windows accumulated on the carpet and the tops of the dressers, whose drawers had to be forced, making the silverware rattle, the same laundry hung for days from the clothesline, and the eyelashes in the photos became heavy with sleep. On Sunday mornings, during mass time, I heard the whimpering of the fox, forgotten like the laundry that blew in the wind, and the buzzing of insects that emerged from the damp underside of plants, fluttering their colorless wings in the sickly air. The floorboards creaked in time with the rocking chair, as if they walked forward each time my feet pushed, and I suddenly realized that the steps leading up to the attic creaked in the same way, I veered my gaze from the church tower, where the bells were soundlessly shaking, and found the seamstress's son looking at me from the threshold with the meek expression he had when he played with me in the yard by the kitchen, fearfully submitting to my whims.

He brought with him the absence of the sea, for the sea only exists (without actually appearing) in pictures and photographs, and when they tell me my brother Jorge is in Tavira I know they're lying, because the beach is a photographic trick, just as seagulls and fish are mere silhouettes created by skillfully positioned hands between a light source and a wall. The seamstress's son gazed at me from the doorway, the rocking chair clacked against the floorboards, the silt of the past weighed in the attic with its chests of drawers, bidet stands, baskets, the musty smell of hatboxes, and suitcases with old blouses and raincoats, while below us the clocks' heart ticked backward in time. I pulled down my hair's curls, thinking that my sisters would return from church and find him there with me, listening to operas on the gramophone, I wanted to say "Get out of here, you didn't draw me the sea," but I didn't talk to anyone except in the letters that I sent to my brother Jorge in Tavira and that never got answered, and so I stared at him as I used to stare, when I was little, at the earthworms that patiently tunneled through clods. I felt that his arrival signaled the close of a cycle in me and that, as had happened to my father, there was nothing for me to do but lie down, forget Monsanto, and die, as the farms of Benfica and the ivy of my childhood are dying, and something grabs us deep down, like the anxiety of regret. I remembered his mother pedaling the sewing machine next to the window, I remembered the murmur of the lindens, I remembered the soup that the old woman ate while darning, and the threads that got tangled in her hair, and her son, stepping toward me, "Hi Julieta," and I, "Why didn't you draw me the sea?" My brother Fernando was sleeping in his room, the garden was full of light since they'd cut the climbing plants, a different silence inhabited the shrubs, the absence of the palm tree enlarged the horizon, houses and garden apartments with slate balconies stretching from the Rua Emília das Neves and the Estrada de Benfica to the villas of Portas de Benfica and the black neighborhood of Damaia, the remains of the Catholic school, Colégio Lusitano, transformed into a cooper's workshop and a shelter for beggars, with coatracks buried in the grass, the littered reeds by the stream next to the train tracks where no train passed by and where the corpse of the delivery boy had rotted for weeks, "Hi, Julieta," and I, "You didn't draw me the sea because the sea doesn't exist, the sea's a big lie, you hid the waves behind porches and sunflowers and butterflies," a blackbird alighted on top the cage, where the fox was stretched out with its snout next to its bowl, "It's perfectly obvious that she's not my daughter, so stop lying," yelled my father in his office, "I ought to do her in, and you too," and sobs, and slaps, and more shouts, and my brother Jorge, "Dad gets these funny ideas, you know how he is," and the seamstress's son, "Of course the sea exists, I just didn't know how to explain it, if you have a pen, I'll show you," when our mother brought me my lunch she had a lump on her forehead and a gashed cheek, she set the tray on my bed and went back downstairs without kissing me or caressing me, and I asked, "Is our mother not my mother, Jorge?" the corpse of the delivery boy had bloated to the point of ripping his shirt, it was students from the school who found him lying there, curdling, and my father, "She's not to leave this house, I demand that she never leave, that no one ever see her, or hear about her, or have any inkling that she exists," the blackbird flew away from the cage, and I, "If our mother isn't my mother, then I'm motherless and fatherless," I put an aria on the gramophone while he grabbed a pencil and began drawing a beach on the wall, with dunes, rocks, beach tents, and boats, and I, as the tenor's voice came in over the violins, "The sea's green, you have to paint it green," and my brother Jorge, "Even if they weren't your parents, you'd still be my sister,"

Deer jorji I'm yore sister arnt I?

and that was the last blackbird I ever saw, the birds were finished in Benfica, like the palm tree at the post office, the flocks, and the farms, *the birds are finisht jorji Ive never seen a howse so emptie and sad but yore my bruther arnt you?*

"and I, who am your sister, am your sister, aren't I? swear on Grandma's health that I'm your sister," and to the seamstress's son, "Take your time, the mass lasts more than an hour," and he, anxious to please me, marking up the wall from the window to the door, "I'll make it green if you have some colored pencils," and there was a box of gouaches in a basket, he wetted the paints with his saliva and painted green waves on my headboard as the bulldozers mowed down the tombstones in the abandoned cemetery, and I, cranking the gramophone, "How pretty,"

Deer jorji now I no wut the see is like now I no wut Tavira is like its a seeshell I have in my tummy and it wispers and groze and tawks to me

he painted the headboard, painted the windowpanes, painted the ceiling, and painted my body, and I heard the gurgling of water in the cliff, I didn't hear the music, I didn't hear the fox, I didn't hear the shrubs, I heard the gurgling of water in the cliff,

jorge jorge jorge jorge jorge

"I'm your sister, aren't I? Repeat that I'm your sister even if Dad and Mom aren't my dad and mom,"

"You're my sister, Julieta,"

Deer jorji the see is me it hugs me

and he, while continuing to cover the walls with fish and seaweed, "Do you have a waltz, Julieta, or a fox trot, or a tango?" and a building was going up behind our house, with concrete already fleshing out the skeleton of iron, and balconies were appearing, the builder gazed up at it from his car, we're going to be surrounded by windows, blinds, and curtains, Monsanto will be blocked from view, "Am I your daughter, Mom? Am I your daughter?" and she went back downstairs without talking to me, office buildings, apartment buildings, towels hung out to dry, neighbors, hairdressers, florists, saunas, photo booths,

Deer jorji because of the see because of this seeshell in my body there going to take me to Gwarda I dont want to go

the doors of the cuckoo clock slammed in the living room, there was a rowboat and a street of Peniche on the ceiling, women sitting on the front steps of their houses, the braying of engines, the sun, and the seamstress's son left before mass was over, he had green hands, green stains on his coat and tie, a green spot on his chin, *green, jorji, green, anita isnt my sister, maria tereza isnt my sister, fernando isnt my bruther, our muther isnt my muther, our father isnt my father, but you*

"I'm your brother, Julieta"

green

no one knows who it was, no one will ever know, my brother Fernando, "You little whore,"

Deer jorji they want to take the see from me, dont let them, when they askt me who it was I didnt tell, Ile only tell you, the see is crying

and the sheets were green, and the pillow, and my chest, and my shoulders, there was greenness over the green grass outside, the brown bushes were green, and the fox green, and the clocks green, and my family's fury green, and the music green, and the night green until Sunday, when he came by, green, and had there been a blackbird on top the cage, it would also have been green,

green

the sea is green in Guarda, the sea is green

and my sister Maria Teresa who wasn't my sister asked "Who was it?" and my sister Anita who wasn't my sister asked "Who was it?" and my brother Fernando who wasn't my brother asked nothing, and my father who wasn't my father, who had never been my father, shook his horsewhip, "The redhead can't be my daughter, so tell me who she belongs to, wife"

Not to our family, I don't belong to our family, dear Jorge, only to you in Tavira, where you hear seagulls and waves without ever seeing them, and he painted Peniche's bathing huts on the stairs, in the hallways, in the bedrooms on the second floor, in the dining room, on the photos, on the cuckoo clocks, and he opened the shutters, and the wind from the beach blew through my red hair

green

the wagtails had perched on the chinaware, the curtain rods, the picture frames,

and when they came back from mass I was standing in the foyer as in a turret, opening my white arms bristling with feathers and covered by orange freckles

green

to embrace the sea.

4

And I said to my nephew "I don't want any more cobalt, let me die in peace," and it wasn't I who spoke but another woman that used my clothes and my name, another widow, old and ugly, with unfamiliar hands that wore my rings, with darker eyes than I've ever had, and strange wrinkles, almost no hair, another woman who was already dead, whereas I still have at least five or ten or twelve days, sitting in this sick person's chair for fear of lying down, because what began in bed also ends there, and I don't want to end, I can't stand the idea of ending, and if I said "I don't want any more cobalt, let me die in peace," I wasn't speaking of dying but of August with you and my grand-children in the Algarve, lazy afternoons, a book on the terrace, your smile, I was speaking of having all my teeth again and of not resembling my father's aunts, whom we visited at Easter in apartments as still as a manger scene, with them playing the piano and calling my name, an invalid coughing on a sofa, I pulling on my father's coat, "I want to go home," and the sound of the piano followed us down the stairs and into the car, the sound of the piano in my insomnia all night, and an aunt grabbing my chin with her owlish claw, "Would you like a cookie, dear?"

"So send the visitors away, Sofia, and let me die in peace above the new market," going in and out of coma like someone who rises to the surface before drowning for good, without my sister's voice on the telephone at suppertime, "It's thundering, do you hear it? It's not that I'm afraid, but don't hang up yet," she likewise alone, already missing a breast and living in a build-ing like mine, simultaneously modern and old

(walls, ceiling, floor, and rooms with no mystery, overlook-ing a Benfica that's no longer ours or yet anyone else's, a Benfica of strangers who haven't been here long enough to plant their childhood and regrets)

because we who are from here but are not from here, who are from a here that no longer exists, have filled up these buildings with the silt of mementos and albums and letters and faded pictures from the past, and our present is occupied by these ruins of memory, not only the memory of those who preceded us, but the memory of ourselves, because we also forget, because names and images and faces get lost in a fog that makes everything equally blurry, leaving us a today that's inhabited only by death and its certainty, and my sister, "It's not that I'm afraid, but don't hang up yet," with her voice and my silence being but ghosts of voices and silences known only to us, like the silence and voices of the birch trees in the yard, the silence of the arbor by the pond, the silence of Mortágua, the silence of São Martinho do Porto and my father saying "Sweetie pie," I look at his features and remember "Sweetie pie," they can talk about my appearance and how I look better and how I've gained back some weight, but I only hear him saying "Sweetie pie," my father, who was destroyed by the spot on his lung before his house was sold

(the house with Dutch timber work, coach houses, the barn, the cow shed, the greenhouse beyond the dining room, the house),

the house my mother got rid of in the year of the Revolution to move into a condo near mine, where there was no room for the rose garden or the farm or the plaster statues on stone benches, and when the house began to be demolished, our family quietly, discreetly, began to die, dividing the porcelain, the pictures, and the silverware that only made sense all together, in the places where I first saw them and where, within me, I still see them, and one early morning her maid frantically rang my doorbell, "Your mother's in a bad way, ma'am," I slipped a coat over my nightgown, and when I got there the doctor who lived on the ninth floor was putting away his stethoscope, we dressed her and perfumed her bedroom, and I remembered that when my father was in his final agony, not breathing and then suddenly breathing again, his entire body united in revolt against his own death, my mother said to me without any tears, "Your father's a very large tree that can't easily be knocked down," and I, who also did not cry, loved them more that day than I'd ever loved them, "You, Mother, are a tree as large and strong and victorious as he is"

(the hyacinths in the flower beds bowed low, how the hyacinths in the flower beds bowed low)

and we'd been in Algiers, we'd come back from Algiers, and for many years we were happy, until Benfica became a land of exile in our own land, they leveled the orphanage, they leveled the houses of Avenida Gomes Pereira and Avenida Grão Vasco, the milkman's cart disappeared, along with the cows, the produce, and the corn of Poço do Chão

(the clinking bottles, do you remember the clinking bottles, do you remember the white foam?),

they demolished my house on the Calçada do Tojal in whose attic I spend my summers, even if I'm at Balaia Beach, in the attic that looks out onto Monsanto, where my father fought, in the attic playing records on the old horn gramophone and writing this book that someone will finish for me, and the women who visit me belong to the same race of exiles, foreigners in a foreign land that is nevertheless theirs, and that's why I tolerated them in my living room, all deathly afraid, and that's why I didn't get angry at their ominous whispers, their frowns, their anxiety on my and their behalf, "Poor Maria Antonia, and what a loss for us," and I thought, Poor me, fair enough, but when you die there won't even be any more woods, just another neighborhood on top of these neighborhoods, more rooftops on top of these rooftops, chimneys on top of these chimneys, with our square block lying under so many other square blocks that there'll be no reason for it to endure, where are the wisteria, the lindens, the elms, where are the asthmatic geese that flee from us, from us who've become a worn-out and different us, poor you who remain, who get lost on streets where there used to be fields, who get lost at intersections where corn has stopped rustling and olive trees don't sag, my sister-in-law grabbed my hand, and it was as if we were running, dressed in pink, down the Estrada Militar, lined by willow trees, with army trucks rumbling toward the barracks in a whirl of dust

(mulberries, Graça, the taste of mulberries, the flavor of sorrel)

and I held on tight to her sleeve, imagining that we might still be able to go there, but we couldn't, how hard it is for my back to bend, for my arms to move, for my legs to walk, on the site of the Estrada Militar there are no more soldiers marching behind an officer and a drum, just shanties of blacks and Gypsies, Gypsies and blacks, with no light but the gleam of their teeth and the foaming drool of dogs as scrawny as they are, huts made of boards, cardboard, barrel staves, and planks from scaffolds, barefoot women heating up pots on stones, children with faces like puddles, blind people, mud everywhere, even in September,

poor you, who will have to go into the church where I'll be sealed in a coffin, and as you push open the door, the flames of the votive candles will flutter toward your mourning (which will last as long as a mass plus a burial) and force you to consider, Who's next, Manuela? Who's next, Luísa? the cemetery full of husbands who did not wait and who are not waiting, "Do you hear the thunder? It's not that I'm afraid, you know I'm not afraid, it's useless to be afraid, but talk to me, stay on the line a bit, don't hang up yet," in Ericeira I would light the stove before dusk, the wind in the pine trees terrified me, through the living room window I saw the hill slope down to the dunes, and the sand glistened, the waves broke my bones against the embankment, my nephews rode their bikes toward the water that the red flag prohibited, on top of the cliff there was a deserted café with its name in large pallid letters, São Lourenço Beach was still not frequented by vacationers, just a few seagulls, no swimmers, no bathing huts, just teenagers hopping among the rocks to get away from their parents, and my fellow widows talking to me of canasta and of excursions to Sicily, to Yugoslavia, to Leningrad, to Egypt, "How about it, Maria Antonia?" and I nodding yes, imagining a busload of my visitors knitting their way around Europe, to Sicily, of course, to Yugoslavia, of course, Leningrad, naturally, it has a splendid museum, Egypt, the Pyramids, the Sphinx, and why not an excursion to Benfica, and why not an excursion to what we once were, weddings, processions, carnival balls, hockey games, my father's German shepherd howling in its cage, and after my visitors left, with their Sicilies and their museums, my nephew, observing the market with his back to me, said "If you don't want any more radiation, then fine, it's up to you," and I asked "How much time?" and he, rearranging the bibelots, "I don't know," and then I saw him sitting under a withered walnut tree at Hyacinth Park, he, who had lived and worked in London, who received eight television channels, had a Spanish maid, and didn't even know there was a Hyacinth Park, garden apartments with wilted dahlias on the slope of Alcântara, the drunk boarder bursting into the sewing room swearing "I can fly," the seamstress threatening him with her iron, and then, calming down, "I'm sorry, ma'am, but my nerves are shot from having to deal with this and other troubles," and my nephew with his briefcase on his knees, waiting for nighttime to go home as I wait for daytime to die, because the one thing I'm sure of is that I'll die during the day, early in the morning, with a neighbor doctor—summoned so urgently he won't have had time to comb his hair—listening to my unmoving heart and supposing that he hears it, when what he'll really be hearing is the elevator cable, and with me will die the characters of this book that will be called a novel, which I've

written in my head, fraught with a fear I don't talk about, and
which one of these years someone, in accord with the natural
order of things, will repeat for me in the same way that Benfica
will be repeated in these random streets and buildings, and I,
without wrinkles or gray hair, will water my garden with the hose
in late afternoon, and the palm tree at the post office will grow
again before my parents' house and the zinc windmill searching
for wind, and my sister, a widow like me whose left breast was
amputated because of a cancer like mine, a cancer, a cancer, "It's
not that I'm afraid of thunderstorms, there are lightning rods
after all, and it's useless to be afraid, but don't hang up yet,"

(I promise I won't hang up, I'll stay on the line, we're very
large trees that can't easily be knocked down, we're the last trees
in this treeless neighborhood except for those in the woods that
have miraculously resisted the demented fury of builders, perhaps they'll be tiled over, or framed by aluminum-enclosed balconies the way the orchards and cows of Poço do Chão were
framed, raising all around us a present without a past, a species
of future in which only faucets will be entitled to shed tears, we
are very large trees, Mother, we are trees, but explain to me where
our roots can survive when the earth has all been asphalted, carpeted, and parqueted, when even the cemetery ground has been
paved by stones, when not a square foot of grass is left for my
now frail body, reduced to a shadow that stubbornly protests,
and when this condo shrinks to the exact size of my dread, which
is why I invented the Rua Ivens, which is why I invented Tavira
and Esposende and Johannesburg and Loures, which is why I
invented Alcântara and the river and the trains and Peniche,
and I don't know if the Tagus still exists, or the beach at Cruz
Quebrada, or the sewers that spew out this city I hate from having loved it so much, but I didn't invent Mortágua, I didn't
invent São Martinho do Porto, I didn't invent Benfica, no, not
Benfica, I didn't invent Benfica, I didn't invent my father's final
agony, I didn't invent my mother's passing, I didn't invent my

own death, I'll stay on the line, I'm not leaving, I won't hang up yet, but how convey to you, sister, the terror that awaits me if I don't talk of feelings, I hate the intimacy of sorrow, I hate whatever is maudlin in fear and obscene in despair, nor have I ever laughed much, I think I don't know how to laugh, when my daughter giggled for the first time I felt afraid for her sake, she tottered toward me with her hands pressing the wall, come here, little girl, come here, Sofia, I won't hang up yet, I'll stay on the line, even if we're not very large trees, it's hard for us to be knocked down, and even if they knock us down, we'll remain in photos, in scrapbooks, in mirrors, in the objects that prolong and remember us, in the clocks, my God, that will cease their ticking in the moment when we cease, and you smiling at me with the only smile that during all these years has ever, forgive me, made me cry)

and my nephew in the chair next to me, forgetting about the new market, "How are you feeling, Aunt Antonia, did you sleep all right?" and I, who could no longer walk, "I sleep all the time," I sleep more and more, and when I wake up they try to make me eat, but the food won't go down, and your cousin, "How's that, Mom?" and I pretend to thank her, but my jaw won't chew, they feed me intravenously and I watch the drops enter my arm, and when they think I can't hear, my sister born in Algiers asks "Why so much suffering, why does she have to suffer so much?" but I don't suffer, I'm not suffering, I'm painting the sea right here in my home, I'm taking down the photos of happy moments from their hooks, along with the oil paintings, watercolors, and prints we got as wedding presents, including "William Tell Sends Out His Boat" and "William Tell Threatens the Governor," one of which fell on the floor and broke when we moved here, I'm taking down the photos and paintings and prints and hanging up fish, sea waves, masts, and my nephew, "I'm going to give you some pills that are easy to swallow and will help you sleep," and I, "I'd like to have my teeth back, to have hair, to lose this color, to be me," and my daughter, "You look better today, Mom," and my youngest sister, "I think so, too," and yet they wouldn't let in my girlfriends with their travel plans, "She gets tired, the cobalt has depleted her strength, as soon as she improves we'll call and arrange an outing, a movie, a canasta game," and the girlfriends, "Of course, of course, it takes time to convalesce, we'll wait for your call," and whispers, sympathetic kisses, footsteps trailing away, the door opening and then closing, until it's just the two of us, daughter, as on the day you were born, not in this condo, which didn't even exist, or in the house, which exists no longer, but in a white delivery room whose white sheets and white light blinded me, and first it was my thighs that got wet before I knew it, and it wasn't blood but water, tank water or aquarium water, membranous water that gently flowed under my bottom, and after the water it was a weight in my body's center, tentacles slowly drawing away like a corpse's retracting limbs, and then the first pain, like a cramp ravaging my womb, arteries pounding, veins swelling, cartilage resisting, the pain subsiding, my body relaxed, and then another pain, It's August twenty-fifth, I thought, the sign of Virgo, intelligent, orderly, methodical, unadventurous, "Bend your chin against your chest and push," the pain was white, white like the delivery room and the room's brightness and the sound of the shot by which my grandfather killed what was killing him inside, it went away and came back, dissolved and reappeared, extinguished and flashed, "Push harder," "I'm pushing, doctor, I'm pushing," while wondering why I should expel the life that was in me, my grandfather stuck a pistol in each ear, his own pistol and my father's pistol, but only his left hand pulled the trigger, and not one syllable of the letter he left us was intelligible, strokes and dots, strokes and dots, strokes and dots that were shouts, "Push harder, push harder, harder, harder, harder, harder," my legs held by clamps, the midwife miles away from me, and I exhausted, "Push, bend your chin against your chest

and push," perhaps you didn't want to be born and they forced
you out of me, perhaps you held on to me so as to drag me along
as they dragged you out of me, August twenty-fifth, the sign of
Virgo, but what planets, where was Mercury? one pain on top
of another, like the buildings of Benfica that have sucked up our
life and the past, "I don't want any visitors, or any pills, or anything to eat," my grandfather slumped over his desk, the re-
volvers on the floor, a sneeze of a thousand tiny drops on the
paper, "Push harder," buildings on top of storks, on top of
palm trees, on top of the horizon of Monsanto, and my father,
"Sweetie, sweetie pie, sweetie," push harder, "I don't want any
more IV, Dad, I don't want any more cobalt, I don't want to
look better, I don't want to have gained weight," you didn't want
to live and I forced you, you wanted to stay in me, but I sent
you away, and a voice, "I already see its hair, keep pushing," and
with my chin against my chest I saw the blood and the baby,
head upside down, greasy and slippery and dirty with me and
with her, all wrinkled, and linked to me by a cord, "Sweetie pie,"
said my father, "sweetie, sweetie pie," and my sister on the telephone, "Don't hang up yet, I'm afraid," and my sister who was
born in Algiers, "Why so much suffering, for God's sake?" and
they took me to my room on a bed with wheels that squeaked,
and they brought you all washed and dressed and with black hair,
and your eyelids were puffy like clams, it was late afternoon, soon
it would be dark, and I asked them to leave you with me, they
turned on the light over the headboard, they raised my bed with
the crank of the gramophone in the attic, and an opera or a tango
or a waltz started playing, and you looked peaceful and calm and
didn't cry, the smell of an apple tree outside brought back to
my memory the soft, intense, weightless, bittersweet aroma of
the arbor, the lindens, the immortelles, and the hyacinths in the
backyard on spring mornings, illuminating the hallway indoors,
I cuddled the baby girl as she slept or got used to the world, I
pulled her closer to me, sweetie, sweetie pie, sweetie, my grand-

father stock-still, his blanket sliding down his knees, and I, "How much time?" and my nephew, "A long time, Aunt Antonia, a very long time, with no more injections, no more IV, no more cobalt," and my hair once again brown and full and lush, they placed the metal tray with my dinner in front of me, vegetable soup, fish, a stewed pear, a bottle of still water, and when the nurse, wearing a cap, opened my door I said, "Don't take the baby, because she'll grow up and I'll lose her, I'll have her for such a short time before she's no longer mine," and I unbuttoned my shirt, pulled out my breast, slowly leaned you into it, tickling your forehead, your cheeks, and your nose with my nipple, and when I inserted myself into your mouth, the smell of the apple tree shaded your face, the certainty that I would never ever die made my blood surge, I felt on my skin, or under my skin, the teeth you still didn't have, and while I emptied myself into you, daughter, I realized I was being born.

5

The fox died on the day after I found nothing to eat in the pantry and the day before I was visited by the now old red-haired man, who rang the bell at the gate,

waited, rang again, waited again, pushed against the chipped and rusty latch that gave way with the sound of a bone when snapped, and then walked up the weed-infested gravel path with a kind of bashful reticence, each hesitant step seeming to excuse itself,

an old man who stopped before the house, trying to decipher the interior through the warped blinds, and then reached out his hand not to the electric buzzer, which at any rate didn't work, but to the iron knocker shaped like a closed fist with a ring on the middle finger that struck against an iron coin, producing an urgent sound that echoed in the attic's stagnant air,

some twenty-four hours after I had stood up from the rocking chair to look through the window that faced Monsanto Park, looking not at the hill with the prison on top, but at the clumps of surviving lilies in the garden, and that's when I saw the fox lying in its cage, flat out on the cement, in whose cracks sprouted short tufts of moss,

and I realized it wasn't sleeping, I realized it had died next to its empty bowl, and I realized that its screeching howls during the night had been its way of bidding farewell to an absurd existence, as deafeningly absurd as my own,

and I kept watching it from the top of that house so unsteady it wobbled, as if it were made of moldy cardboard boxes, topped by once red roof tiles that the pigeons, having moved to Venda Nova or Amadora, no longer splotched with their hard-wax droppings, and I kept watching it without going down the stairs, without going out into the yard, without going to where it lay, without anything in me that resembled dread or alarm, certain that everything around me would disappear, inviting me to disappear, too,

and that afternoon, when I got hungry, I looked for something to eat in the pantry and the kitchen but found only empty tin cans and jelly jars with crusts of sugar that my fork couldn't pry away from the glass, of which they now formed an inalienable part, as if they were defects in its manufacture,

and when I placed a cup beneath a faucet and turned it on, there was a slow gurgle in the pipes, a solitary muddy drop fell into the drain, and I thought, They cut off the water, they cut off the electricity, they cut off the gas, they must have forgotten I exist, if they ever knew I did, given that my life has been a perpetual absence, an irrevocable nothingness since the very beginning, and I didn't even feel bitter toward my parents or my siblings, for I understood their embarrassment and their fear,

and while the boxwoods shrank and the profile of Monsanto glowed orange in the twilight, I used the water that was left in the fox's bucket to make an infusion of leaves from the loquat tree by the kitchen, which survived in spite of being infested with parasites,

and I passed through the rooms, I passed through the silence of the clocks and photos, the saints of the small shrine, the cumin seeds peeking out of the sofa upholstery, I went up to the second floor, where my brothers and sisters had their beds, and in the room between them was my parents' bed, with the tarnished silver cross of an ivory rosary hanging from the middle of the headboard,

and besides the bed there were paintings, dressers, clothes decomposing behind the wardrobe mirror,

and besides the furniture there was the paralysis of silence: the threatening silence of my father and the fearful, nervous silence of my mother, whose pajamas and nightgown had lain side by side in terror and hatred, and by the time I'd reached the attic the sky over Monsanto had turned completely black, not with the black of nightmares, just indifference, and I rummaged through the stack of records between the rocking chair and the mattress for the overture to *Aïda*, I wound up the gramophone, I changed the steel needle for another, equally dull needle, I placed it on the outside groove, I listened to the music that emerged from the horn as if from me, I looked at the whirlpool of windows that the neighborhood had become, and I think I fell asleep,

Jorge,

because when I stood up from the rocking chair it must have been about ten or eleven A.M., with the sun still shining in the yard by the kitchen but already grazing the iron spikes in the gate, and that's when I noticed the red-haired man, as old as my mother and my father would be if they weren't now mere voices from the past,

and I saw him ring the bell that refused to ring, I saw him on the gravel path, I saw him marvel at the crumbling shutters, I saw him contemplate the fox's corpse, which was beginning to stink, I saw him strike the fist of the knocker against the coin on the door, and I stood there as if I had not seen him, whom I recognized as the same man that before my mother's funeral had placed a bouquet on the doormat and hurried away, as if he'd left a message or were carrying out an order, and he was much younger then, and much better dressed,

the same man whom no one else in the house had seen, and by the time someone found his bouquet and tossed it into the hearse, he was vanishing down the Estrada de Benfica in a streetcar or a taxi, returning to the home where he lived with his wife and children, or alone, and there was still the palm tree, there were still the storks, the white breasts of swallows in May, the abandoned cemetery, and the red-haired man ran away from his furtive chrysanthemums as if he hated them, or else hated that place, but this time he didn't go away, he stayed there, determined though feeble, wearing a shabby coat and eroded by the years, a quasi widower waiting on the doormat like a dog awaiting its disappeared owners,

and so I finally walked down to the front door, listened to the heaving gills or paper lungs through which old people breathe, surely more like gills than lungs, old people having an amphibious quality that sets them clearly apart from us, and out of curiosity or pity I turned the key, and the daylight lit up the foyer, the tall porcelain jar in which the umbrellas of the dead were buried up to their handles, and the stuffy air of the living room, reminiscent of a forgotten museum,

and he, all embarrassed, searching for a pretext to justify his visit, "Excuse me,"

and while I marveled at how much he resembled me, he insisted in a low voice, as if the words were hurting him, "Excuse me, I'd just like to have a few words with you,"

and I, thinking that he'd brought me the birds and waves of Peniche that the seamstress's son had drawn for me during mass over the course of several months, when I learned that the sea made me swell and that it cried, "Can you draw me the ocean?"

and he, startled, "The ocean?"

and I, "The ocean,"

and he, "The ocean?"

and I, as if the seashell of my womb had awoken with an echo of tears, "The ocean, the ocean, can you draw me the ocean?"

and he, moving his freckled hands that I imagined to be clumsy and unhappy, "You want me to draw the ocean?"

and the church bell rang half past some hour or other, the sun moved beyond the roof toward Rua Cláudio Nunes, whose bars hummed with blowflies and chicken livers in clay dishes, and I, "The ocean, that's right, haven't you ever seen the sea?"

because after my brother Jorge went away, the only times when I didn't get everyone frantic and furious with my screaming were when someone painted dunes and boats around the house, and the old man, turning his hands one way and then the other, "You really want me to draw you the ocean?"

and I, "Isn't that why you came, to draw the ocean? Didn't you bring your box of gouaches?"

and he, "I'm sorry, I forgot, but if you have any gouaches, I'll paint you the sea right now,"

and I led him into the kitchen, offering him the rest of my loquat leaf tea in a clay mug, since not an unbroken teacup remained in the sideboard, and I dragged him to the living room, I opened the curtains, I sat on the sofa and had him sit on the leather armchair that was used by my father, whose sweat from the nape of his neck had stained it, and the red-haired man breathed with effort, as if to exist were a voluntary, laborious act, he observed me with the turkey eyelids of old people and moved his jaws like a puppet from a fair, saying "So you want the ocean, so you want the ocean, so you want the ocean," such that the ocean, from being repeated, became devoid of meaning, devoid of the lifeboat's siren, of the sea swallows on the rocks, of the fog and the water's roar,

and I suddenly missed the seamstress's son, who during mass on Sunday would paint waves all over the house, on the walls, the sheets, the pictures, the floor, and the bed, and he painted himself, and he painted me, and the old man indignantly said "What?" as if the greenness had to do with him,

and I, surprised at his indignation, "He painted the waves on my body, he painted Peniche on my chest, on my back, on my shoulders, and my thighs opened up with rowboats and seashells, but then I was sent to Guarda, where they took the sea away from me, they took away the waves as soon as the sea came crying out of my womb," and he said

"What?"

with vociferous rage, as if he were my master or my father, as if my life concerned him as much as it did me, so that I asked, "What do you have to do with me and the sea?"

and quiet now, on the verge of a decisive phrase but desisting, without the courage to explain, he mumbled "Nothing,"

and as the fox's stench entered through the broken windowpanes I realized he was lying, that he had mumbled "Nothing" because he couldn't bring himself to tell the truth, and I compared his hands with my hands, his face with my face, his hair with my hair, I sensed he wanted to leave but lacked the strength, and I repeated, "What do you have to do with all this?"

and he, "Nothing, forgive me, I don't have anything to do with it,"

as if his words had sharp edges that hurt him, as if each syllable left a trail of blood, and I suddenly understood the reason for my past and for my entire existence, my years in the attic, my father's resentment, my brothers' and sisters' anxiety, my mother's dashed happiness, and I raised my fist to his head, nearly touching his nose with my nose, and asked "Was it because of you that my family kept me confined? Was it because of you that they wouldn't let visitors see me? Was it because of you that they sent me to Guarda and didn't teach me to read or write and never let me go out? Was it because of you that they forced me to rot here on the Calçada do Tojal? Was it your fault that I ended up all alone, without water or electricity, waiting to starve to death like the fox in the ruins of this house, since my father isn't my true father? Aren't you the one who made me inside my mother, just like the seamstress's son made the sea of Peniche and a seashell that cried inside me?"

and he, chewing his gums, almost inaudible, "Yes,"
and I, "Yes?"

and he, taking scorpionlike steps over the carpet, much older than when he had sat down, "Yes,"

and now the sun lit up the cage and the whole yard, the bushes, the grass, the gate, and beyond the gate the enclosed balconies with clotheslines that were surrounding and smothering me, and beyond the enclosed balconies the hill of Monsanto with the prison and electric poles, and beyond the hill and the clouds Peniche, and Tavira, and the sea, the sea I never saw except when it cried inside my body, the sea, the fishermen's trawlers, the sea swallows, the sea,

the sea and he pacing from room to room, talking to nobody unless himself, "I thought no one knew, I thought no one ever suspected anything,"

and we were in the kitchen, next to the yard with chickens, and I picked up a brick, and my brother Jorge, wearing breeches, "Kill him,"

and the red-haired man didn't cluck, he just stared at me, with his chin hanging down over his tattered tie, "Kill him,"

and my brother Jorge, who still hadn't gone off to the military academy, pointed his finger and said "Kill him"

while my bother Fernando called the cook, "Come quick, Cidália, Julieta's trying to kill the speckled hen,"

and the red-haired man, "This was all so different fifty-seven years ago,"

and the cook, with an eggbeater in her hand, "Stop it, Julieta, stop right now or I'll tell your mother,"

and while he looked at me, shifting his weight in shoes that looked as old and wrinkled as he was, I raised the brick over his head, I said "Father," I think I said "Father," my voice was a hateful bark, "Father," a disillusioned, embittered, and furious bark, "Father," I said, "Father, Father,"

Father, Father, Father

and the fox's corpse, my grandmother's corpse, and the corpses of my brothers and sisters infected Benfica, infected the neighborhood, infected Monsanto, and the church bell, and the palm tree that wasn't there, and Rua Cláudio Nunes, and Amadora, and the sky,

I raised the brick over his head, "Come quick, Cidália, and look what Julieta's doing," and my brother Jorge, "Kill him, kill your father, kill him,"

but I just let him wait there, already dead, deader than if I smashed his head with a brick or a log or a stone, I ran up to the attic, turned the crank on the gramophone, and played a waltz (or a bolero or two-step or tango or fox trot or march) so loud that I couldn't hear my own screams.

6

As trees fall I fall and falling fall as the leaves and shadows fall soft and slow and I hear them weeping and talking to me and don't answer as I fall because if I answered what would I say but that I'm sinking as my father and my mother and my husband sank before me becoming suddenly still and as white as the light in this house so white that over the white furniture the mirrors return their silence and tears and tomorrow they'll rise up with me and with no words but the priest's they'll turn my face toward the sun.

7

I was in my brother Jorge's room, the closest one after Teresa's room to the stairs leading to the ground floor, when I heard voices overhead. At first I thought that the pigeons had returned, puffing their crops and twitching their wings on the eaves and the roof of the attic, or that the bougainvillea had revived and was whispering in the windowpanes as the October wind blew,

but then, as I looked for records in the trunk my brother had filled over the years with newspapers, school books, beach photos, love letters, recipes, galena stones, and mica stones,

I realized it wasn't pigeons or the bougainvillea I heard, nor was it furniture or floorboards creaking with boredom in the afternoon silence, it was the voices of people talking in the attic, the voices of a woman and two men inquiring, answering and explaining, footsteps shuffling across the floorboards at the bidding of a heavier voice that coughed and that was the axis around which the other voices turned,

and as I moved toward the door, trying to make out their words, the voice that coughed said to the other two, "The house has been unoccupied since my cousins died, years ago, as you can tell from the dust and the state of disrepair, so you could either, as I see it, knock all this down and put up a twelve-story high-rise, or else fix the place up and have yourselves a first-rate house, wait till I show you the downstairs, the lawn, and the yard by the kitchen, this place may seem damp and dark, but don't be fooled, when the blinds are raised light comes in everywhere, and the location is fantastic, not to mention the view, and the peace and quiet,"

and I to myself, How did they get in without me noticing, how did they climb the stairs without me hearing them, how did they enter the attic without asking my permission?

and I heard an object break above me, a flowerpot, or the gramophone, or a glass vase, and I wondered, What cousin is this who became owner of the Calçada do Tojal and wants to sell off what's rightfully mine, who only now, after all these years, has come here with these strangers to expel me, to rummage through my clothes and my loquat teas and my attic, to take over the nook where I burrow like a rodent in the ground,

and the cougher, "Gems like this place don't turn up every day, solid construction, a good piece of land, and from here it's a cinch to get anywhere in Lisbon, even in rush hour,"

and I, afraid they might see me, wondered, What should I do, go upstairs and kick out the would-be buyers and the man who claims to be my cousin? But he has no idea I was ever born, he only knows about my parents, my sisters, and my brothers, he'll think I'm a trespasser, he'll demand proof of identity that I don't have, he'll expel me, he'll call the police to have me arrested since there's no document that tells who I am, and I'll be sent to court, and the court, after hearing lawyers and doctors and social workers and witnesses, will lock me up in a state institution in Sacavém or Alverca, to die among already dead widows and retirees,

and a female voice, "We could put in more windows, Alberto, and redecorate the interior, which looks hideous, I'm sure the kids would absolutely love it after being cooped up in an apartment in Carnaxide,"

and a male voice, less enthusiastic, more pragmatic, "Yes, but that takes money, and lots of it, the problem with these houses from the beginning of the century is that the original building materials are no longer available and you spend a fortune just on basic repairs, rewiring and new plumbing, not to mention the hassle of getting building permits from City Hall,"

and the cougher, "Let me put your mind at rest, I can assure you that the wiring and plumbing are in tip-top condition, with a little bit of paint here and there you'll have a dream house, I'd live in Benfica if my wife weren't so stubbornly set on Lapa,"

and the female voice, "Is the furniture included in the price you mentioned?"

and then they came down the stairs to the second floor, with the two men talking all the while, and I, to keep out of sight, went from Jorge's room to Maria Teresa's, with its ethereal fragrance as of a sacristy,

and I wondered, Where's my father's gun? If I find his gun, I'll shoot them down, they have no right to buy and sell what belongs to me, if only I could play *Norma* on the gramophone, if only I could sit in the rocking chair and forget about them as I forget about whatever scares or troubles me while gazing at the hills of Monsanto, the prison, and the blue trees in the distance,

and the intruders visited my sister Anita's room with its narrow bed, dolls with porcelain faces, and printed cotton curtains that fluttered like a lake's eyelashes, not an adult's room but that of a child, as if it had never known death, suffering, or mourning, with girlish furniture, fluffy cats, class photos with five rows of uniforms and braids looking at the camera with round innocence, the only room in the house with life, scented with clove and lavender, an island of warmth that had always been off-limits to me,

and I thought, They're not going to take my sister's room from me, I won't let them steal her dolls, I'll look for the pistol, load the barrel with bullets, and blow out their brains, I'll kill them as I killed the chickens with a brick,

and I thought, I hate you thieves, I hate you, I hate you,

and the male voice, "It reeks of mildew in here, and it's impossible to air out because the window latches are frozen shut, who would ever sleep amid all this junk?"

and the female voice, "I just love these dolls, they're so exquisite, I don't know why it is, but nowadays everything is made without any taste or craftsmanship, all plastic and all exactly alike,"

and I took off my shoes in Maria Teresa's room so that they wouldn't hear my footsteps, I walked down to the ground floor, afraid to look for the pistol since a squeaky hinge might give me away, the man asked, "Who's that?" and the woman, "Don't tell me the house is haunted, I'd rather not live with ghosts," and my supposed cousin, "Don't be silly, ma'am, I didn't hear a thing, you're just not used to the place, but as soon as you move in and change a couple of windowpanes you'll feel right at home,"

and I thought, If only Jorge would show up from Tavira to chase them out with his horsewhip, bolt the door behind them, and then go with me up to the attic to listen to a tango or a two-step,

but nobody came up the gravel path and no key jingled in the lock: the house accepted the strangers, forcing me to flee from the cougher, who praised the layout of the rooms, the stonework, the furniture, the pictures of Christ in agony, and the other man, "They're not bad, they look like me when my mother-in-law visits," and the woman's voice, "My husband's lying, in fact he's crazy about my mother, they always gang up on me," and the man's voice, "That's all I can do, Rita, if I dared to contradict her, she'd strangle me," and the cougher, already on the landing that leads to the kitchen, his shoe pressing on the loose floorboard that no carpenter had been able to fix, "I understand all too well, my mother-in-law has made my life sheer hell," and the woman's voice, "What bugs me about men is that they're all alike," and the cougher, letting the matter drop, "From the verandah you can see the yard by the kitchen, perfect for a vegetable garden, because it gets sun all afternoon,"

and I remembered how when I was little the cook planted asparagus and squash, and a coop was built to keep the chickens from pulling up the seedlings, but my sister Anita, feeling sorry for the animals, would let them out, and the cook would run from the stove to shoo them away from the devastated plants with her apron. Besides the loquat, there used to be a tree from China whose leaves fluttered like sequins against the wall, and in November we could hear the bronchitic toads in gaps where the mortar had worn away, their singing would wake me up at night, and our neighbor the brigadier, who wore a beret and had flown from Lisbon to Paris in a canvas contraption at the beginning of the century, complained to my father that the toads were a nuisance, the tree from China was chopped down, the toads languished in the sun, but the tree's roots kept growing, causing a corner of the house to slant upward, like a packet boat in a field of thyme and saffron, which I was now forced to abandon by the voice that commented on the pantry, the casseroles, the dishes and silverware strewn over the kitchen counter, the dish towels, a braid of onions hanging from a beam, and the woman's voice, "Just how long has the house been vacant?" and the cougher, "Since before I had the title registered in my name, and that was ages ago, of course there may have been an occasional tramp or Gypsy," and the woman's voice, "I doubt that tramps or Gypsies were here, because the house doesn't look like it's been scavenged," and the man's voice, "Still worried about phantoms, Rita? Not even they would want to live in this mess," and the cougher, "I come by once a month to check up on the place, and I can assure you that no one has been living here,"

and I fumed, thinking, You liar, thinking, You swindler, thinking, This is the first time you've come to the Calçada do Tojal, thinking, I wonder what would happen if I suddenly jumped out and told them who I am, thinking, It's useless, thinking, They'd look at me with bewilderment, thinking, They'd make fun of me, thinking, They'd kick me out, into a neighborhood I don't know, into a city I'm a stranger to, and the woman's voice, "I'm not worried about ghosts or phantoms, I'm not that crazy, but some creature or other is in this house," and the man's voice, "Your imagination, Rita, you'll never grow up," and at that moment it began to rain. It wasn't a hard rain, not the kind to pelt the roof and windows with its metallic fingers, but a weightless blanket of water, a fabric of silvery pollen under the blue sky that would hardly moisten the gravel path or the grass in the yard, a light March or August drizzle that wraps us, without touching us, in a lilac aura, and I remembered my widowed mother gazing at winter from her chair in the living room, I remembered my father in his office tapping the horse-whip against his thigh, I remembered my sister Maria Teresa and my sister Anita talking in whispers, and my brother Jorge saying "Don't worry, Julieta, I like you a lot," so that when the cougher asked, "Would you like to see the living room?" I felt like calling Jorge, I felt like begging him, Help me, and the man's voice insisted, "Sometimes you're just like a little kid, Rita," and I ran to the foyer, the woman said, "Somebody's escaping, I swear there's somebody escaping," and I heard no more, because I gently closed the door behind me and scrambled down the path to the Calçada do Tojal. The rain's transparent threads danced, and the stones in the sidewalk were soft and firm under my heels. A little dog sniffed my ankles, yelped once or twice, and turned away, already bored. In what looked like a café or a bar a radio played one of the waltzes I used to play on the gramophone, on Sundays during mass time, while I waited for the seamstress's son to come and draw me the waves of Peniche. Perhaps that's why I didn't miss the Calçada do Tojal, the cuckoos hanging from their spiral springs, or the hills of Monsanto slipping into night in the distance. And so I began to walk to Venda Nova, oblivious of the people whose paths I crossed and who turned to stare at me, the waltz faded behind me, a drunk in a tuxedo and a top hat mumbled a sentence I didn't catch, and by the time I reached Amadora it was so dark that even my shadow had disappeared. But there were lit windows and the weight-less October rain rising in the darkness. The blackness kept me from seeing the rowboats, the lifeboat, the trawlers, the sea swallows, the dunes, the Roman bridge, and the outdoor café of Tavira, it kept me from discerning the wagtails on the rocks, the baskets of fish, the sun on the waves, and the crabs at low tide, it kept me from making out my brother Jorge waiting for me with a smile, but there was no point in calling out to him, since I already felt close to him, since I felt close to the sea.